THE WORLD'S GREATEST
CULTS

ACKNOWLEDGEMENTS

Corbis UK Ltd 129
Owen Fraken 141
Mitchell Gerbr 79
Hulton-Deutsch Collection 56, 73, 102
Mimmo Jodice 30
Roger Ressmeyer 15
Janez Skok 153
Bruce Adams
Eye Ubiquitous 47
Roger Wood 29
Corbis-Bettmann 67, 107, 131, 136, 140, 152
Hulton Getty Picture Collection/Sheila Gaiman 76
Rex Features 181
SIPA 11, 184

THE WORLD'S GREATEST
CULTS

Nigel Cawthorne

CHANCELLOR
PRESS

This edition published by Chancellor Press,
an imprint of Bounty Books,
a division of the Octopus Publishing Group Ltd,
2-4 Heron Quays, London E14 4JP.

Printed in 1999

ISBN: 0 75370 088 3

Printed and bound in Great Britain by
Mackays of Chatham

Contents

Introduction

The author G K Chesterton once said that if people stop believing in religion they don't believe in nothing, they believe in everything. This is an apt motto for our atheistic age. The collapse of organised religion in the West has resulted in strange cults springing up like weeds. Their soil is the intellectually unassailable triumph of materialism, the sterility of consumerism, the loneliness of being just one among so many billions on this planet, the demystification of death and the difficulty that science has in conveying the answers that it may have to age-old questions. Their seeds are ancient eddies in the mainstream of thought, secret knowledge that has somehow remained concealed from humankind down the ages and the ever-optimistic hope that if God is not going to come and save us some alien in a spaceship will.

But cults are nothing new: they were the minority religions of the ancient world to which modern mystics hark back. They also exist within the mainstream religions, such as when some charismatic leader decides to steer his flock off on a new course. However, that new course increasingly results in death – homicide or suicide and sometimes both. But somehow cults manage to go on recruiting . . . even when their leaders are shown to be conmen and their core beliefs to come straight from the pages of a science-fiction comic.

Cults nevertheless continue to fascinate. To an outsider, they bear astounding testimony to the sheer depth of human gullibility. After all, if you don't want to get involved with cult, the rules are simple. Never join anything that does not first tell you what it is about. If you have to wait until you are initiated before you are told, you will find that there is an inner circle that holds in the secrets . . . and another inner circle inside that. Never join anything that demands that you hand over everything that you own. Avoid leaders who want you to do hard, manual labour all day while they ride around in fancy cars and yachts. Never join anything whose price for admission is that the leader gets to sleep with you or your wife – or, for that matter, your children. Avoid worshipping trees, because you'll only get splinters. Never go near anyone who wants you to drink poison. And it is best to steer clear of people who like fooling around with nerve gas and nuclear weapons. Now that's not difficult, is it?

Unfortunately, there are lots of people who can't follow these simple rules: they join cults. There are so many cults that exist in this world that there is simply not enough room to mention them all here; it seems that there are just too many weird and wonderful things to believe in. However, those presented here constitute the world's greatest.

If you are approached by a cult that has not been mentioned in this book, consult the checklist of rules above. And if in doubt, keep your money in the bank and your clothes on.

1 ❖ Aum Supreme Truth

Tokyo's subway system is the biggest underground railway in the world. It runs for nearly 400 miles (644km) and carries some 9 million passengers a day. Early in the morning of 20 March 1995, five members of the Aum Shinri Kyo 'Supreme Truth' cult got on five different trains at the extremities of five lines. At 8.15am, the height of Tokyo's morning rush hour, these trains would converge on the Kasumigaseki, the centre of Japan's government. Four or five stations before it, the five cult members surreptitiously dropped vinyl bags that they had been concealing behind the newspapers that they were holding. With the sharpened tips of the umbrellas that they were carrying they pierced the bags. Then they slipped off the trains and disappeared among the crowds on the platforms.

As the packed trains sped on towards their destinations, a solution of 30 per cent sarin leaked out of the bags. Sarin is a nerve gas that was developed by the Nazis in Germany. It is colourless, odourless and can kill any living being with 100 feet (30.5m) in a matter of minutes. Soon the deadly gas was rising around the ankles of the commuters.

The Aum Supreme Truth cult's leader Shoko Asahara had ordered the gas attack. His aim was to paralyse the government of Japan as a first step in his plan for world domination. He failed. But 12 innocent people died and 5,000 more were hospitalised.

It is easy to dismiss Shoko Asahara as a madman. A half-blind, overweight hippie conman and murderer, he admired Adolf Hitler and believed that he was the reincarnation of Imhotep, the Egyptian architect who built the pyramids at Sakkara in the twenty-seventh century BC. A sage and a scribe, Imhotep was known as the 'Great Physician' and the cult that grew up around him survived well into Roman times.

In 1995 Asahara was 41 and had built up a following of between 3,000 and 10,000 people. His followers were not just the no-hopers picked up off the streets that many cults depend on: among his flock were the brightest and the best. The murderers whom he had deployed on the subway trains were: Ikuo Hayshi, a 48-year-old cardiovascular surgeon who had studied in the USA before joining Aum; 37-year-old Yasuo Hayashi, an electronics engineer and key member of Aum's Ministry of Science and Technology; 31-year-old Masato Yokoyama, an applied-physics graduate; 30-year-old

Kenichi Hirose, who read advanced studies in superconductivity before joining Aum; and 27-year-old Toru Toyoda, a graduate student who had studied particle physics at Tokyo University before dropping out to follow Asahara.

Their leader's education was far more esoteric. The fourth son of a weaver of *tatami* – the straw mats used as flooring in Japanese homes – Shoko Asahara he had been educated at a school for the blind. Then named Chizuo Matsumoto, he had been born blind in the left eye and partially sighted in the right. At school, having some sight gave him a tremendous advantage over the other pupils, whom he began to bully and dominate. He even threatened the teachers.

Coming as he did from a lowly background, he had a burning ambition to be rich. He also wanted to be a leader: he talked of becoming the prime minister of Japan one day and stood regularly for election as the president of the student body. However, he was always defeated in the school elections because everyone was afraid of him. He used the fear that he engendered in the other students to extort money from them and had amassed the equivalent of over £20,000 by the time that he left high school. He planned to go on to study at the prestigious Tokyo University but failed the entrance exam. It was a terrible setback and he instead went to work in a massage parlour, where he was arrested for hitting a fellow employee.

Soon afterwards, he met a pretty, college-educated girl called Tomoko. They married in January 1978. Six months later, the first of their six children was born. With money from Tomoko's family, Chizuo set up the Matsumoto Acupuncture Clinic. It prospered and Chizuo branched out into quack remedies. He began marketing what he called 'Almighty Medicine' at the equivalent of £5,000 for a three-week course (the 'medicine' later proved to be merely tangerine peel dowsed in alcohol). Dressed in a white coat, with a stethoscope around his neck, Chizuo touted his wares around Tokyo's posher hotels. He convinced elderly people that he could cure rheumatism, but the police were not so sure. In 1982 they arrested him for fraud. He was fined the equivalent of £625 – small beer compared to the £125,000 that he had made from the scam.

Although he was now making more money than his father had ever dreamed of, something was missing: Chizuo yearned for some spiritual dimension to his life. He was not alone – millions of other young Japanese people who had grown up with Japan's booming, post-war economy were also searching for enlightenment.

Chizuo began taking an interest in all forms of mysticism, from fortune-telling to geomancy. And he began performing bizarre experiments, burying food and magnets around his home which, he believed, gave him the psychic power to read other people's auras. He joined a religious cult called the Agonshu. Although essentially a Buddhist sect, the Agonshu had its own satellite-TV station, which it used, it said, to beam out 'healing power'. Its followers could develop their psychic powers, it claimed, if they severed all contact with their families.

Chizuo seized the opportunity to embark on his own spiritual voyage. He meditated for 40 minutes a day for 1,000 days and emerged enlightened. In 1984 he registered Aum Inc – Aum being named after the Hindu mantra *om* – and opened his own, one-room yoga school, which sold his concoctions as a sideline. It was called the Aum Association of Mountain Wizards and offered a haven from the stress of the relentless pace of Tokyo life. The pressures of work meant that many young people in Japan had been brought up scarcely seeing their parents and although Chizuo was only 29 he became the father that they had never had.

Ever eager to enhance his spiritual powers, Chizuo set off for the Himalayas to walk the same path as Buddha. There he claimed to have discovered visionary powers which enabled him to read people's minds and to see their past lives. In the future, he believed, he would be able to fly.

When Chizuo returned to Japan, he told the cult magazine *Twilight Zone* that he was a messiah and claimed that he could levitate for three seconds, though his flight capability was increasing all the time. In fact, his levitation was a simply yogic trick, but a photographer managed to catch him on film in mid-hover and the magazine ran the picture. The attendance at his yoga school consequently rocketed and soon he opened a chain of schools across Japan.

Up until this point Chizuo was probably merely a conman, but then his dark side began to assert itself. He claimed that a mystic whom he had met while he was in the mountains had told him that Armageddon was coming at the end of the twentieth century. Then, while he was meditating, a voice had come to him, telling him that God had chosen him to be the leader of God's army. It was now that Chizuo Matsumoto adopted the exotic-sounding name Shoko Asahara.

He began writing books. The first was called *Secrets of Developing Your Supernatural Powers*. In it, the 'Venerable Master' claimed to be able to teach people how to read other people's minds, make their wishes come true, take trips into the fourth dimension, develop X-ray vision and levitate. In order to prove the truth of his claims, Asahara put the picture of him levitating that had been published in *Twilight Zone* on the cover. The advertisement for the book read: 'Spiritual training that doesn't lead to supernatural powers is hogwash!'

Shoko Asahara, leader of the Aum Supreme Truth Cult

With the flood of new recruits that the book brought him, Asahara cranked up his whole operation. The Aum Association of Mountain Wizards became Aum Supreme Truth. His three-day yoga courses, which cost the equivalent of £25, were dropped in favour of a £250 ceremony in which the great guru injected 'divine energy' directly into a follower's head. Followers were also told that straightforward cash donations would aid their spiritual development. And they were asked to give up their time to hand out leaflets advertising Asahara's books.

At the core of the cult was a New Age mixture of Eastern religion and mysticism. The central tenet was the forthcoming apocalypse. Asahara drawing together the Hindu god of destruction, Shiva, Christian ideas of Armageddon, the apocalyptic prophecies of Nostradamus and the Buddhist concept of *mappo* – the time when the world will collapse into chaos. He predicted that Japan would re-arm itself in 1992, sparking World War III. A nuclear holocaust would follow, which would destroy the world in 2003. This catastrophe could be prevented, Asahara told his followers, only if 'Buddhas' – enlightened ones – taught by himself took over every country in the world. He spelt out his vision in more detail in his book *Day of Annihilation*. Even if World War III did come, it would not be the end of the world, he said. Nuclear annihilation was no problem for those who were enlightened. His followers would emerge from the rubble of civilisation as a post-holocaust race of superhumans.

Asahara, it seemed, was well on the way to becoming a superhuman himself. He claimed to be able to meditate for an hour under water without breathing (somehow, however, he neglected to inform the *Guinness Book of Records* of his feat).

The cult began a recruitment drive in every city in Japan, using magazine advertisements, mailshots and telephone marketing. Videos of Asahara were shown at 'truth meetings' – recruiting drives in which recruiters told visitors that they had been initiates in a previous life. Initiation took the form of bizarre rituals. In some, locks of Asahara's hair were boiled up to make tea, which was then drunk. In others, initiates had to drink Asahara's blood and semen. New recruits were then enrolled in expensive courses designed to raise them to new levels of consciousness.

Aum's US branch simply told followers to cleanse themselves by donating large quantities of money to the cult. More money was raised by selling Asahara's beard clippings or his dirty bath water, which he called 'Miracle Pond'. When the supply failed to meet the demand, Asahara instead sold tap water; called 'Nectar Water', Asahara explained in his book *Declaring Myself Christ* that he had transformed it into a mysterious fluid that emitted light. It cost a good deal more than ordinary water, of course.

In 1988 Aum set up its headquarters in a compound on the slopes of Mount Fuji. Followers paid the equivalent of £1,250 to attend week-long seminars held there. They slept on the floor and ate one bowl of boiled vegetables a day, drinking filthy, stagnant water that had been blessed by Asahara. The rotund guru himself kept up his strength with massive meals consisting of the finest foods.

He told his followers that they would have to cut their ties with their families in order to discover the truth. Those who had brought children were separated from them. Any child who was unfortunate enough to be born in the Aum compound was not given a name, only a designation letter. The children received no formal education and were left to their own devices in the most squalid of conditions; they were, however, taught to admire Hitler.

Followers were told that the price of truth was to surrender everything that they owned to the cult. They had to divulge the details of their bank accounts and PIN numbers. Once inside the cult, they were cut off from the outside world. Letters went unanswered. Recruits were given new names and deprived of sleep, making them highly suggestible. Asahara made no secret of the fact that he was using brainwashing techniques, justifying himself on the grounds that he was the 'spiritual dictator of the world'.

In Asahara's philosophy, pleasure – the pleasure of his followers, at least – was bad karma. That's why they got such rotten food and lived under such harsh conditions. The smallest act of disobedience would be punished with a beating. More serious offenders were locked in tiny cells, with a video of Asahara being played at maximum volume, 24 hours a day. Or else they would find themselves in solitary confinement, in pitch darkness, and were forced to fast for a week. Children as young as ten were punished in this way. Devotees were forbidden to have sex. Anyone who did was forced to wear a dog collar and beg for scraps, or was hung by the feet at their master's pleasure. Masturbation was punished with a week's solitary confinement.

Strangely enough, this treatment did not seem to put anyone off. Soon Asahara was making so much money that he was investing his profits on Tokyo's buoyant stock exchange. He applied for Aum Supreme Truth to receive religious status, which would have given him substantial tax exemptions. But the authorities were worried by complaints from the parents of some of his followers, who said that the cult had robbed them of their children, and did not comply. Asahara then began a campaign of protests, lawsuits and the hounding of government officials. The authorities crumbled and gave him his tax exemption.

The press next tried to take him on. Taro Maki, the editor of *Sunday Mainichi*, began running a series of exposés on Asahara and Aum. Asahara struck back with a book called *The Insanity of the* Sunday Mainichi: *Taro Maki's Ambitions*. The *Mainichi*'s offices and the neighbourhood around Maki's home were furthermore plastered with fliers defaming him, and Maki's family was harassed by late-night phone calls. But the police were afraid to act against Asahara. Buddhism had been suppressed before World War II, and any move against a quasi-Buddhist organisation, it was felt, would be seen as a return to the bad old days.

Asahara claimed that Aum was the fastest-growing religion in the history of Japan, with some justification. Young people were particularly attracted to it. The cult's stern code of discipline emulated the rigid school system in which they had been brought up. And Asahara's apocalyptic vision echoed the fantasy world that they knew from computer games, cartoons and ultra-violent comics. Young scientists dropped out of university in their droves in order to join Aum, which seemed to offer a spiritual dimension beyond the rigid materialism that they had been taught.

Hideo Murai, a brilliant astrophysicist and computer programmer, left a highly paid job in the R&D programme of Kobe Steel to become Aum's chief scientist. He saw parallels between Aum and Isaac Asimov's *Foundation* series. Asahara had been hooked up to a faulty EEG machine and had been shown to have been 'brain dead: the machine registered little or no brain activity. Asahara argued that this was a good thing, because with no brainwaves of his own he could absorb other peoples'. In other words, he could read their minds. Within Aum, Murai developed electrical caps that gave the wearer an unpleasant shock every few seconds. The caps were supposed to synchronise the wearer's brainwaves with those of the master. This process was called the PSI – 'Perfect Salvation Initiation'. Caps were given out free to members of Asahara's inner circle, who rented or sold them to others at extortionate prices. Children had to wear PSI caps, too, and were punished if they removed them. Other machines were similarly developed to be sold to the gullible.

Things were becoming decidedly wacky, and when one of Asahara's followers expressed a wish to leave the cult the guru took exception and had him dunked in freezing water in order to remove the heat from his head that was plainly clouding his judgement. The unfortunate died from hypothermia. A fellow follower was appalled by this. Although he tried to keep his misgivings to himself, after a gruelling interrogation he, too, confessed that he wanted to leave. There was a struggle and the man's neck was broken. Asahara ordered his body to be burnt and the ashes scattered. Fearing for their son's safety, the dead man's parents contacted the police. A search found nothing.

When a young lawyer named Tsutumi Sakamoto took up the case of 23 families who had lost children to the cult, Asahara ordered that he should be killed. His top aides, including Murai, accordingly murdered not just Sakamoto, but also his wife and baby son. Their bodies were buried in remote graves, their teeth having been smashed so that they could not be identified from dental records. When the job was done, Asahara reminded his henchmen that the punishment for murder under Japanese law was death. If anyone betrayed the group they would all die together.

Soon afterwards, Asahara went to the recently reunited Germany to establish a branch of Aum. He was greeted by members of the government. But Taro Maki sent a *Mainichi* reporter after Asahara. At a press conference in Germany the reporter accused Asahara of murdering Sakamoto. Asahara replied 'If I was going to kill someone, I would kill Mr Maki.'

But the evidence of its involvement in the Sakamoto murders was stacking up against Aum. A cult badge was found at the scene of the crime. Only a hundred had been made. Asahara quickly put them into mass production and marketed them across Japan. Then he ordered the killers to burn off their fingerprints.

Asahara still nursed his ambition to become prime minister of Japan. In 1990 he and 25 of his followers ran for parliament. This was not as strange as it sounds. A secretive Buddhist sect called Soka Gakkai, which

had been formed during the 1930s, had begun to come to political promi-
nence during the 1960s, aided by the Japanese law that limits the investigation of religious organisations. By the 1990s, now calling itself the Clean
Government Party, it had 63 seats in parliament. In 1994 it merged with the
New Frontier Party and effectively held the balance of power.

Aum spent the equivalent of £5 million on the electoral race and used
every dirty trick in the book, but Asahara was still trounced at the polls.
Voters were understandably fazed by the fact that they were not voting for
26 different candidates, but for one – Asahara – 26 times over (the other
Aum candidates all wore Asahara masks). Asahara had been predicting his
biggest victory to date and this was his first real setback. Polling figures revealed that not even all of his own followers had voted for him. Perhaps
worse still, their electioneering had brought many of his followers into contact with the real world again. A number of his top aides defected; one even
took the equivalent of £1 million of Aum funds with him as his 'golden
handshake'.

The morale of those left behind was sorely dented. But Asahara was
not downhearted: if the Japanese electors did not know what was good for
them he would have to take more extreme measures. While Asahara
preached, in his Buddhist way, that killing cockroaches was bad karma, he
promised that killing the enemies of Aum – and despatching them to hell
– would take believers one step closer to nirvana. His young followers took
him seriously and began to discuss the possibility of producing a variety of
hi-tech weaponry.

Asahara himself favoured weapons of mass destruction. He had long
been predicting the apocalypse, and instigating biological warfare seemed
one way in which he could manufacture an Armageddon of his own. After
a world-wide trawl of the available literature in the field, Aum scientists
began cultivating the botulism bacterium, which is 16 million times more
toxic than strychnine. Apart from radioactive isotopes, it is the most toxic
substance known to humanity.

While Asahara and his aides went on a much-publicised retreat for a
comet-watching seminar on the remote island of Ishigaki, his followers
sprayed the parliament building in Tokyo with botulism. Asahara had
thereby aimed to wipe out the government of Japan in a single stroke. It
did not work. Sloppy cultivation had killed the bacteria and the Japanese
government survived unharmed. Although this was another setback, it
was not a total disaster: the retreat had attracted thousands of new followers and Asahara netted the equivalent of over £1.2 million.

He began to plan to expand Aum world-wide. His first stop was India, but the people there had seen too many gurus before and were not impressed when Asahara declared himself to be the Buddha. He also had dealings in Laos and North Korea, but had the greatest success in the former Soviet Union. Broadcasting twice daily on the state-owned Radio Moscow – a privilege that he paid the equivalent of £500,000 a year for – he soon had three times as many followers in Russia than he had in Japan. They were organised by Kiyohide Hayakawa, Aum's chief engineer, whom many cult followers believed was the real power behind the throne. His book, *Principles of a Citizen's Utopia*, was a declaration of war on the Japanese state. Hayakawa used Aum's Russian operation to recruit military scientists, buy weapons and get himself some badly needed military training.

Back in Japan, Aum founded a hospital, whose patients were subject to the tender mercies of the cardiovascular surgeon Dr Ikuo Hayashi. He had joined the cult following a car crash. He had fallen asleep at the wheel and the resulting accident put a mother and daughter in hospital. He then became depressed and turned to the sect for help. Soon he was putting the bizarre treatments recommended by Asahara – such as swallowing hot water or string and jumping – into practice on his heart patients. The hospital where he worked had to let him go.

Asahara set up a clinic that Hayashi and his wife, Rira, an anaesthesiologist, ran. During just eighteen months nine people died in the clinic – a remarkably high mortality rate when you consider that the clinic only had nine beds. Asahara claimed that the death rate was high because the clinic took in a large proportion of terminal cases. Hayashi blamed it on a mysterious force. But there was nothing mysterious about it: the place was filthy and home to numerous cockroaches, which the staff refused to killed because of the Buddhist injunction against taking life. The nurses were ignorant of the most elementary rules of hygiene and one dead patient was left unattended in the ward for a week. For his part, Dr Hayashi prescribed odd Aum treatments, including dropping severely ill patients into baths of scalding water. (Dr Hayashi also experimented with mind control. He would implant electrodes into cult members' heads and administer powerful electric shocks that often resulted in memory loss.)

Patients' families were not allowed to visit them and they were pressurised into joining Aum, being told that they would only be cured if they gave all of their worldly goods to the sect. If that failed, patients' signatures would be forged on freshly drawn-up wills and other documents, and their condition would subsequently deteriorate rapidly.

Running a hospital also gave the cult access to drugs, which were used to endow initiates with mystical experiences or to induce paranoia, with which to scare the uncertain into joining Aum. Asahara himself became a frequent user of LSD, which did little to help his mental stability.

Asahara suddenly advanced the schedule for the apocalypse: it would now occur in 1997, he said. The cult's scientists were exhorted to speed up their production of weapons of mass destruction before Japan was wiped out by the Americans in a sneak nuclear attack. As they had failed to make a biological weapon, the Aum scientists tried their hand at producing chemical ones. The nerve gas sarin was chosen because it was both easy to produce and could kill vast numbers. The scientists built a chemical plant at which to mass-produce sarin in the Mount Fuji compound.

Asahara was interested in small arms, too. He bought a failing engineering works, looted its machine tools and bankrupted the company. The tools were taken to Mount Fuji, where, in Aum's new factories, Hayakawa and Murai aimed to mass-produce AK-74s – the successors to the famous Kalashnikov AK-47, the world's most popular assault rifle. Laser- and nuclear-weapons' programmes were also started.

All of this activity was funded by Asahara's other business acquisitions. The Aum empire was now so large that it was listed on the Tokyo stock exchange. Aum had opened a chain of computer shops, fast-food restaurants, beauty salons, coffee shops, dating agencies, construction companies and on-line services. Asahara's aim was to build not just an army, but also an alternative society. These businesses brought in huge amounts of money, which was no big trick as they were staffed by Aum members who received no wages. They also acted as recruiting centres. Cut-price financing hooked the unwary. In order to pay off what they owed, debtors simply had to join Aum and hand over all of their worldly goods. And being a religious corporation, Aum was exempt from tax. The business could not fail. By 1995 Aum was a billion-dollar enterprise.

While the cult's followers lived on practically nothing, Asahara enjoyed a luxurious lifestyle, running a fleet of Rolls-Royces and Mercedes-Benzes. The collapse of property prices in Japan furthermore meant that the sect could go on expanding.

Aum attempted another biological *coup d'état* by spraying botulism into the atmosphere at the wedding of Prince Naruhito in 1993. It again failed, so the Aum scientists turned to anthrax. As an experiment, Aum's chief microbiologist, Seiichi Endo, pumped a mist of anthrax spores out of the eighth-floor laboratory of the Aum building in eastern Tokyo. Neighbours complained of the stench and lost their appetite; pets grew sick and small birds died. Fortunately, the spores had not been incubated properly before they were released and there were no human fatalities.

However, anthrax spores can live in the soil for decades, so it is still possible that there could be a deadly outbreak of the disease.

But for the moment anthrax, along with botulism, had failed as a weapon of mass destruction, so teams of Aum members were despatched to Zaïre in search of the deadly ebola virus. Meanwhile, Aum was stockpiling hundreds of tons of chemicals for use in its chemical-weapons programme.

While Aum scientists worked on laser and microwave weapons, security at the Aum compounds was tightened. Beatings became more frequent and the treatment of ill and older people became more inhumane. Soon followers were simply disappearing: bodies were incinerated in giant microwave ovens; the remains were treated with nitric acid and flushed down the sewers. And Aum hit squads set out to murder or abduct any former members of the cult who were now working against it.

By the end of 1993 Aum's multi-million chemical plant had been completed. Using a method that the cult had learned in the former Soviet Union, Aum's chief chemist, Masami Tsuchiya, began synthesising sarin. Asahara, who was now complaining about being sprayed with nerve gas from helicopters and planes, wanted 70 tons of sarin – enough to kill millions of people – plus a stockpile of other deadly nerve gases.

Having failed to purchase a nuclear bomb in Russia, Hayakawa headed for Australia, where he bought a ranch and began mining for uranium. The operation was eventually closed down by the Australian authorities, who were appalled by the careless way in which Aum members carried lethal chemicals on commercial airlines and who had quickly marked Asahara and his henchmen as undesirables. But the closure did not occur before the scientists had tested Tsuchiya's sarin on a flock of sheep. One of the believers was shocked, pointing out that killing animals contravened the precepts of Buddhism. She was reassured by the chief chemist, who told her that all further tests would be carried out on human beings.

In the towns where Aum had compounds, it was not popular. Followers played mantras at full blast all the time, paraded through the streets in their white robes and polluted the neighbourhood with toxic waste. And locals grew sick of being questioned constantly by distraught parents who were looking for their missing children. In Matsumoto, a front company had been used to buy a plot of land for Aum. When the local residents found out what was really going on they complained, only to be subjected to a campaign of harassment. The man who had sold it the land took Aum to court for making the purchase under false pretences. Asahara decided to launch a nerve-gas attack on the courthouse and thus to kill the three judges who were deciding the case.

On 27 June 1994 a converted refrigeration truck full of nerve gas turned up at the courthouse in Matsumoto, but the court had already risen for the day. The truck then drove to the residential area where the judges lived and pumped out a cloud of sarin gas. However, the wind changed suddenly and the judges did not die, although they became critically ill. Eight other people were killed, however, and more than two hundred were hospitalised. The sarin had not been prepared properly, otherwise many more would have suffered an agonising death.

The police found chemicals in the house of one of the victims and arrested him. He protested that he was an amateur photographer and used them for his hobby. Even though the poor man had been hospitalised – along with his two daughters and his wife, who had lapsed into an irreversible coma – he was vilified by the media and his neighbours as 'Dr Gas'. However, one person was more understanding: 'His Holiness, the Master Shoko Asahara' sent a package of books and invited him to bring his wife for free treatment at the Aum hospital.

The media also received a package. It was from an anonymous informant who blamed Aum for the attack and warned of a future attempt – perhaps on a crowded subway. On numerous occasions Asahara publicly mentioned sarin in his sermons, but no one took any notice. An even more glaring clue as to Asahara's intentions was a gas leak at the Aum facility at Kamikuishi, which injured a number of cult members just two weeks after the Matsumoto attack. When the emergency services turned up they found dangerous chemicals strewn all over the place, but Aum guards quickly ejected them. A week later, another leak killed all the plants nearby. Still nothing was done.

Aum scientists began making dynamite, and even bought supplies of materiel from the US Department of Defense. Aum purchased two remote-control helicopters – designed to photograph inside the craters of volcanoes – as a delivery system for the sarin. Two inexperienced operators crashed the drones within minutes of their delivery, however.

Despite such instances of ineptitude, Asahara decided that they were now armed sufficiently and started to train an army. He sent young female believers to the bars that were frequented by members of Japan's Self-defence Force (SDF) to recruit new members. SDF veterans were then used to train Aum members in remote camps. Aum troops were told that their army would be armed with superweapons: plasma guns that would vaporise anything in their path, satellites that would reflect searing beams of sunlight down onto their enemies and bombs that would consume all the oxygen in the atmosphere. If true believers had been following the meditation techniques taught by Asahara they would, of course survive these terrors, he promised. (Although these weapons may sound far-fetched, a team of Aum scientists had actually built a working prototype of an electromagnetic rail gun, the weapon with which the USA had planned to knock out any incoming nuclear warheads in the 'Star Wars' Strategic Defense Initiative.)

In preparation for his *Putsch*, Asahara wrote a constitution for his projected new 'Supreme State' and organised a shadow government, including ministries of health and welfare, justice, science and technology, as well as a ministry of construction with which to supervise the reconstruction of the post-apocalyptic Japan. At the head of it all was the 'Holy Monk Emperor', Asahara himself.

The 'Holy Monk Emperor' claimed that he was above all earthly desires. But that did not stop him from having sex. He did not enjoy it, of course, but felt that it was his duty to initiate the young girls who joined the sect, he said. In his quarters was a bath that took nine at a time. When his closest aide gave birth to twins, he replaced her with a 17-year-old who rose rapidly up the executive ladder.

As well as producing chemical weapons, small arms and dynamite, Aum plants were manufacturing massive amounts of drugs – LSD, mescaline, PCP or angel dust, methamphetamine and 'truth serum'. These were used to recruit members, control the intransigent, brainwash the independently minded and – along with 1960s'-style light shows and loud music – give initiates 'mystical experiences'. Every cult member was in a permanent, narcotic-induced haze and Aum was producing so many drugs that it began selling the surplus to Japan's Mafia, the *yakuza*.

The conduit was two former *yakuza* bosses who had joined Aum. One of them, Kiyohide Nakada, bought guns from the Mafia and utilised the expertise of Mafia gunsmiths at the Aum small-arms plant. He also recruited rightist *yakuza* gangs to fight alongside Aum against the Japanese state. The *yakuza* members were furthermore employed to kill cult members or their families for their life assurance or inheritances. Aum reaped millions in this way, while the *yakuza* was used for debt collection and to keep complaining neighbours quiet.

The other former *yakuza* boss, Tomomitsu Niimi, became Aum's 'Minister of Home Affairs', responsible for security. He maintained discipline within the cult with a rod of iron. Devotees could even be punished for having the wrong blood type. Increasingly, the punishments meted out by Niimi resulted in death.

Those who had fled the cult and would not return, as well as relatives of members who had money, were abducted by Niimi's snatch squads. Some disillusioned cult members did manage to report what they knew to the police, but the police were pitifully inadequate when it came to handling the situation. Japan had no national police force, only local forces which were more used to enforcing minor city ordinances than investigating major crimes.

The feeble National Police Agency (NPA), which was supposed to oversee the local forces, was, however, forced into action when phosgene gas was pumped into the flat of Shogo Egawa, a journalist who had set out to investigate Aum. NPA agents surreptitiously took samples of the soil and vegetation around Aum's Mount Fuji compound looking for chemicals. A police informer was sent to the compound. He later he collapsed in the street and died; he had been given an injection of the lethal nerve gas VX. Aum had already infiltrated the police, so it had known that he was coming.

Aum's own 'ministry of intelligence' also infiltrated other government organisations. It recruited members from those who held sensitive posts, planned the kidnapping of the families of men in important positions and staged daring, intelligence-gathering raids. Some high-ranking civil servants were cult members. Aum also had members in the judiciary and the armed forces, who leaked classified material to them. Members working in industry handed over details of the latest laser and nuclear technology to Aum simply by copying sensitive computer files to discs and then giving them to the cult. Cult spies stole data on explosives, rocket propulsion and laser-guidance systems. Army commanders were bugged. For years, Aum members dressed as telephone engineers tapped phones, something that the NPA was reluctant to do.

Aum's Russian branch became increasingly important to the cult. The AK-74s were now coming off the production line and Aum had a growing number of troops who were trained to use them. The former Soviet Union was their sole source of heavy military equipment, however. Aum bought a military helicopter in Chechnya and had it shipped in parts to Japan, but Aum technicians failed to reassemble it. And a nuclear bomb was still on Aum's shopping list.

Yet an orthodox priest had now managed to infiltrate the organisation and was exploiting the disillusionment among the cult's members. The suicides of two cult members had furthermore generated a great deal of bad publicity. Although Russian members were subdued with drugs and brainwashed during gruelling initiation rites in which they had to eat their own vomit, they grew scared of the amount of chemicals – particularly phosgene – that were being stored in their headquarters and began to desert the cult. The Russian branch was damaged further when Aum's 120-strong orchestra escaped the guru's clutches. (Its members had been employed to play music that Asahara said that he had heard in another dimension, which he hummed to them. Their master's mystical music turned out to be a collection of snatches stolen from Beethoven and Tchaikovsky.) The orchestra's members were imprisoned in the cult's Mount Fuji compound, starved of food and put through an induction programme that involved drugs and vibrating mattresses. Fearing that they were going to be gassed, two members escaped and managed to telephone the Russian embassy in Tokyo. Reluctantly, Asahara was forced to let the orchestra go.

Sarin was now being manufactured by the ton, and the Aum members who made it, like other Japanese factory workers, sang a 'company' song praising the product that they were producing. Then, in January 1995, production had to stop. The newspapers were carrying stories that sarin had been found in the samples of topsoil that the police had taken from around the Mount Fuji compound. This linked Aum with the gas attack at Matsumoto. The chemical factory was quickly transformed into a shrine and the media were invited to inspect it. Explaining the presence of sarin in the soil around the compound, an Aum spokesman said that the government had been spraying the cult with it. Asahara compared this alleged action to the FBI's attack on David Koresh's Branch Davidians at Ranch Apocalypse in 1993 and said that he himself was dying from the effects of mustard gas having been sprayed at him by the Japanese government. Aum also sued the head of a local fertiliser factory for spraying sarin and other chemicals on its members.

Aum next published lists of its prominent enemies, starting with Emperor Akihito, President Clinton and Madonna; Freemasons and Jews were also denounced. A private hit list was prepared, too. Rival gurus were killed with VX.

The Kobe earthquake occurred in January 1995, as well. Just as he had predicted, this was the beginning of the end, Asahara said, and quickly published a book, *Disaster Nears for the Land of the Rising Sun*, to tell the world so. A flier advertising the book asked where disaster would strike next. On the back of the flier was a map of the Tokyo underground system. The Kobe earthquake had been triggered electromagnetically by the US military, Aum scientists claimed. Murai accordingly set about trying to devise his own 'earthquake machine'. Meanwhile, Asahara upped production at the cult's firearm and explosives factories.

Security was tightened still further. People who wanted to leave the cult were locked in tiny metal containers, so small that they could not even sit up. Those who posed a security risk were tortured to the point at which they were turned into vegetables. When one leading donor escaped, her brother, a public notary, was abducted and killed. Aum was blamed for his death and the Tokyo Metropolitan Police Force (TMPF) – the country's elite – now felt compelled to act.

But Aum planned a pre-emptive strike against the police and mounted a laser on a truck, planning thereby to attack the TMPF's headquarters. The laser was not powerful enough to do any damage to the building; the aim was instead to blind a large number of police. However, the laser gun broke down, so gas attacks were now planned.

On 5 March 1995 Aum carried out a practice attack on a Tokyo underground train. It took place at midnight, when the train was the least crowded; nevertheless, 11 people were hospitalised. On 15 March an attack was launched on Kasumigaseki Station using biological weapons. As well as being home to the Japanese government, the Kasumigaseki area of Tokyo also boasted the building that housed both the headquarters of the TMPF and the National Police Agency. Again the biological weapons failed.

The TMPF's plans were now well advanced: it had borrowed gas masks and anti-chemical-and-biological warfare suits from the army and was preparing a simultaneous raid on all the Aum facilities in Japan on 20 March.

But Aum had its plans, too. By travelling the subway, its members realised that they could release sarin on six trains that would arrive at Kasumigaseki Station within minutes of each other, just precisely the time when the most police would be arriving for work. Hundreds, perhaps thousands, of commuters would also be killed.

While Aum members were warned of the impending attack by the TMPF on the Internet, the police in Osaka jumped the gun and arrested four cultists who were suspected of being involved in an abduction. Fearing that the sect had been alerted to its plans, the TMPF postponed its raids.

Aum members were now making their final preparations for the sarin attack. They sent out a loudspeaker van denouncing Aum in the name of the rival cult Science of Happiness. They also staged a firebomb attack on Aum's Tokyo headquarters, leaving behind a number of Science of Happiness leaflets. For good measure, Aum slapped a writ on Science of Happiness for defamation.

At the Mount Fuji compound, bags of sarin solution were prepared, while the hit squad practised piercing similar bags filled with water. Then each attacker took a pill made up of the sarin antidote, pyridine aldozine methioxide or PAM. They were given their final briefing in front of an image of Shiva, the Hindu god of destruction. At the last moment one of them dropped out, so that in the event only five trains were hit, instead of six.

The first that anyone knew of the gas attack was when a passenger pushed the emergency button on a train at Tsukiji, four stops before Kasumigaseki. Three people collapsed on the train, five on the platform. More escaping passengers collapsed in the streets outside. The victims were eerily silent: the sarin had paralysed their larynxes, then their lungs.

On the Hibiya line there was full-scale panic at the station before Kasumigaseki. Although the victims stumbled, or were carried, off the train, it pulled out of the station and was only halted when it reached Kasumigaseki. A leaking package on the train on the Chiyoda line was removed by two members of staff, who subsequently died. The train was evacuated at the next station.

The train on the Marunouchi line was also allowed to continue after the first victim had been helped from the train by staff. Another victim collapsed at the next station. The station-master and his assistant removed the suspect package and the train was allowed to continue. They, too, fell ill and by the time that the train was stopped one person was dead and hundreds had been injured. A station-master removed the sarin package from the train travelling in the other direction on the Marunouchi line with a dustpan and brush, but only after it had travelled through Kasumigaseki, had reached the end of the line and was on its way back. It passed through Kasumigaseki three times before the subway system was closed down at 9.30am, one hour and twenty minutes after the first victims had collapsed.

At first the word spread that there had been some sort of explosion on the underground, and hospitals began to receive burn victims. They were completely baffled by the symptoms of the victims who were coming into the emergency rooms. It was only at 10.30am that a military doctor recognised the symptoms of nerve gas, and PAM was prescribed. By that time some of the doctors and nurses were also developing symptoms, and patients' clothes were therefore burnt in case they carried traces of the gas.

As the death toll mounted, it became clear that the victims were not the police or government officials that the cultists had been targeting. They were ordinary commuters. Asahara told the killers that this was not important: Aum had simply given the dead the opportunity of moving on to a higher spiritual level. To those outside the cult, the arbitrary nature of the attack made it all the more frightening.

Aum was immediate suspected of perpetrating the attacks. Its leaders vigorously denied it. They were Buddhists, they said, and consequently could have nothing to do with killing. They pointed out that sarin could only be made by experts – like those in the US Army. Aum spokesmen also accused the Japanese government of carrying out the attacks in order to smear the sect.

Meanwhile, Aum's stockpiles of gas and chemicals were disposed of, weapons were melted down and machinery dismantled. Aum's key personnel went into hiding. Documents and membership lists were destroyed. And Asahara disappeared.

Aum was forewarned of the police raid on the Mount Fuji compound two days after the gas attack. A thousand police in riot gear burst in soon after dawn. They found people who had been incarcerated and starved and others who were too drugged to speak. Malnourished children were released, many wearing electrode caps. In a basement the ashes of numerous murder victims were discovered. The chemicals had not been concealed well, and from what they found the police reckoned that Aum was capable of making enough sarin to kill 4 million people. They kept quiet about the biological weapons that they discovered, however, fearing that the news would cause nation-wide panic.

The cult continued to deny everything and filed a suit against the police for the equivalent of £200,000 in damages. In a video broadcast on Japanese TV, Asahara accused the USA of trying to gas him and his followers. Meanwhile, the sales of gas masks rocketed, as did those of the book *Deadly Perfume*, a science-fiction novel about gas attacks on the Paris Metro and London Underground. Subway systems around the world went on the alert.

Hundreds of police raided other Aum premises across Japan and began to track down Aum safe houses. Aum's offices in New York were searched and the Russian branch was closed down, with the cult being ordered to pay the equivalent of £2.5 million in compensation to the parents of members.

Then the cult struck back. The head of the National Police Agency, who was in charge of the investigation, was shot outside his apartment building. This inflamed the police, who plastered Japan with wanted posters and instigated a nation-wide dragnet for the cult's leaders. Soon many were behind bars. None, however, were charged with the sarin attack; they were all held on other charges, usually of false imprisonment, harbouring suspects or even minor traffic violations. But Asahara was still at large. He even managed to publish a new book, *The Pity of a Ruinous Nation – Japan*. It warned of another 'horrible event' soon to hit Tokyo that would 'make the Kobe earthquake seem as minor as a fly landing on your face'. The event, he said, would occur on 15 April 1995.

The threat alone was enough to paralyse the city, but the day passed without event. Four days later, however, there was a gas attack on the

Yokohama subway, which hospitalised six-hundred people. Yet the perpetrator was not an Aum member. He was a small-time gangster with 'personal problems' who had used mace. Two days after that there was another gas attack in Yokohama. The whole of Japan was soon in the grip of paranoia concerning gas attacks.

While the police grew increasingly frustrated, the *yakuza* took action. It purged Aum members from its ranks and a *yakuza* hitman stabbed the cult's chief scientist, Hideo Murai, to death in front of a TV camera outside Aum's Tokyo headquarters. Fumihiro Joyu, the former head of Aum's Russian branch, then became the public face of the cult. His purple pyjamas and slender good looks quickly turned him into a sex symbol, and young women flocked to Aum's headquarters in the hope of catching a glimpse of him.

The cult's children were taken into protective custody and gradually deprogrammed. Many disillusioned members left the cult, but some accepted Aum's propaganda that it had been framed by the authorities. By the end of April no cult member had yet been charged with any sarin-related offence. Aum went on the offensive, demanding that the police issue a report of their investigations. It also issued a writ suing a newspaper for linking the cult's name with the Matsumoto attack.

On 5 May 1995 a package left in the toilets at Shinjuki underground station in Tokyo burst into flames and started belching noxious flumes. Fire-fighters wearing breathing apparatus quickly extinguished it. It was a national holiday and the station was packed. The packet was found to contain sulphuric acid and sodium cyanide, which, when mixed, produce hydrogen cyanide (hydrogen cyanide had once been marketed under the tradename Zyklon B, the gas that had been used in the Nazi death camps). The packet had been placed so that the station's ventilation system would blow the deadly gas over the nearby platform and thus kill an estimated 20,000 people, but fortunately the fire brigade had managed to extinguish it first.

All this time the police knew where Asahara was: he was holed up in a secret hideaway in the Mount Fuji compound. Yet they did not arrest him. First they wanted to round up the rest of his henchmen and build up a cast-iron case against Aum. When they finally arrested him, on 16 May, they did so in a blaze of publicity, with the TV networks being on hand to broadcast the event live. The image of the purple-robed Asahara being led out of the compound was displayed on the huge TV screens that grace the sides of buildings in Tokyo. The following morning a letter bomb arrived at the office of the governor of Tokyo, maiming the secretary who had opened it. The perpetrator had already been arrested.

Asahara was accused of being the mastermind behind the sarin attack. He denied it, asking how he, a blind man, could have done such a thing. Nor had he ordered his followers to make sarin, he said, but there were so many of them that he could not know about everything that they got up to. Some of Asahara's followers regarded this statement as an act of betrayal, and when four more failed cyanide attacks were made on the Tokyo subway jailed cultists revealed where the final caches of sodium cyanide and sarin were hidden.

Over 350 cult members were arrested, although nearly half of them were later released. Aum's leadership was charged with the production of illegal drugs, kidnapping and murder. Asahara himself was served with ten indictments, including twenty-three counts of murder.

The cult had been deprived of its leader and many of the cultists left Aum. The cult's religious status was lifted, its bank accounts were seized and Aum was ordered to pay the equivalent of £4.8 million in compensation to its victims. But still the murderous cult has not been banned and Aum Supreme Truth still soldiers on. It runs a chain of shops across Japan, selling computers and cult memorabilia, and it attempts to recruit new members via the Internet. An anonymous programmer has even written a computer game called Kasumigaseki, which is based on the sarin attack on the Kasumigaseki subway station.

The trial of Asahara is set to run for years. The police remain reluctant to investigate Aum's activities. The cult's stores keep its coffers well lined. An Aum band, called Perfect Enlightenment, performs songs using Asahara's words as lyrics and recruits to Aum's meditation centres meditate in front of Asahara's image.

2 ❖ Cults of the ancient world

Cults existed long before the great religions that we know today. In primitive, hunter-gather societies, people venerated the animals that they hunted because their lives depended on them. Cultic shamans would dress in animal skins and act out the chase. And in sacred caves, far from their normal dwellings, primitive artists painted anthropomorphic images of the animals that they worshipped. When people settled down in early agricultural communities, they venerated the gods of weather, who brought them rain for their crops, and the plants that provided them with food.

The cult of the tree

The cult of the tree spread across the ancient world. One branch of the cult was represented by the ancient Druids, who worshipped the oak whose acorns were ground to produce flour.

The cult of the tree reached its apotheosis in the ninth century BC, in ancient Mesopotamia. In 884 BC the bloodthirsty tyrant Ashurnasirpal II became emperor of Assyria. He used captives taken from his ever-expanding empire to rebuild the city of Calah, now Nimrud in Iraq, and made it his capital. On the surviving walls of his great palace are murals that tell the story of his numerous military campaigns. Several panels depict Ashurnasirpal, who considered himself to be the most powerful man in the world, on his knees before a tree. It is thought that the tree represented the goddess of fertility, and Ashurnasirpal was sometimes portrayed approaching it with a distinctly phallic-shaped watering can.

It is not known exactly what form tree worship took, but the Bible calls it the 'unspeakable abomination'. Trees were cut down in the forest and brought to the city, the Bible says. They were nailed upright and decorated with silver and gold. (It seems that this 'unspeakable abomination' is still practised in almost every household across the Christian world on Christmas Eve.) Tree worship continued throughout the Babylonian era and survived in the Middle East for at least two centuries after Christ's birth.

The cult of the dead

In ancient Egypt, the members of the cult of the dead worshipped Osiris, the lord of the underworld who decided which souls would go to paradise. Rites involved ritual ploughing and an annual trip down the Nile to the place where Osiris was supposed to have been murdered. Each year, followers of the cult would bury cloth effigies of the god. They would also unearth the effigy interred in the previous year at a time when the corn would be sprouting. With death comes renewal, seemed to be the message. The cult of the dead had a large female following because Osiris was believed to be virile, even though he was dead – a fact celebrated in the priapic puppets that women cultists carried in procession.

Human sacrifice in Central America

The Egyptian cult of the dead had none of the barbaric aspects associated with the cult of the dead in Central America, where, from the earliest times, the peoples of the region practised human sacrifice. In a cave in the Tehuacán Valley, 100 miles (161km) south-east of Mexico City, the headless corpses of human sacrifices from 7000 BC have been found. Their religion

Osiris, the Lord of the Underworld, who decided which souls would go to paradise

celebrated savagery. Temple artwork often depicts the dismembered body of Coyolxauhqui, the moon goddess who, with her brothers, the 400 stars, plotted to murder their mother, Coatlicue, after she had conceived Huitzilopochtli, the god of war. But when Coatlicue died Huitzilopochtli emerged from her womb fully grown and armed. He slaughtered the stars, killed Coyolxauhqui and dismembered her body. Cosmologically, this myth explains how the sun (Huitzilopochtli) seems to extinguish the stars and the moon. It is also a symbolic model for how the Aztecs suppressed their enemies.

The decoration of the elaborate ball courts found at Veracruz show that the captain of the losing team was sacrificed by the winning captain. Sacrifices were always carried out in the same way: their hearts were cut out of victims' bodies while they were still alive. Sacrifices would take place on top of great, pyramid-shaped temples, using a special sacrificial knife and a bowl in which to hold the heart and blood. The temples also had vast skull racks, where the heads of victims were kept.

The last great civilisation in the region, that of the Aztecs, was the most bloodthirsty of the lot. The Aztecs conducted wars simply to supply their temples with the huge number of human sacrifices that they required. They believed that the sun god would be too tired to rise each morning if he was not nourished by gallons of blood and stacks of fresh human hearts.

When King Ahuitzolt opened the Great Temple at Tenochtitlán, the

Dionysus, the Greek God of wine and ecstasy

Aztec capital, 20,000 captives were sacrificed during the dedication. This was not as cruel as it sounds, as the Aztecs believed that those sacrificed in this way were guaranteed a place in heaven. But when the Spanish witnessed the extent of the butchery during the festival of the Aztec war god Huitzilopochtli they were so terrified that they turned on the Aztecs and slaughtered them and then razed the city of Tenochtitlán to the ground. The modern-day Mexico City is built on its ruins.

The cult of Dionysus

In ancient Greece, the cult of Dionysus was celebrated in a much more life-giving fashion. Dionysus, the Greek god of wine and ecstasy, and the illegitimate son of Zeus, was a lusty fellow. His mother, Semele, the daughter of the king of Thebes, died before he was born. Zeus' jealous wife, Hera, had persuaded Semele to ask Zeus to prove his divinity by revealing himself to her in his true form, whereupon she was killed by a lightning bolt. Zeus then plucked the unborn Dionysus from her womb and implanted it in his thigh in order to carry Dionysus to term. Dionysus is therefore known as the 'twice-born' god.

Hera was still bent on Dionysus' destruction and introduced him to wine when he was a youth. In an effort to save him, the Anatolian mother goddess, Cybele, took him to India, where he was introduced to the joys of sex by satyrs and maenads. When he returned to Greece he introduced drunken orgies.

The cult that surrounded him was popular among women. At festivals, Dionysus was symbolised by a giant, erect phallus. The rites were drunken and often frenzied. Participants were masked to represent nature spirits – and to conceal their identities – and their inhibitions were shed. Bacchus was the Roman equivalent of the Greek Dionysus. Bacchanals became so frenzied that in 186 BC the Roman Senate banned them because they constituted a threat to good order. However, there was a rival to Bacchus in the last days of the Roman Empire.

The cult of Cybele

At the end of the third century BC tree worship came to Rome in the form of the cult of Cybele, the great mother goddess. Her consort – and, in some versions of the myth, her son – was Attis. When Cybele and Attis were to be married his hermaphroditic father, Agdistis, grew jealous and cursed Attis. Attis consequently castrated himself under a sacred pine tree and bled to death. Agdistis was overcome with guilt and persuaded Zeus to prevent Attis' body from decaying.

During Hannibal's invasion of Italy, in 204 BC, the Romans believed the Sibylline prophecy that if they brought the symbol of Cybele – a small, black meteorite – to Rome from the home of her cult in Pessinus, near modern Ankara, victory would be theirs. That is what they did, and Hannibal was defeated in 202 BC.

However, the Romans were horrified by the Cybelline rites that accompanied the stone. Each year, followers cut a pine tree from the forest and erected it in the cult's temple. On the Day of Blood, 24 March, new priests castrated themselves in front of it. Older priests let their blood, while other followers slashed themselves with knives, so that their blood splashed onto the tree. Romans were forbidden to join in, but many enjoyed watching the gory spectacle.

Bull cults

Roman blood sacrifices extended only to bull cults. Initiates would sit in a pit covered with a wooden grating; a bull, adorned with gold, would be sacrificed on the grating, so that its blood splashed over the initiates below, thereby baptising them. This ritual continued until the fourth century AD, when the first Christian emperor, Constantine, banned human and animal sacrifices across the empire.

In Crete, the death of Dionysus – who was torn apart by Titans on the orders of Hera – was commemorated by devotees ripping a live bull to pieces. The heart and other parts of the bull were then eaten; the testicles were particularly prized. In AD 160 a cultist named Carpus carried a pair of bull's testicles from Vatican Hill in Rome to Lyons in Gaul, so that he could present them to the temple of Cybele there.

The most famous bull cult was that of the Minoans in Crete, where the Minotaur – half man, half bull – roamed the labyrinth beneath the palace of King Minos at Knossos. The Minotaur was the son of King Minos' wife, Pasiphae, and a bull that the god Poseidon had sent for Minos to sacrifice; when Minos failed to do so, Poseidon made Pasiphae fall in love with it.

Every nine years the Athenians would send seven young men and seven virgins to Crete as a tribute. They would be locked in the labyrinth for the Minotaur to consume. The Athenian hero Theseus, with the help of King Minos' daughter, Ariadne, eventually killed the Minotaur.

The cult of Mithras

The Roman cult of Mithras sprang out of the ancient Persian religion Zoroastrianism, and involved the worship of the Persian god of light, Ahura Mazda; Mithras was his servant. Membership of the cult was confined to men and it was particularly popular among Roman soldiers. Worship took place in underground shrines in which a sacred fire, representing the sun, was kept burning night and day. Interestingly, the festival of Mithras was celebrated every year on 25 December.

The Essenes

Interest in the Essene cult revived in 1947, when the Dead Sea Scrolls were found in a cave near the headquarters of the cult, which had been abandoned in AD 70. The forerunner of many modern-day cults, the Essenes believed that Armageddon was on its way. In preparation for the Day of Judgement, they took vows of poverty and chastity and withdrew into the desert, away from mainstream Jewish life. There were strict levels of initiation into the cult.

The Essenes believed that they were the sons of light and that, in the final battle, they would be pitched against the sons of darkness. Armageddon would last for 40 years. John the Baptist was almost certainly an Essene, and it is thought that the cult had a considerable influence on early Christianity. Having been formed in around 200 BC, the Essene cult died out in around AD 200.

3 ❖ Early Christian cults

The early Christian Church could itself be thought of as a cult. It was certainly considered so by the Jews and the Romans. As Christianity spread, different ideas began to take hold in different places and soon there were cults within the cult.

The Montanists were the first Christian offshoot to call for a return to the beliefs and practices of the original Catholic Church. They did so in AD 156, only a century and quarter after Christ had died.

In AD 325 the newly converted Emperor Constantine called the Council of Nicaea to hammer out a set of core beliefs that Christians would have to abide by. The first cult to go was Arianism, which taught that only God the Father was God. Although he had created the universe through God the Son, Arianism held, there was a time before that when God the Father was alone and had created God the Son out of nothing. (Arianism remains one of the key elements in the beliefs of Jehovah's Witnesses.)

After the Council of Nicaea the Gnostics were persecuted. The Gnostics emphasised the importance of a direct knowledge of God – *gnosis* is Greek for 'knowledge'. They mixed Christianity with the ideas of Plato and the Zoroastrian belief that the world is made up of opposing forces: light and dark, good and evil, spirit and matter. They also believed that humans were spiritual beings who were forced to dwell in the material world, which they experienced through the senses. But once they had attained the *gnosis*, as revealed by Christ, they could learn to know the ideal world that was inhabited by God. Some Gnostics believed that a state of ecstasy provided divine illumination, others that one could only get there the hard way, through fasting and meditation.

Gnosticism was itself riven by cults. One of the more extreme was represented by the Manichaens, who followed the third century AD heretic Mani (whose name has given us the word 'maniac'). Mani was a follower of Mithras before converting to Christianity. In AD 240, at the court of the Persian king, Shapur I, he developed his own religious philosophy. He followed the Zoroastrians in their belief in a universe that was divided into light and dark and good and evil. Satan, he said, was born out of the darkness and had stolen part of the light – or goodness – from early humans. Mani dedicated himself to the bringing of the light and set out the ways in which he thought that human beings could rid themselves of the darkness.

Mani's followers practised extreme asceticism. They were forbidden to kill any animal or plant for food, and, if possible, they should not break even a single twig.

Mani travelled to India and China to spread the word, but when he got back King Shapur had been replaced by Bahram I. The Zoroastrians opposed Mani's ideas and Bahram had him arrested in AD 276. Mani was crucified and his corpse flayed.

Some cults had strayed so far from mainstream Christianity that they abandoned the idea of a male God, instead identifying a female force behind the universe, which the Greeks called *Sophia* – another Greek work for knowledge.

As the persecution of the Gnostics began, they became an underground sect which employed secret passwords, signs and handshakes with which to identify members. But by AD 500 Gnosticism had disappeared completely. We only know what they believed in because 12 leather-bound books of their writings were unearthed in a cave in Egypt in 1945. The books narrowly escaped destruction when the mother of the two brothers who discovered them began using them to light her stove. Even when it was realised what they contained, knowledge of their existence was suppressed for decades by the Roman Catholic Church, which still regarded their doctrines as being dangerous.

After the Council of Nicaea the great theologian St Augustine, bishop of Hippo, defined the central tenets of Christianity. As a youth, Augustine had himself been a cultist, a practitioner of Manichaeism. When he became a Christian, he was, at first, a Monarchianist. The Monarchianists were a cult which condemned the Christian Trinity because it implies that there are three gods rather than just one. Those who believed in the Trinity, however, condemned the Monarchianists because their position implied that God suffered on the cross.

Augustine accepted the Trinity later in life, but went on to attack Pelagianism. Pelagius was a Scottish or Irish monk who held that it was possible for humans, albeit with a great deal of effort, to live sinless lives. This was not so, said Augustine: everyone – even new-born babies – was tainted by the original sin that had been bequeathed to them by Adam (after all, children are produced as a result of sexual intercourse, which is sinful).

The battle raged on among Christians for centuries, with Augustine's views eventually winning the day. However, this left theologians with another problem: if Christ had been born without sin his mother, Mary, must also have been born without sin. So in 1854 the Roman Catholic Church officially declared the immaculate conception of the Virgin Mary. There were even moves afoot in some quarters to make her the fourth member of the Trinity, but that might take another thousand years or so.

By the twelfth century the doctrine of the Roman Catholic Church was pretty much settled, but the Church itself was a mess. Services were conducted in Latin, which few of the congregation could understand. Most people were illiterate and could not read the Bible for themselves. But they could still see that the Church was corrupt. The clergy enjoyed a life of luxury and many priests lived openly with their mistresses, ecclesiastical marriage having been banned.

In 1176 a wealthy French merchant called Peter Waldo decided to clean things up. He was even given a dispensation to preach by the pope, provided that he obtained a licence from his local bishop. However, as the bishop in question, the bishop of Lyons, was one of the fat cats whom Waldo wanted to denounce the licence was refused, and in 1184 Waldo and his followers were excommunicated.

The Waldensians then became peripatetic evangelical ascetics. Over the years they became more radical. They rejected the ideas of purgatory, transubstantiation, invocation, excommunication, confession, absolution, penance and the purchase of indulgences. They celebrated only baptism, marriage and the Eucharist, the latter once a year, on the Thursday before Easter. They translated the Bible into French and – heresy of heresies – allowed women into their ministry.

The Waldensian heresy proved popular, so Pope Innocent III formed the Poor Catholics to counter it, which aped the Waldensian popularism while remaining faithful to the edicts of the Church. When that did not work, the Church resorted to persecution and imprisoned and burnt Waldensians as heretics. Augustine had already ruled that it was perfectly acceptable to use force in order to save people from heresy: after all, you might burn their bodies, but you would save their immortal souls. Waldensian cells survived in remote settlements in the Alps, however. By the sixteenth century there were still enough to them to form an alliance with their natural heirs, the Calvinists.

The persecution of the Waldensians came about largely because a more heretical cult had sprung up. During the twelfth century the Crusades were in full swing and travel between the east and west increased enormously, with the result that and ideas that had been long suppressed in Europe began to surface again. Among them was Manichaeanism.

Manichaeanism flourished in and around the city of Albi, in southwestern France, before spreading to Italy, Spain and Flanders. The cult's followers were called *Cathari*, which means 'pure ones' in medieval Latin, or Cathars. They took Zoroastrian dualism to its extreme. As the material world exists on the dark, evil side of the universe, Jesus Christ, who exists on the good side, could not have been born into it, they believed. Consequently, he could not have been crucified, hence the cross had no significance. The trappings of the Church existed in the material world, too, so it followed that the Cathars could not accept any of those.

The human soul, they believed, belonged on the good side of the universe, but it was trapped on the bad side. Cathars were consequently against marriage, sex, eating meat, drinking wine and anything else that brought material comfort or sensual pleasure – though they did eat fish, in the mistaken belief that fish do not multiply by means of copulation. The laity, or 'believers', was not required to hold too fast to these rules, but complete abstinence was required of the *Perfecti* ('perfect ones'), who formed the inner circle of the sect.

Fearing persecution, the Cathars kept their faith secret, but when the pope found out about it he sent Cistercian monks to try to convert them. The Cistercians met with little success, and were mocked in the streets of Toulouse; Count Raymond VI of Toulouse, who controlled the Cathar regions of southern France, was himself a Cathar. Pope Innocent III sent an envoy to meet him, who was assassinated. The pope responded by ordering a crusade against the Cathars, the first in Europe.

In 1208 20,000 crusading knights under Simon de Montfort attacked the towîn of Béziers. When soldiers asked the papal legate, Arnaud, abbot of Cîteaux, how he could distinguish between a Cathar and a good Catholic, Arnaud replied 'Kill them all; God will know his own'. They did. But the slaughter of the entire population of Béziers only sharpened the Cathars' resolve; they fought on for another 40 years. For those who believe that the world is an evil place death holds little fear and many Cathars performed the rite of *Endura*, a sanctified form of suicide through fasting. *Perfecti* who were given the choice between converting to Catholicism or being burnt to death chose martyrdom.

The Cathars' last stronghold was the fortress of Montségur in the Pyrénées. Thought to harbour treasure, including the Holy Grail, it came under repeated attack. In March 1244, after a ten-month siege, the Cathars surrendered. Two hundred men and women walked out of the fortress singing, straight into the massive funeral pyres that the crusaders had prepared for them. No treasure was found.

Secret cells of Cathars endured for another 50 years. Some fled to the Balkans, where they survived until the fifteenth century, when they were finally absorbed into Islam.

4 ❖ The Knights Templar

The Crusades were responsible for the foundation of the Christian military order, the Knights Templar. In 1118 the French nobleman Hugues de Payns and eight other veteran crusaders established the Poor Knights of the Temple to protect Christians travelling from Jaffa to the city of Jerusalem, which the crusaders had captured from the Muslims 19 years earlier. Since then Christians had been harried by hostile Arabs. De Payns named the organisation after Jerusalem's Temple of Solomon, where it was first quartered.

In 1128 Pope Honorius I officially recognised the order, which was now known as the Knights Templar. The Roman Catholic Church encouraged the Templars, as the order seemed to provide a way in which to curb the excesses of the crusaders, who were described by St Bernard of Clairvaux – the head of the Cistercians – as 'unbelieving scoundrels, sacrilegious plunderers, homicides, perjurers and adulterers'. Indeed, many of those crusaders who were recruited into the Templars had previously been excommunicated.

Knights Templar had to swear an oath of fraternity, poverty and chastity. They were not even allowed to kiss their mothers, and in order to ensure that there was no hanky-panky they had to sleep fully clothed in lit-up dormitories. St Bernard absolved them of the sin of killing, provided that they killed the enemies of the Roman Catholic Church; he called the Templars 'Christ's legal executioners'.

The Templars took a vow never to retreat, whatever the odds, and gained a reputation for being ferocious in battle. Like many modern-day cults, they were told to cut themselves off from their families, and members handed over all of their worldly goods to the order when they joined it. This policy made the Knights Templar immensely rich. As the order had been founded to aid travellers, it also set up a banking system, so that funds could be safely transferred from place to place. It invested in real estate, too. Soon the Templars' distinctive, circular churches and strongly defended fortresses spread across the Mediterranean, and then across Europe.

By the end of the thirteenth century the Crusades were effectively over, and the Knights Templar thus deprived of their original purpose.

However, the ending of the Crusades also freed the order from the massive cost of maintaining an army in the Middle East. Impoverished European kings began to eye up the huge wealth amassed by the Templars and soon turned against them.

The secrecy surrounding the order had encouraged rumours of idolatry, homosexuality and devil worship. In 1307 Philip IV of France, who was in debt to the Templars' bank, ordered the arrest of the Templars on the grounds of heresy. He then forced Pope Clement V – the first of the popes to be exiled to Avignon – to give him permission to seize their property. In the following year Edward II seized Templar property in the British Isles, and the London Temple, the order's English headquarters, was closed.

The Roman Catholic Inquisition – a body formed to suppress heresy – then began to torture confessions out of the Templars. It was soon compiling a lurid dossier on the activities of the order, which allegedly included homosexuality, urinating on the cross and worshipping Satan in the form of a black cat, which the Templars kissed under its tail. According to some Templars' confessions, they also worshipped a pagan idol called Baphomet, a goat endowed with a woman's breasts and boasting an erect penis. It wore a five-pointed star or pentagram around its neck, and oil, said to have been rendered from the flesh of dead infants, was massaged into its skin. Baphomet was, in fact, a simple corruption of the name Mahomet (Mohammed), the founder of Islam. Indeed, 200 years in the Middle East had rubbed off on the Templars. Many spoke Arabic and at least one had converted to Islam. The English Templar Robert of St Albans had even commanded a Muslim army.

In France, 36 Templars died under torture, and in 1310 54 were burnt at the stake. In 1312 Clement admitted that there was no evidence of heresy within the order. Nevertheless, Philip of France insisted that he close it down. The surviving Templars were allowed to join other orders or else to go free, but the order's grand master, Jacques de Molay, was imprisoned for life on the strength of his confession, which had been extracted under torture. He suddenly retracted it, insisting that the Knights Templar was blameless. Consequently burnt at the stake, before he died de Molay cursed Philip and Clement; both expired within the year.

5 ❖ The Rosicrucians

The Rosicrucians, it could be argued, belong to cult that does not exist. Largely a fictional invention, it seems to have taken 400 years before it had any members. The earliest reference to the cult was made in a Protestant pamphlet published in Kassel, Germany, in 1614. It was called *The Universal and General Reformation of the Whole Wide World; Together with the* Fama Fraternitas *of the Laudable Fraternity of the Rosy Cross, Written to All the Learned and the Rulers of Europe*. This pamphlet purported to be the manifesto of a brotherhood of alchemists, which said that although they knew how to turn base metal into gold they were much more interested in spreading spiritual and philosophical wisdom.

The founder of the cult was claimed to be Christian Rosenkreutz – *Rosenkreutz* is German for 'rosy cross'. The pamphlet said that he was born in Germany in 1378 to a poor, but noble, family. His family could not afford to take care of him and sent him to a monastery, where he learnt Latin and Greek. A monk took him on a pilgrimage to the Holy Land. In Damascus, the boy impressed the wise men of the city with his medical and healing skills. They taught him science and mathematics and then directed him to a city called Damcar, which has never been identified and is probably mythical. There he was taught many secrets, including those of alchemy.

Travelling on to Egypt, Rosenkreutz learned natural history and read the occult and metaphysical works of Hermes Trismegistus. Collected between the first and third centuries AD, these fused Greek ideas with those of ancient Egypt. In Fez, Morocco, Rosenkreutz learnt magic and the Kabbalah. The Kabbalah was said to have been handed down by God to Moses at the same time as the Ten Commandments. It was too sacred to be spoken about directly or written down, however, so Moses hid its ancient wisdom in the first five books of the Bible. The purest and worthiest of Jewish scholars have been trying to decipher it ever since.

The first stab at understanding it was made in the *Sefer Yezira*, or 'Book of Creation', in around the fourth or fifth century AD. During the thirteenth century the Spanish Jew Moses de Leon wrote the *Sefer ha-Zohar*, or 'Book of Splendour', which he claimed was based on an ancient manuscript in his possession. Between the thirteenth and fifteenth centuries interest in the Kabbalah spread across Europe, but suffered a setback when the Jews were expelled from Spain in 1492.

During the Italian Renaissance, ancient ideas, such as Gnosticism and Hermeticism, were rediscovered, and a Florentine mystic named Pico della Mirandola came up with a Christian version of the Kabbalah, which stressed the underlying unity of Christianity, Judaism, paganism and Greek thought. By the time that the *Fama Fraternitas* was published, the Christian Kabbalah – essentially a form of magic – was popular throughout Europe.

According to the *Fama Fraternitas*, Rosenkreutz was rather troubled by what he had learnt about magic and the occult. But he realised that he could use his knowledge in the service of the Christian faith and that it could be the basis of a great revival of spirituality. When Rosenkreutz returned to Europe everyone laughed at the ideas of spiritual renewal that he had brought with him. The only thing that they were interested in was his knowledge of alchemy. Everybody wanted to know how to change base metal into gold, but Rosenkreutz refused to show them. Plainly, the world was not yet ready for the great reformation of thought that he had in mind.

Rather than let what he had learnt go to waste, Rosenkreutz decided to write it all down, so that the truth could be revealed when people were more receptive to it. Along with seven monks from the monastery in which he had been brought up, he set about the task and built a temple in which to house the fruits of their labours.

When the job was done, the order broke up to enable the brothers to carry the medical knowledge that Rosenkreutz had learnt to every corner of the earth. They agreed that they would not charge patients for their healing work. They would operate in secret, abandoning their monks' habits and wearing the dress of the countries to which they travelled. They adopted the initials RC – short for the Latin *Rosae Crucis* 'rosy cross' – as their password, vowing not to acknowledge the existence of the cult until the password was given to them. Each year they would reassemble at the temple, and before each of them died they would pass on all that they had learnt to a worthy successor.

Rosenkreutz himself died in 1484, at the age of 106, according to the *Fama Fraternitas*. But the order, it said, continued from generation to generation, as each of the brothers passed on his knowledge.

In 1604, the *Fama Fraternitas* said, the brothers – who now included the author of the *Fama Fraternitas* – unearthed the door to a mysterious tomb, with the words 'I will reappear after 120 years' written on it in Latin. The tomb had seven sides and was lit by a brilliant light from within. Inside, they found Rosenkreutz's corpse, which had been perfectly preserved. In its hand was a book. Satisfied that they had fulfilled the legend on the door – presumably a prophecy left by Rosenkreutz himself – they sealed up the tomb again. Now, they decided, the world was ready for their message of spiritual renewal, and they threw open their ranks to new membership.

In 1615, the year after the *Fama Fraternitas* was published, it was followed by *The Confessions of the Rosicrucian Fraternity*. This spelt out the Rosicrucian message in more detail: the brotherhood consisted of fundamentalist Christians, it said, and it condemned Mohammed and the pope. The German astronomer Johannes Kepler had spotted some new stars in 1604, the year in which Rosenkreutz's tomb was said to have been opened; this was the sign, it stated, that society was at last ready to hear the Rosicrucian message.

In the following year *The Chemical Marriage of Christian Rosenkreutz* was published. It was a strange, magical tale surrounding the purported attendance of Rosenkreutz at the wedding of Frederick V of Bohemia and the daughter of England's king, James I.

These three works were all produced anonymously. The Lutheran priest Johann Valentin Andreae, however, finally admitted to writing *The Chemical Wedding* – though, as a Christian, he distanced himself from it, claiming that it was purely a satire that he had written when he was young and foolish. But it is now thought that he alone, or in collaboration with the circle of other mystics and intellectuals who gathered around Christoph Besold, a professor of law at TŸbingen University, wrote all three Rosicrucian pamphlets.

Whether the pamphlets were spoofs, satires or a sincere attempt to alter the intellectual and moral agenda, they were a gift to conmen. One Dutch gentleman paid the equivalent of £650 to join the sect, only to find out subsequently that he had been duped. Another shyster pretending to be a Rosicrucian went about selling 'transformation powder', supposedly demonstrating how to make gold. It was, of course, a con.

But two respected philosophers, the German Michael Maier and the Englishman Robert Fludd, began to write more about the Rosicrucian order, though both denied being members. Maier said that would-be recruits were secretly observed for five years before they were contacted by the Rosicrucians. Many were rejected. Those who were recruited were sworn to secrecy.

Interest in the Rosicrucians was really aroused when *Fama Fraternitas* went on sale in Paris. Posters went up across the city purporting to have come from the Brotherhood of the Rosy Cross. They promised to bring universal peace and wisdom, as well as everlasting life, to those who joined the order. The brethren themselves preferred to remain invisible, however, and the posters gave no details of how to join. Suitable candidates would be contacted in due course, it was promised. The posters caused a sensation. Rumours spread that the brotherhood had legions of followers in Germany, Holland, England and other hotbeds of Protestantism. Yet Paris was a Catholic city and the Roman Catholic Church quickly condemned the cult, but in doing so gave credence to its existence.

Stories abounded of strange apparitions, gold coins that turned into slate once the customer left the shop and hotel guests who vanished without a trace when their bill came. According to the Church, this was plainly the work of the devil: the Rosicrucians had made a pact with Satan, the Church said. They could be transported by magic to anywhere that they wanted to go; with their knowledge of alchemy, they had unlimited supplies of gold; they could hold a listener spellbound in any language that they chose and were the masters of disguise. Many Parisians took to sleeping with loaded muskets beside their beds.

Anti-Rosicrucian pamphlets were circulated. In this atmosphere of paranoia, the philosopher René Descartes feared for his life and went to great lengths to distance himself from the Rosicrucians. He had heard about them earlier, in Germany, and had tried to contact them in vain; eventually he concluded that the whole thing was an elaborate hoax. After months of uproar no Rosicrucians appeared, and the Parisians, too, thought that they had been the victims of a hoax – perhaps as the cover for some fiendish, Protestant plot. The coat of arms of Martin Luther featured a rose and a cross, it was noted. Then again, roses and the cross are strewn throughout Christian allegory – the rose often being taken to symbolise the Virgin Mary, or her womb, and the cross Christ. And in alchemy the cross symbolised the four alchemical elements, while *ros* – the Latin for 'dew' – was known to be one of the vital ingredients needed when turning base metal into gold.

Both Maier and Fludd died without apparently having been contacted by the order, and with them Rosicrucianism disappeared for nearly a hundred years. During the eighteen century a number of rival Rosicrucian societies sprang up, each claiming to be the original and only one and tracing its provenance not just back to Christian Rosenkreutz, but also to the Egyptian pharaohs and beyond. This time their members declared themselves.

In Breslau, Germany, Sigmund Richter wrote down elaborate rules and rituals for his followers. One German lodge insisted that its members carry a black, silken cord at all times with which to strangle themselves if they felt the urge to divulge the cult's secrets. Clearly, this was a stricture that Richter did not observe.

In 1743 the Comte de Saint-Germain, who was reputed to be a

Rosicrucian, held the salons of London spellbound. He was an accomplished musician, a polymath and, some said, barking mad. He claimed to be 2,000 years old and rumours were rife that he could produce gold and precious gems at will. He was, of course, very handsome, and women throughout the courts of Europe swooned when he appeared. Men, too, were impressed by him. Even Voltaire described him as a 'man who never dies and knows everything'. There may have been something to this: he died in 1784 in Schleswig, but was spotted at the execution of Marie Antoinette in 1793 and continued to put in earthly appearances up until 1820.

In Amsterdam, the Order of the Asiatic Brethren of the Rosy Cross was founded under the auspices of Baron Hans Carl von Ecker and Eckhoffen, and was notable for the elaborate uniforms of the different grades of its members. Way ahead of its time, the order accepted Jews, Arabs, Iranians, Armenians and Orthodox Christians, provided that they paid the hefty membership fees. The price tag naturally increased the higher the rank and baron von Ecker did very nicely.

In 1782 *The Rosicrucian Unveiled* was published. Its author, who used the pen name Magister Pianco, said that he had spent vast sums of money and years of devoted study in climbing the ranks of his lodge, only to discover that his bully of a master had no divine revelations to offer.

This did not put an end to the Rosicrucian craze, but simply encouraged more swindlers to take up the lucrative scam. Conmen were soon marketing pieces of the 'philosopher's stone', which was reputed to turn base metal into gold. Others offered membership . . . for a price. Any sincere remnants of earlier Rosicrucian lodges had been absorbed into Freemasonry long ago. The Freemasons' Rose-Croix Eighteenth Degree, which operated as an independent Masonic discipline under Sir Thomas Dunckerley from around the end of the eighteenth century, seems to have incorporated many of the principles of Rosicrucianism.

During the 1850s the former French cleric Eliphas Lévi claimed to have discovered a connection between the Kabbalah and the Tarot. The 22 trumps in the Tarot deck corresponded to the 22 letters of the Hebrew alphabet and the 22 paths in the tree of life spoken of in the Book of Creation. Lévi claimed never to have been a Rosicrucian, but his theories inspired a new interest in the cult.

In 1888 a poet and numerologist, Marquis Stanislas de Guaita, set up the *Ordre Kabbalistique de la Rose-Croix*. It had a supreme council of twelve, but no other members. In 1890 one of the 12, Joséphin Péladan, set up his own rival Order of the Rose-Croix of the Temple and the Grail. Péladan was a charismatic figure who usually dressed in a monk's robe or a medieval doublet; he also immersed himself in the artistic life of Paris. He lectured on mysticism in art, staged occult plays – including two that he claimed were the missing works of the Greek playwright Aeschylus – and wrote occult books, including the popular works *How To Become A Magus* and *How To Become A Fairy*.

In England, in 1865, Robert Wentworth Little and a group of fellow Freemasons formed the *Societas Rosicruciana in Anglia*, in association with a German organisation. The society combined neo-Christian philosophy with mystical beliefs in reincarnation, clairvoyance, alchemy and magic. During the 1870s it had 144 members in England and 500 world-wide, but it foundered when some of its followers became influenced by the new cult of Theosophy and defected in 1887 to form the Hermetic Order of the Golden Dawn.

Rosicrucianism had yet to catch on in the USA. One group, called the *Fraternitas Rosae Crucis*, based in Quakertown, Pennsylvania, claimed to date back to 1858. But it was not heard of until 1907, when R Swinburne Clymer declared himself its chief magus. In the same year Carl van Grasshof, a member of the Theosophical Society in Los Angeles, converted to Rosicrucianism, changed his name to Max Heindel and wrote *Rosicrucian Cosmo-Conception*. Heindel banned his group's members from consuming meat, tobacco and alcohol at their base in Oceanside, California. Apparently he wanted them to live longer, even though they believed in a reincarnation. The year 1907 was a busy one for American Rosicrucians: it was also the year in which the *Societas Rosicruciana* was founded in upstate New York by Sylvester C Gould.

H Spencer Lewis, who founded the Ancient and Mystical Order of the *Rosae Crucis* (AMORC), claimed that American Rosicrucianism had started in 1693, when a group of German mystics came to Pennsylvania to try to isolate the 'elixir of life' which was said to flow in the Wissahickon river, near what later became the Germantown area of Philadelphia. The lodge apparently closed in 1801. However, Lewis claimed, Rosicrucianism followed an ancient, 108-year circle of death and rebirth and happily, in 1909, while on a trip to France, he was led back to it. He then spent six years studying in France, before returning to the USA to establish AMORC. When he published the order's first manifesto, in 1915, he claimed that AMORC already had 300 members.

Lewis asserted that AMORC was the one true Rosicrucian order, and quickly out-distanced his rivals by staging a display of alchemy before an invited audience that included a journalist from the *New York World*; it apparently worked. Instead of secretly observing potential recruits for five years in order to see whether they were worthy of membership, Lewis put recruiting ads in the papers. For as little as $5 down and $1.50, he promised that applicants could learn the secrets of life and join a select group that included the Pharaoh Akhenaten, Jesus, Plato, Aristotle, Cicero, St Thomas Aquinas, Francis Bacon, Benjamin Franklin and Claude Debussy.

Members received a membership card, a secret password, a magazine and diagrams showing secret handshakes. But enlightenment did not come easy and for an extra $2 a month members could buy a home-study course which would supposedly improve their intuition, concentration, memory, health, personality and influence over other people. Once they had completed the course, members who could not get to a lodge could initiate themselves. All that they had to do was to stand in front of a mirror and trace out a cross on the glass. They then had to say 'Hail, Holy Cross' and meditate for three minutes. Finally, they were required to touch themselves on the forehead with their forefingers and said 'Peace'.

Lewis died in 1935 and his son, Ralph, took over. When Ralph died in 1987, a devotee named Gary Stewart stepped into his shoes. By that time AMORC boasted a membership of 250,000 in 27 countries, as well as an annual turnover of the equivalent of over £1 million. Its headquarters, Rosicrucian Park, turned an entire city block in the city of San Jose into a Disney-like version of ancient Egypt.

Today, AMORC's only serious rival internationally is the *Lectorium Rosicrucian*, the International School of the Rosy Cross that was set up in The Netherlands by the brothers Z W and J Leene. It has branches in over two dozen countries, including the USA and Britain, and its magazine, *Pentagram*, is published in ten languages. J Leene, using the name J van Rijckenborgh, has written numerous books, among them *The Elementary Philosophy of the Modern Rosycross*; *The Universal Gnosis*; *The Egyptian Arch-Gnosis*; and *The Secrets of the Brotherhood of the Rosycross*. For the supposed guardian of secret knowledge, he seems to be a bit of a blabberer.

6 ❖ The Freemasons

Although the Freemasons claim an ancestry that goes back to the building of Solomon's Temple in Jerusalem – some even say that Adam was the first Mason – the cult seems to have sprung up among guilds of medieval stonemasons. The term 'freemason' makes its first appearance in the records of the City of London in 1375. At the time the bulk of the population was peasants, who were tied to the land. The masons were a cut above the rest because their craft enabled them to roam from place to place and from project to project. At the site at which they were working there was a lodge where the stoneworkers could stay until the cathedral or castle was completed. As the projects got bigger the lodge was not a building, but rather the body of masons who worked together on one commission.

Because they travelled around, masons seemed exotic to the generally static population. They were also trained in a craft whose skills did indeed stretch back to ancient Egypt and beyond. Their skills were their livelihood, so the masons had good reason to keep them to themselves. An untrained man who only pretended to know the craft could wreak havoc on a project, so the masons used secret passwords, signs and special handshakes as a means of recognition.

During the seventeenth century the Freemasons began admitting honorary members, who had nothing to do with stoneworking, to their lodges. In 1619 the City of London's Masons Company founded a sister organisation, called Acception, which admitted 'accepted members' at twice the normal fee.

By the turn of the eighteenth century there were four lodges in London and the movement was growing apace. The Grand Lodge was set up in 1717 as a governing body to supervise the cult's transition from a historic craft guild to a broad social movement.

By this time the rites and rituals of the Masons had become regularised and remain similar to this day. The lodge met in private, often in the back room of a tavern, where business was conducted and ideas freely exchanged. But the ceremonials took place in a special lodge room, which had been decorated for the purpose. While the master and officers of the lodge gathered in the lodge room, the initiate entered an anteroom, where the tyler – an archaic spelling of 'tiler' – waited with his sword drawn.

The initiate was then instructed to remove his jacket and bare his left breast – presumably to demonstrate that he was not a woman (women are not usually allowed to join the Masons). The candidate then emptied his pockets of money; he was told that he should remember that he entered the order poor and penniless whenever he met fellow Masons in straightened circumstances. The left leg of his trousers was then rolled up above the knee and his right foot was 'slipshod' – that is, the initiate put on a slipper instead of a shoe. (Only those who have been initiated know what this rite means, but it is thought to have some connection with the founder of the Jesuits, Ignatius de Loyola, who had a bad foot.)

A Freemason showing the uniform worn by members

The initiate was next 'hoodwinked', or blindfolded, to remind him that he entered the order in a state of ignorance. A noose was then put around his neck – probably to remind him of the punishment that was meted out to those who reveal the order's secrets – and he was led into the inner chamber. At the door, an officer barred his passage by holding a dagger to his chest. With the blindfold having been removed – representing moving from darkness into the light – the initiate lay on the floor in the symbolic coffin of the Masonic martyr Hiram Abiff, who died rather than reveal the Masons' secrets. The candidate next answered a series of ritual questions. Then, kneeling before the master, he swore not to disclose any of the secrets of Masonry. If ever he were to do so, he accepted that his throat would be cut and his tongue torn out by the root and buried in the sand of the sea at the lower water mark. The noose and blindfold were then removed, and the new Mason was told of the significance of the ceremony. Finally, he was taught the secret step, the sign, the password and the handshake.

Now, as then, the new recruit thereby becomes a first-degree Mason or apprentice. He is given a set of tools, each of which is thought to have a symbolic value. The chisel represents the gift of learning; the hammer the power of conscience; and the 24-inch (61cm) ruler the 24 hours of the day. He can now also wear a Mason's apron.

After his initiation, the apprentice must dedicate himself to study. Once he has made sufficient progress he becomes a second-degree, or 'fellow Craft', Mason. Then he receives a plumb line symbolising rectitude, a square representing morality and a level signifying equality. Eventually, he becomes a third-degree, or 'master', Mason and is given a trowel, which represents brotherhood (because a trowel is used to apply the cement that holds the blocks of stone together).

During the eighteenth century there was a vogue for the esoteric, and the Masons began to discover ties linking them to ancient cults – the Rosicrucians, the Knights Templar, the Cathars and the Gnostics. Some Masons even say that Adam's fig leaf was the first Masonic apron. Masons furthermore saw a connection with Pythagoras, the sixth-century BC Greek philosopher and mathematician. After they had completed five years of study, Pythagoras initiated his students into an inner circle, when they were shown the connection between numbers and the mystical meaning of the universe.

The Masons also have another legend, concerning the biblical figure Hiram Abiff. Abiff was the grand master of a lodge of Dionysiac architects sent by King Hiram of Tyre to help King Solomon build his palace and temple in Jerusalem. He developed a system of signals and passwords which his foremen used to assess the level of a craftsman's skill. Three low-ranking craftsman tried to force Abiff to tell them what the password of the master's degree was. When he refused, they killed him. This story illus-trates the seriousness with which Masons take the vow of secrecy.

A number of fashionable aristocrats were attracted to the Craft, in-cluding members of the British royal family. Since 1737 at least sixteen royal princes have been Masons, four of whom went on to be crowned king. But clergymen, intellectuals and free-thinkers joined the Masons, too, perhaps because the society's secrecy rules allowed them to discuss sub-versive notions behind closed doors.

In 1723 the Masons' *Book of Constitutions* was compiled by Dr James Anderson, a minister of the Church of Scotland. It specified that the order was open to men of any religion or opinion. The *Book of Constitutions* was published in Philadelphia, in 1734, by the master printer and Masonic grand master Benjamin Franklin.

By the end of the 1730s Masonic lodges were spread across Europe. Freemasonry was particularly popular in France: by 1742 there were 22 lodges in Paris, and by the time of the French Revolution there were probably as many as 100,000 in France. Indeed, many respected historians believe that the revolution was fomented in Masonic lodges.

The Masons certainly played a part in the American Revolution. The first colonial grand master, Daniel Coxe, proposed a plan to confederate the American colonies as early as 1732. George Washington, John Hancock, Benjamin Franklin, Paul Revere and many other key figures in the revolution were Masons. General Lafayette, the young French marquis who rallied to the American cause, was also a Mason. So was Benedict Arnold, whose name Americans consider to be a byword for 'traitor'.

One American officer, Colonel John McKinstry, was captured during the War of Independence by Native American Mohawks who were allied to the British. They tied him to a tree and were about to burn him alive when he made a secret Masonic sign. One of the Mohawks then put a stop to the execution. His name was Joseph Brant; educated in Europe, he had been initiated into the Masons in London. He delivered McKinstry to British officers whom he knew to be Masons and they subsequently returned him to an American outpost.

Masonic lodges have long been perceived as presenting a political threat. In 1735 they were banned in The Netherlands; similar bans followed in Sweden and Switzerland. Masonry was outlawed in Austria during the reign of the Archduchess Maria Theresa because the Masons would not let her join their society. The Austrian lodges were later re-opened and a former slave from North Africa, named Angelo Soliman, was initiated in the prestigious True Harmony Lodge in Vienna in 1781.

Masonry has often faced attack. During the eighteenth century, for example, pamphleteers regularly claimed that the Masons were in league with the devil and that their rites involved sodomy and flagellation. In 1738 Pope Clement XII denounced Freemasonry and excommunicated all those who had been initiated into the Craft. The papal ban was lifted only in 1965. The Roman Catholic Church opposed the Masons' encouragement of men of different ranks associating together. The Masonic oath of secrecy was furthermore said to be an affront to the confessional, where everything was supposed to be revealed to the priest. In Catholic countries the secular authorities also cracked down on Masons: some were arrested and tortured, but the movement was now too well established to be stamped out.

In the USA public opinion turned against Freemasonry after the revolution, when a man named Captain William Morgan was abducted. An itinerant stonecutter who was not an initiate, Morgan seems to have discovered a number of the Masons' most closely guarded secrets. In 1826, in Bavaria, upstate New York, he approached the publisher of the local newspaper, Colonel David C Miller. Together they began work on a book that would reveal all. The local lodge got wind of this plan and decided to put a stop to it. Morgan was arrested and jailed for a debt of less than $3. The following night four Masons went to the jail, paid off the debt and bundled Morgan into a waiting carriage. He was never seen again.

Miller printed 50,000 handbills appealing for information about the abduction and 'possible murder' of Morgan. Although Morgan had probably simply been given enough money to keep him quiet and had then been dumped across the Canadian border, lurid tales about his ritual execution at the hands of the Masons began to circulate. The Masons were condemned from the pulpit and John Quincy Adams, the sixth president of the United States and a distinguished congressman, proposed that Freemasonry be abolished. Prominent politicians distanced themselves from the Craft and membership figures plummeted.

In 1832 William Wirt ran for president as the candidate of the Anti-Masonic Party. He won in the state of Vermont. In all, he received 1,265,755 votes, 8 per cent of the national total. However, his achievement marked the height of the backlash against the Masons. By 1848 the Masons had raised the money to build the Washington Monument, which had been proposed by Congress on 14 December 1799 only hours after Washington's death. The cornerstone was laid in a full Masonic ceremony, but a renewed bout of anti-Masonic sentiment halted the monument's construction in 1855. Work was resumed in 1879 and the monument was completed in December 1884 with the final addition of a 100-oz (2.8kg) aluminium capstone. It was placed on the very top of the monument, in a Masonic dedication ceremony that took place on a platform 572 feet (174m) above the ground.

Freemasonry, in the USA at least, has never looked back since, and the United States now boasts some 16,000 lodges and several million members.

During the late nineteenth century a series of books published in France claimed that Freemasonry was a hive of Satanism and debauchery. The Nazis turned against it, too, during the twentieth century, paranoically condemning it as part of an imaginary plan for world domination, the world-wide Jewish conspiracy. They were aided in their anti-Masonic propaganda by a French historian named Bernard Fay. In 1943, Fay helped to produce a film called *Forces Occultes*, which purported to show how the Masons had started World War II. The Nazis made Fay head of France's national library, the *Bibliothèque Nationale*, where he researched the membership of the Craft. He came up with 170,000 names and thanks to his efforts 117 French Freemasons died and 520 were deported. At the end of the war

Fay was sentenced to life imprisonment, but he was subsequently given a presidential pardon and released after seven years. France's National Front leader, Jean-Marie Le Pen, still commands a large, anti-Masonic following.

In Spain hundreds of Masons were executed under General Franco. Others fled abroad and had their property seized. Freemasonry was only permitted again in Spain during the 1970s.

Freemasonry has long been entwined with Italian politics. During the nineteenth century its secret network of members and anti-clericalist stance made it the perfect vehicle for the Italian nationalism which culminated in the unification of the country. More recently, it was brought to the world's attention in 1981, when Roberto Calvi – who was known as 'God's banker' because he organised the financial affairs of the Roman Catholic Church – was found dead, hanging under Blackfriars Bridge in London. He was a member of a mysterious lodge of Freemasons called P-2 – *Propaganda Due* – which was accused of acting as a state within a state. Not only were its leaders prominent members of the establishment, but some also had links with organised crime.

Italy's prime minister, Giovanni Spadolini, described P-2's right-wing political aspirations a 'creeping coup'. No one can be sure of how exactly much of a political threat it posed. That the lodge was a government-in-waiting may well have been one of the grander delusions of its head, Licio Gelli. It used its political influence mainly to obtain favours and to cut through red tape. Businessmen used P-2 as a way of securing contracts and dealing with Italy's labyrinthine bureaucracy.

In fact, few of the members knew of P-2's larger agenda. Gelli and his deputy, Umberto Ortalini, were highly secretive, holding their initiation ceremonies in anonymous hotel rooms. It was only when the scandal broke and the membership lists were published that members discovered who their fellow members were. Although they came from all of Italy's political parties, ranging from the socialist PSI to the neo-fascist MSI-DN, members tended to be rightward leaning. Gelli himself held duel Italian-Argentinean natiónality and had been a friend of Argentine dictator Juan Perón.

The Masonic lodge P-2 was part of the Grand Orient rite of Freemasonry. However, when Gelli took over during the 1970s it was expelled, and when the scandal was revealed orthodox Freemasons denied any connection with it. The existence of P-2 only became known to the public in 1981, when investigating magistrates in Milan tried to untangle the affairs of the disgraced Sicilian financier Michele Sindona. Sindona had used the contacts that he made through P-2 to build up a financial empire.

He was an expert in evading Italy's banking laws by setting up foreign companies through which money could be laundered. One of his P-2 contacts was Roberto Calvi.

When these activities were revealed Calvi fled to London, where many people believe that he was murdered in a ritual Masonic execution. Sindona was arrested in New York – for fraud and for staging his own kidnapping – and was jailed for 25 years. Gelli fled to Switzerland, where he was caught trying to take $55 million out of a fraudulent bank account. Before he could be extradited to Italy, however, where he faced charges of political conspiracy, criminal association, extortion and fraud, he escaped from the Swiss maximum-security prison in which he was being held with the help of a warder, who drove him across the French border to a waiting private jet.

Freemasonry has spawned a number of spin-off organisations. One of them is the US *Phi Beta Kappa*, which was founded by Thomas Jefferson and friends in William and Mary College, Williamsburg, Virginia, in 1776. Originally organised along Masonic lines, the rites and secrecy associated with the Craft were dropped during the 1850s and it became an honorary society whose entry requirements depended on scholarship. There are now some 180 chapters of *Phi Beta Kappa* and it publishes *Key Reporter* and the *American Scholar*. Yet even this benign organisation was once feared as a threat to democracy and it was banned in the state of Michigan for a time.

In 1776 the charismatic Count Cagliostro turned up in London, along with his ravishing wife, Lorenza Feliciani. Where they came from no one knows. Some thought that Cagliostro was Polish; some a Spaniard; some an Arab. When he was asked, he said that he had been born in the Red Sea, within the shadow of the pyramids. He was certainly wealthy, but no one knew where his money came from. Some said that he was a Sicilian conman; some that he had robbed and murdered an Arab prince; some that he had married into wealth in Mexico. When the French parliament questioned him on the source of his riches he said 'What does it matter . . . provided I regard religion and obey the law'. In any country, he said, bankers gave him what he needed. That was the only answer that he would give.

Within a year of his arrival in London Cagliostro he had been initiated into the Masons. Being something of an entrepreneur, he then went to the Continent and set up his own lodge, which he called the Egyptian Rite. Cagliostro's version of the Craft varied considerably from standard Masonic practice. Equality was definitely out: as the 'Grand Cophta' – or 'Grand Coffer', to those who thought that he was a conman – he sat on a throne. Unlike the Masons, the Egyptian Rite allowed women to join it.

Their initiation involved Cagliostro blowing on their faces. He also performed weird rites involving swords, invocations and the Kabbalah. Children were hypnotised and allegedly given the gift of prophecy. The secret of Cagliostro's wealth, some thought, may have been the philosophers' stone, which he claimed to possess. In order to keep himself solvent he often sold of little chunks of it. Cagliostro set up branches in The Netherlands, Germany, Poland and Russia. But he seems to have over-reached himself when he attempted to establish the Egyptian Rite in Rome. He was arrested and appears to have died in jail.

The Egyptian Rite was not the only lodge to admit women. In 1710, the 17-year-old Elizabeth St Leger became a Freemason in Ireland. She had fallen asleep in her father's library and awoke to hear a lodge meeting going on. She tried to creep away, but was caught by a guard. Although her brothers insisted that she be put to death, the secrets of the Craft were instead preserved by means of admitting her to the lodge. In 1770 the landlady of the Crown tavern in Newcastle eavesdropped on the lodge meetings that were held there and then placed advertisements in the newspaper offering to make the secrets of Freemasonry known to her sex.

In France, a female movement called Adoptive Masonry was set up so that women could join in the fun. Marie Antoinette attended lodge meetings and after the queen had lost her head Napoleon's wife, Josephine, was enrolled as France's grand mistress. In the USA, in 1867, the Order of the Eastern Star was established for the female relatives of Freemasons. The order still flourishes, but no amount of equal-opportunities legislation can force US Masons to open their own lodges to women. The sons of Masons can join the Order of DeMolay and Order of Builders; their daughters the Order of Job's Daughters and the Order of the Rainbow. Such offshoots are not permitted in Britain, however.

If the Masons themselves were not secretive enough, another, more shadowy, cult that was formed in Bavaria during the 1780s is still a gold mine for conspiracy theorists today. This is the Order of the *Illuminati*, which was established by an idealistic law professor named Adam Weishaupt. Its manifesto talks of equality and brotherhood, but the order was actually established to oppose what Weishaupt regarded as an organisation that was dedicated to world domination: the Jesuits, who certainly dominated Bavaria at that time.

The *Illuminati* were organised so that only the innermost circle – the Areopagites – knew that Weishaupt was the leader (you could only become an Areopagite after gruelling years of study). All forms of communication were in code and members and lodges were given code names that were borrowed from the ancient world. The *Illuminati* were encouraged to spy on each other and report their findings to their superiors. The order devised its degrees to seem like a natural progression from the three degrees of Freemasonry, and Weishaupt furthermore used Masonic lodges as a recruiting ground.

By 1794 the order had several thousand members in Austria, Switzerland, Bohemia and Hungary, as well as in Bavaria. But when Duke Carl Theodore came to power in Bavaria he and banned both the Freemasons and the *Illuminati*. His men raided the home of an *Illuminati* member and seized incriminating documents (Weishaupt's brand of liberal free-thinking seemed dangerously close to anarchism back then). The documents also contained chemical experiments – for alchemy or bomb-making, perhaps. The papers were then published, along with a letter disclosing that Weishaupt had arranged an abortion for a woman who was carrying his child. This was an effective personal smear on Weishaupt, who was in hiding in Regensburg. But there was worse: a lot of the documents were in code. This implied that all sorts of secret practices were going on, and soon more than 50 publications appeared condemning the *Illuminati* as Satanists.

The Freemasons had already been implicated in the French Revolution – the Masonic triangle appears in the emblems of a number of revolutionary groups. But the Masons were widespread and the *Illuminati* were not, which made them seem all the more shadowy and sinister. Even Count Cagliostro condemned the *Illuminati*, along with the Masons, from his jail cell in Rome.

In 1797 a book called *Proof of a Conspiracy against All the Religions and Governments of Europe, Carried On in Secret Meetings of Free Masons, Illuminati, and Reading Societies, Collected from Good Authorities* was published. Despite its cumbersome title, it became an international best-seller. Thomas Jefferson read it and pointed out that Weishaupt lived under the 'tyranny of despots and priests', commenting that such secrecy would not have been necessary in the United States. Washington, however, condemned the activities of the *Illuminati*.

The *Illuminati*, as far as one can tell, had died out by the beginning of the nineteenth century. But conspiracy theorists still see their hand everywhere. In 1967 the right-wing John Birch Society in the USA republished *Proof of a Conspiracy* and since then there has been a spate of books explaining how the *Illuminati* are trying to achieve world domination. The key to these theories is found on the US dollar bill: on the back of it there is an all-seeing eye on top of a pyramid, which is supposed to be the symbol of the *Illuminati*.

Although the *Illuminati* probably exist only in the eyes of conspiracy theorists, the Masons have gone from strength to strength. While British Masons still have just three orders, US Masons, such as the members of the Ancient and Accepted Rite of Masonry, boast thirty-three degrees. Some have wonderful titles, such as sublime prince of the royal scent, grand elected knight kabosh and perfect master. Those who are at least thirty-second-degree Masons are eligible to join the Ancient Arabic Order of the Nobles of the Mystic Shrine, or the Shriners. This cult was set up in New York during the 1870s by the actor William Florence. While touring France, Florence had attended a party given by an Arab diplomat and subsequently became enthralled by Eastern rituals. The Shriners are most notable for the exotic costumes that they wear to their conventions. They are easy to mock, but the Shriners, and similarly bizarre groups, raise millions of dollars for charity – which is a great deal more commendable than releasing nerve gas on to the subway.

It is also worth remembering all the famous men who were Masons. Apart from the USA's founding fathers and a number of British kings, the list includes Christopher Wren, Voltaire, Mozart, Liszt, Haydn, Goethe, Alexander Pope, Walter Scott, Rudyard Kipling, Robert Burns, Mark Twain, Oscar Wilde, Winston Churchill, Charles Lindbergh, Sam Houston, John J Pershing, Douglas MacArthur, Robert Perry, Admiral Richard Byrd, Buzz Aldrin, Henry Ford, Joseph Smith, John Jacob Astor, Theodore Roosevelt and possibly even also Lenin and the shah of Iran.

7 ❖ The Theosophists

In 1859 Charles Darwin published *The Origin of the Species* and thus drove an apparently immovable wedge between science and religion. The Theosophical Society sought to breach that rift, and by the end of the nineteenth century it had become enormously influential.

The word 'theosophy' comes from the Greek words *theos* – 'God' – and *sophia* – 'knowledge'. The Theosophical Society, which was founded in New York in 1875, aimed to create a universal brotherhood of humankind – regardless of race, religion or class – in order to study ancient religions, philosophies and science and thereby liberate the psychic powers that it maintained were latent in humans. It reclaimed the concept of evolution from what it saw as the brutal materialism of Darwinism, by insisting that

Helena Petrovna Blavatsky, or Madame Blavatsky as she was known. She was the driving force behind the Theosophical Society

humankind was evolving towards a more spiritual existence and individuals towards a higher state through reincarnation. There were already masters, Theosophists said, who held the secret knowledge, but who held themselves back from the bliss of merging into the universal oneness in order to show others the way.

The driving force behind the Theosophical Society was Helena Petrovna Blavatsky. Known the world as Madame Blavatsky, her friends and intimates called HPB. She undoubtedly led a remarkable life, but exactly how remarkable we shall never know. Like many of her circle who claimed to possess the universal truth, she seemed incapable of telling the truth in the ordinary sense, so her life story probably represents a heady cocktail of fact and fiction.

It seems that she was born in the Ukraine in 1831. Her father was an army officer, her mother a romantic novelist. From an early age she claimed that she could make furniture move and objects fly about by touching them only with her invisible 'astral arms'. At 17 she was married off to the 40-year-old Nikifor Blavatsky, a Tsarist general and provincial governor. She said that the marriage was never consummated, and after three months she left her husband and made her way to Constantinople

(Istanbul). The couple never divorced and she kept his name for the rest of her life.

From Turkey, she set off on her travels. It is not quite clear where she went. She simply referred to this period, from 1848 to 1858, as her 'veiled time'. On various occasions she claimed to have visited the Orient, most of Asia, India, Africa, Europe, the United States and Canada, as well as Central and South America. During these trips she allegedly whirled with the dervishes, learnt magic in Japan's mountain-worshipping Yamabushi sector, traversed the Rockies in a covered wagon, discovered the mysteries of the Mayan ruins on the Yucatán, was initiated into Voodoo, became a Druze, slept in the Great Pyramid of Cheops and became an independently wealthy woman by trading in Sudanese ostrich feathers. Or so she said.

Apart from all of that she also found the time to spend seven years in Tibet, living in a remote valley in the Himalayans with a group of *mahatmas*, or masters, who revealed to her the secrets that later became the basis of Theosophy. Yet Tibet had been closed to foreigners since 1792 and there is absolutely no evidence that she went there. She certainly went to Egypt, however, where she began smoking hashish. She took a course in snake-charming and consulted a Coptic magician, whom she later dismissed as a charlatan. After that she travelled around Europe with an Hungarian opera singer, who claimed to have married her. There were several other putative husbands, although she claimed to her dying day that she was a virgin. Yet a child lived with her for a time: Yuri, a hunchback who died in late childhood. The child was adopted, she said.

She briefly managed a factory producing artificial flowers in Tiflis, but the main thrust of her career was in spiritualism, which she practised in Russia. In England, she was the assistant to the celebrated medium Daniel Dunglas Home.

Back in Cairo, in 1871 she formed the *Société Spirite*. Its occult teachings, she said, came from an Egyptian order called the Brotherhood of Luxor, which was so ancient and exclusive that no one had ever heard of it. The *Société* was a failure, so she made her living as a medium until she was exposed as a fraud and fled back to Europe.

In Paris in 1873, she received a message from the spirit world telling her to go to the United States and complied. At a seance in Vermont she met the Civil War veteran, lawyer and newspaperman Henry Steel Olcott, who was covering the event. He was impressed by her large size and her massive, Mongoloid face. She was wearing the scarlet shirt that had been popularised by the followers of Garibaldi and had short, crinkly, blonde hair, which, he said, put him in mind of the fleece of a Cotswold ewe.

They hit it off immediately. Though not as widely travelled as HPB, Olcott fancied himself as a cosmopolitan and a free-thinker. Olcott dropped what remained of his journalistic scepticism when, back in New York, he received a letter written in gold ink on green paper. It said 'Sister Helen will lead thee to the Golden Gate of truth.' It was signed by the grand master of the Brotherhood of Luxor.

Within a year Olcott and Blavatsky were living together in an apartment in Manhattan. He did the cooking and the housekeeping while she ran a salon for those who were interested in the occult and the esoteric arts. He was much impressed by her ability to conjure things out of thin air – though the lights had to be dimmed while she did so – and by the way in which she summoned him by ringing an invisible bell. Olcott suggested that they form an organisation to investigate all things mystical. They toyed with a number of names, eventually coming up with the 'Theosophical Society'.

They appear to have picked their moment well. For two centuries rationalism had seemed to have been on the advance and now Darwin had dealt God, the creator, a possibly fatal blow. But scientific materialism offered people nothing beyond the grave and it was this vacuum that the Theosophical Society and its spin-offs intended to fill.

Using spirit writing, Madame Blavatsky dashed off the occult masterpiece *Isis Unveiled*. The Egyptian goddess Isis had appeared to her several times, she said, but the majority of the book was nevertheless about the masters whom she claimed to have met in Tibet. They had written it and then projected it around the world into her room in New York by using 'astral light, she explained. If this was true then the masters were plagiarists: much of the book is lifted verbatim from other texts. Despite damning reviews, the massive, two-volume, 1,300-page *Isis Unveiled* was an instant best-seller. It maintains that all human religions and philosophies originally sprang from a single, hidden source. That source was 'universal science'. Knowledge of it was held by the masters, who were using her, Madame Blavatsky, to convey the truth to humankind, she added.

The success of *Isis Unveiled* gave the Theosophical Society a great fillip. Thomas Edison and Adner Doubleday, the latter the celebrated Civil War general and supposed inventor of baseball, both joined. Lodges were opened in London and Bombay. However, Blavatsky's occult credentials soon came under attack from her former spiritual mentor, the medium Daniel Dunglas Home. Blavatsky's private life also came under scrutiny and it was rumoured that she was about to be charged with bigamy. Olcott and Blavatsky set off for India.

Although the two Theosophists had formerly poured scorn on the idea of reincarnation, once in India, where the concept was widely accepted, they took it on board, too. After all, it explained how the masters had amassed their secret knowledge: they had built it up over the course of their successive lives. Two of the masters became particularly important to Blavatsky. One was Master Morya, whom she claimed that she had met in England during the 1850s when he was already 125 years old. The other was Master Koot Hoomi, who had also spent time in Europe, where he frequented the beer halls of Munich.

Under the guidance of the *mahatmas*, Blavatsky began to recruit future Theosophists. One, an impressionable youth named Ramaswamier, set out after her when he thought that he was going to visit the masters. Although it was Madame Blavatsky, he believed that he saw a master on horseback. He knew that the figure was a master, he explained, because he had already seen him in an astral projection back at the Theosophical headquarters. Ramaswamier's claims were given wide circulation through Theosophical journals.

Olcott and Blavatsky then had a parting of the ways. Although he dressed like a Hindu and was bearded like a Sikh, Olcott became a Buddhist. He travelled widely, setting up numerous new lodges and recruiting thousands. But he had lost interest in the mystical side of Theosophy and instead concentrated increasingly on social reform and the idea of a universal brotherhood.

Madame Blavatsky, however, plunged deeper into the occult. She used her enormous charms to woo Alfred Percy Sinnett, the editor of the British daily newspaper in India, *The Pioneer*. Already interested in the occult, Sinnett found that letters from the masters fell from the skies whenever he visited the headquarters of the Theosophical Society. And when Madame Blavatsky went to stay at his house in Allahabad more letters mysteriously appeared on his pillow in the morning. In 1881 Sinnett wrote a book extolling both Theosophy and Madame Blavatsky, which aroused interest in England. This did not impress the paper's owners, however, who were conservative Christians, and Sinnett was sacked.

Sinnett, Blavatsky and Olcott then headed for London, leaving Blavatsky's handyman and housekeeper, Alexis and Emma Coulomb, in charge of the Theosophical Society's headquarters, which had recently moved from Bombay to Adyar, near Madras. The Coulombs soon fell out with other members of the Theosophical Society and talked freely to the staff of *Christian College Magazine*, which was run by Protestant missionaries who thought little of Blavatsky. The astral projections of the masters were nothing but turbaned dummies that were paraded on moonlit nights, the Coulombs said. And the letters from the masters that fell from the sky were, in fact, pushed through a crack in the ceiling.

Blavatsky threatened to sue her detractors, but Olcott counselled caution: a court case would put all the claims of the Theosophical Society on trial. Blavatsky never set foot in India again. Worse was to come. The recently founded Society for Psychic Research was eager to prove Madame Blavatsky's outlandish claims for Theosophy and she agreed to co-operate. But then the society sent an investigator out to India. Despite openly admitting being pro-Theosophy, the investigator found that the Coulombs' claims were true, and in a 200-page report added numerous other examples of Blavatsky's fakery – including revealing that the 'master' whom Ramaswamier had seen on horseback was, in fact, a man hired by Blavatsky to play the part. This news distressed one Indian devotee so much that he set out to Tibet to make his own investigation. Sometime later his frozen corpse was found. The resulting scandal would have sunk anyone else, but Madame Blavatsky's greatest triumph was still to come.

After a quick tour of the Continent she sat down and wrote the 1,500-page *The Secret Doctrine*. In this, the tenets of Theosophy were, at last, fully unveiled. Published in 1888, *The Secret Doctrine* purports to have been based on the world's first book, *The Stanzas of Dzyan*, which, unfortunately, scholars through the ages have failed to unearth. The heavens, it says, are full of numerous universes, each containing countless solar systems. Every solar system has its own god; beneath him are seven planetary spirits, each in charge of a phalanx of angels. Evolution takes place in steps, from mineral to vegetable to animal to human to the superhuman, or spiritual being, to come. The first inhabitants of the Earth, the book stated, were descended from the residents of the moon and lived on a continent called the Imperishable Sacred Land. Then came the Hyperborean race, also known as the Boneless or the Sweatborn. They lived at the North Pole (but since they did not have bodies they presumably did not feel the cold). Next came the Lemurians, who were the first to have bodies and reproduce by means of sexual intercourse. Their homeland, Blavatsky said, is now at the bottom of the Indian Ocean.

The fifth of these so-called 'root races' was the Aryans, who spread south and west from northern Asia. Apparently, we are still in the Aryan phase. Madam Blavatsky revealed that there will be two more root races. Then the cycle will be complete and humans will move to another planet to start all over again. Meanwhile, individual humans progress from having physical bodies, through the astral, mental and ethereal states in a series of incarnations. Progress is regulated by karma. Obviously, those with the best karma have arrived at the highest ethereal state. These are the masters.

Even though she had been exposed as a fraud, *The Secret Doctrine* brought Madame Blavatsky many plaudits. New members flocked to the Theosophical Society and Madame Blavatsky formed an inner circle, called the Esoteric Section, as a rival to the recently established Hermetic Order of the Golden Dawn. She established the magazine *Lucifer* and published two more books, *The Key to Theosophy* and *The Voice of Silence*, before she died in 1891. Even sceptical newspapers conceded in their obituaries that she was one of the most remarkable women of the nineteenth century.

Her final work, *The Theosophical Glossary*, was published posthumously. However, during her lifetime she had promised two more volumes of *The Secret Doctrine*, which would finally explain all the secrets of the occult. Some Theosophists are still waiting for them.

Madame Blavatsky had left instructions that after her death the British Annie Wood Besant, the head of the Esoteric Section, should take over as the leader of the Theosophical Society. As a teenager Besant had been obsessed with Anglo-Catholicism and at 20 had married an elderly clergyman. But she was not cut out to be the wife of a country vicar and left him after six years of marriage. She became a socialist, a free-thinker and an atheist. A friend of George Bernard Shaw, she rose rapidly through the ranks of the British Fabian Society and the National Secular Society. As a feminist campaigner she was unsuccessfully prosecuted for selling obscene literature – in the form of a booklet on contraception – through the post.

When *The Secret Doctrine* was published she had reviewed it favourably. Madame Blavatsky had quickly recruited her and had made her head of the Esoteric Section, the occult wing of Theosophy. As the successor of Blavatsky Besant was an inspired choice: she could not be accused of fakery because she professed neither psychic nor spiritual powers. However, she had a rival for the post: William Q Judge, one of the founder members of the Theosophical Society in New York. He headed the American Section and thought that he, rather than the parvenue Besant, should be in charge of the society. He suggested that they share power and then set sail for England to meet Besant.

When Judge turned up in London to discuss the matter Besant received a mysterious letter from the *mahatmas* telling her that Judge was right: he should be in charge. This was very puzzling, as Madame Blavatsky had said that the letters would stop when she died, but they nevertheless kept on coming. They looked just like the ones that had arrived during Madame

Blavatsky's lifetime and were in exactly the same handwriting. Besant was so convinced by the letters that she went public and told a meeting that she had received them from an 'unseen world'. If Madame Blavatsky was a fraud who had written the letters to hers then she, too, was a fraud, Besant said. This statement caused a sensation. Besant had a towering reputation and not even her worst enemy would have called her a liar. People began to believe that the Society of Psychical Research had judged Blavatsky too harshly.

Membership of the Theosophical Society accordingly rose again. A novel called *The Mahatma*, about a master, was serialised in a magazine. *Mahatma* hats went on sale and fashionable Londoners greeted each other by asking 'How's your karma?' Even William Gladstone, the once and future prime minister, was asked questions about Theosophy at a working men's club, according to *The Times*.

By 1894 Judge was trying to force Besant out of the society. Letters from the *mahatmas* now claimed that Besant was controlled by 'dark powers'. Besant retaliated by revealing that the letters were a fraud. Presumably Judge had got hold of the crayons and rice paper that Blavatsky had used, along with the great seal of the *mahatmas*, and after a little practice he had managed to forge Blavatsky's handwriting.

Judge sailed back to the United States and formed the 85 US chapters of the Theosophical Society into the Theosophical Society of America. Besant struck back with a speaking tour of the USA and managed to found 37 new lodges that were loyal to her.

The game was up in England, however. The Theosophical Society had been exposed for the second time as a fraud, so Besant headed to Adyar, where the Indian wing of the organisation was still expanding. Besant became a passionate advocate of Indian independence, establishing the Indian Home Rule League and becoming the president of the Indian National Congress. The Theosophical Society in India turned itself over to humanitarian work and social reform. It established a number of schools, including the Central Hindu College, where Mahatma Gandhi and Pandit Nehru learnt much of the background of Hinduism. Although critical of Theosophy, Gandhi acknowledged that it was Besant who had brought the idea of Indian home rule to every household in the Subcontinent. She bought a newspaper with which to propound the idea of Indian independence, renaming it *New India* and making it one of biggest-selling dailies in the country. During World War I she was even interned for her anti-British views, but was released after three months as a result of the public outcry.

Having been estranged from one Anglican priest, she then became involved with another: the Reverend Charles W Leadbeater, who had early been expelled from the Theosophical Society for telling the boys in his charge that it was alright to masturbate. (Besant miraculously came up with a letter from the masters saying that Leadbeater was right.) Together they wrote a number of books which turned the Theosophical Society more towards Esoteric Christianity than the Esoteric Buddhism that was Olcott's legacy. (However, Besant did write *An Introduction to Yoga* and translated the Indian scripture the *Bhagavad-Gita* into English.)

In 1908 Leadbeater became entranced by the 14-year-old Jiddu Krishnamurti, apparently because of his remarkable aura. Leadbeater announced that Krishnamurti would become the long-awaited fifth Buddha, the living incarnation of a master and a new world teacher. The wisdom that he would deliver, Leadbeater believed, would begin a new root race as described in *The Secret Doctrine*. Besant adopted Krishnamurti and established the Order of the Star in the East as a vehicle for his mission. This caused dissent among many Theosophists, who accused Besant and Leadbeater of trying to start a new church, the antithesis of everything that Theosophy was supposed to stand for.

The head of the German chapter, Rudolf Steiner, quit Theosophy in order to start Anthroposophy. Rather than evolving towards becoming God-like beings, such as the masters, Steiner taught that human beings had once, in the dim and distant past, possessed those divine qualities and should now struggle to find them within themselves again. Through Christ, Steiner said, people could ascend to higher spiritual levels, but the two evil powers of Lucifer – through human pride – and Ahriman – through the material world – held them back. Steiner introduced a spiritual theory for what is now known as organic farming – with natural' times for sowing and harvesting being prescribed and chemical fertilisers being prohibited. He also pioneered 'child-centred' education, with his Anthroposophical theories emphasising the importance of awakening the talents that lay within the child rather than imposing learning on it.

Leadbeater was indeed trying to start a new church and in 1916, he founded the Liberal Catholic Church. For her part, Besant persisted with Krishnamurti. But as the boy grew up he began to have doubts about the destiny that Leadbeater and Besant had thrust upon him. In 1929, at a Theosophist summer camp in front of Besant and 3,000 others, he denied that he was a new incarnation of the Messiah and disbanded the Order of the Star in the East. He became an independent teacher and lectured until his death in 1986. The Krishnamurti Foundation, based in Ojai, California, promotes his work, and his followers call themselves Liberal Theosophists.

Besant never really recovered from this setback. She withdrew to the Theosophist headquarters at Adyar, where she died in 1933. Her body was cremated Hindu-style; it was Leadbeater who lit the funeral pyre.

As well as Anthroposophy, Theosophy had further spin-offs. New Revelation Theosophy, for example, claims that it possesses new teachings from the masters. Another, the Arcane School, was established in California by Alice Bailey. An English Theosophist, Bailey moved to California in 1917, opening a vegetarian café and marrying the national secretary of the Theosophical Society, Forst Bailey. In 1919, while walking in the Hollywood Hills, she said that she had bumped into one of the Tibetan masters, Djwhal Khul, who asked her to be his secretary and began dictating books to her at a prodigious rate. The central tenet of these volumes, which otherwise resembled existing works of Theosophy, is that Christ will reappear as a new world leader and that devotees should meditate in order to prepare themselves for the event.

In 1949 another cult developed from the Arcane School; the new cult ran Full Moon Meditation groups, which meditated every full moon. And the Astara Foundation, which was established in California in 1951 by Robert and Earlyne Chaney, has attempted to return to the early teachings of the Theosophical Society.

It is interesting to note that the influence of Theosophy can furthermore be seen in the works of a number of modern artists, including Piet Mondrian and Wassily Kandinsky.

8 ❖ The Hermetic Order of the Golden Dawn

The pinnacle of late Victorian mysticism was represented by the Hermetic Order of the Golden Dawn. Although the cult never boasted more than 300 members – compared with the Theosophical Society's peak figure of 45,000 – it was extraordinarily influential.

While the Theosophical Society was basically a debating group within which occult and mystical ideas were discussed, the Hermetic Order of the Golden Dawn was a full-blown occult society which practised mysterious rituals and magical rites. Its members included Freemasons, Rosicrucians and Theosophists who believed that they could attain occult powers.

In order to enhance its credibility, any such cult would claim that it could trace its roots back to the beginning of time, but, to all intents and purposes the beginning of time for the Hermetic Order of the Golden Dawn was 1880. It was then that the Reverend A F A Woodford, an Anglican clergyman who was also a Freemason, was said to have come across a pile of manuscripts while rummaging around in a London bookshop. They seemed to have been written in an ancient script. By 1887 they had found their way into the hands of a north London coroner named Dr William Wynn Wescott. He was a Theosophist, a Rosicrucian and a Freemason. Wescott claimed that while leafing through the manuscripts he came across a letter written in German. It said that anyone who wanted to know more should contact the *Sapiens Dominator Astris* – which is Latin for the 'wise one who lives in the stars'. Fortunately, the wise one could be reached via Fr¨ulein Anna Sprengel, and her address in Germany was conveniently provided. Wescott said that he had contacted her and, with the help of the wise one, had deciphered the manuscript. It outlined five rituals which would generate occult power. The wise one then told Wescott to recruit some initiates and try out the rituals.

Wescott accordingly formed the Hermetic Order of the Golden Dawn. After it had been established, Wescott said, Sprengel died and all communication with the wise one ceased. Yet it is highly probable that neither Sprengel nor the wise one nor Reverend Woodford had ever existed, and that the letter was a forgery and that the manuscripts had been produced by Wescott himself. What motive Wescott might have had for founding the order we can only speculate on. It was certainly not money: the membership fee was only two shillings and six pence – 12« new pence – a year, which collectively hardly covered the outgoings on the order's incense, letterhead and ritual wine. Perhaps it made Wescott feel important: during the 1880s and 1890s there were a lot of people who liked dressing up in funny clothes. But Wescott's reasons for establishing the order hardly mattered and from such flimsy beginnings the order flourished.

Wescott recruited a young Scotsman, Samuel Liddell Mathers, to organise the order's rituals for him. Mathers was a very strange man, with peculiar, fish-like eyes. He and his wife, Moina, who was known as Vestigia to the cult, forswore sex and strove to keep themselves 'perfectly clean'. He devised splendid costumes and elaborate rituals from the ancient texts that he studied in the British Museum, and he staged the order's ceremonies with theatrical flair.

The poet W B Yeats was charmed by Mathers and left the Theosophical Society in order to join the Golden Dawn. As a child, Yeats had been interested in Irish folk tales of the supernatural and had witnessed a strange ceremony in which a hooded sorcerer slit the throat of a chicken. As a member of the Esoteric Section of the Theosophical Society he claimed to have learnt how to make a needle that was suspended on a silk thread in a glass case swing to and fro. Though this feat of occult power was hardly impressive, it was a beginning. The Golden Dawn, Yeats hoped, would allow him to communicate with evil powers.

While Yeats was agitating for Irish home rule, Mathers dreamt of restoring a Stuart king to the throne of an independent Scotland, and added the more Scottish-sounding MacGregor to his name. Samuel Liddell MacGregor Mathers – or, as he sometimes called himself, Count MacGregor de Glenstrae – claimed that he was what we would today regard as the equivalent of the original Highlander about whom late-twentieth-century films were made. He said that he was an immortal who had at one time had been James IV of Scotland (all other sources say that James IV died at Flodden in 1513).

Thus claiming royal blood, Mathers acted autocratically and allowed no one to challenge his word. Nevertheless, the Golden Dawn flourished under his leadership. It soon had five temples, stretching from Edinburgh to Paris.

Florence Farr, the beautiful actress and one-time mistress of George Bernard Shaw, became the principal instructor of ritual at the Isis-Urania Temple of the Golden Dawn in London. She claimed to have raised a spirit named Taphthartharath by boiling a pickled snake in a broth of magical ingredients, which included coriander seeds and gum ammoniac. The temple's records do not record what the spirit looked like, nor whether he actually appeared in prosaic, physical form. However, he was made to promise to reveal 'all the mysteries of the hidden arts and sciences' before being allowed to return from whence he came. All present recorded that it was a thoroughly satisfactory experience.

Another important recruit was Annie Horniman, the daughter of the wealthy tea importer who built the Abbey Theatre in Dublin. She became Mathers' benefactor, getting him the job of curator at her father's museum in south London. William Peck, the director of the Edinburgh Observatory, was also a member. So were the Kabbalah scholar and designer of the modern Tarot pack, A E Waite; the writer of occult fiction, Algernon Blackwood; and the psychoanalyst Dione Fortune, who wrote novels concerning the supernatural.

Compared with these luminaries Mathers might have been thought of as a bit of a non-entity, but only Mathers and his wife had access to the 'secret chiefs', the Golden Dawn's equivalent to the Theosophists' masters. Writing in 1896, Mathers said that he did not even know the secret chiefs'

WB Yeats who was a member of the Hermetic Order of the Golden Dawn

earthly names, and that he had only rarely seen them in their physical forms. He made rendezvous with them astrally, he said, and claimed that meeting them was like being close to a lighting bolt, only more sustained. A lesser man, he said, could not have survived even five minutes in their presence.

The secret chiefs dictated their instructions for the order's rituals by means of clairvoyance, directing Mathers to old books, or by speaking to him or to Vestigia in disembodied voices. Of course, this was terrible strain on them, and Mathers and his wife feared for their lives.

In 1892 Mathers and his wife moved to Paris, where, under the guidance of the secret chiefs, they lived it up at Horniman's expense. Mathers also founded an inner circle, called the Order of the Ruby Rose and the Cross of Golden. In order simply to enter it members of the Golden Dawn had to pass all sorts of exams. Within the *Ordo Rosae Rubeae et Aurea Crucis*, to give it its Latin name, there were five more grades with more exams to pass. Naturally, only Mathers and Wescott attained the top grade.

This new order needed fresh initiation rites. These took place in a seven-sided vault whose walls were covered with Kabbalistic and other occult symbols. Mathers or Wescott would lie in what they claimed to be Christian Rosenkreutz's coffin, while initiates swore on pain of a terrible death not to abuse the great power with which they were going to be entrusted. (This injunction did not restrain one member, an electrical engineer named Alan Bennett, who claimed to have developed a glass rod that could paralyse a victim.)

Unfortunately, the authorities for whom Wescott worked were not amused by the idea of a live coroner lying in a coffin and forced him to leave the Golden Dawn. This left Mathers as the head of magic. He derived his powers, he said, from the works of John Dee, the advisor on the occult to Elizabeth I; *The Clavicula of Solomon the King*, a medieval primer on alchemy in the British Museum; and *The Sacred Magic of Abra-Melin the Mage*, an occult work that Mathers claimed to have discovered and translated himself.

Horniman tried to put the order's magic to good use and attempted to cure an epileptic child named Charlie Sewell by giving him treatment on the 'astral plane'. Mathers was on hand to advise. The poor child endured a number of rituals involving golden hexagrams and red crosses; his home was exorcised of black imps and he was laden down with talismans. It is not recorded whether he got better. The infamous Aleister Crowley tried to cure the mother of another member by using a talisman. Unfortunately, the member did not follow Crowley's instructions properly and almost killed the old woman. Once he had done it properly, however, she was cured and lived on until she was 92, according to the occult journal *Equinox*, which just happened to be published by Crowley.

Things then started to get nasty within the Golden Dawn. Crowley accused the Nobel laureate Yeats of attacking him with black magic because he was jealous that Crowley was a better poet. Fortune next reported being plagued by demons conjured up by Vestigia Mathers. Her home was besieged by black cats, she said, and a giant tabby – 'twice the size of a tiger' – appeared indoors, although it disappeared when she stared at it. Fortune then fought a titanic battle with Vestigia on the astral plane. Fortunately, the secret chiefs seem to have changed sides and favoured Fortune. She prevailed, although Vestigia managed to inflict some wounds on Fortune's back, which, Fortune said, resembled the scratches of a giant cat.

All this infighting could have been dismissed as being rather silly if it had not resulted in tragedy. Vestigia had initiated a 33-year-old mentally unstable woman named Norah Emily Farnario into the Order of the Alpha and Omega, an occult offshoot of the Golden Dawn. In the autumn of 1929 Farnario travelled to the remote island of Iona, one of the Inner Hebrides off the western coast of Scotland. She rented a room in a croft, but the islanders shunned the strange interloper and left her largely to her own devices. However, they became concerned when she started babbling to anyone who would listen that she was in touch with the 'world beyond'. Without warning Farnario grew hysterical and packed her bags and tried to leave the island. But it was a Sunday and the islanders, being strict Christians, did not allow the ferry to operate on the Sabbath. Next morning, her landlady found that her bed had not been slept in; her clothes were folded neatly beside it, but there was no sign of Farnario. There was no immediate cause for concern, as the strange women regularly went for walks at night, but when she had not turned up by the following afternoon a search was begun.

Farnario's body was found on the following Wednesday. It was spread-eagled high up on the moor, naked, except for a silver chain around her neck and the black cloak worn by the Order of Alpha and Omega in which it was swathed. The soles of her feet had been cut and had bled, as if she had been running away from something. Her face was contorted into an expression of sheer terror. In her hand was the long-bladed knife that was used in the order's rituals. She had been cutting a cross in the turf when she died. On Farnario's death certificate, the cause of death was simply given as 'heart failure'. Fortune, however, claimed that she had been murdered on the astral plane by Vestigia Mathers. Fortune subsequently left the order to found the Fraternity of the Inner Light.

Horniman also fell out with the Mathers. She stopped the money that was funding their extravagant lifestyle in Paris, so Mathers expelled her from the order. Crowley, the self-styled 'wickedest man in the world', was also causing disruption within the Golden Dawn because of his dangerously uncontrolled behaviour. But Mathers nevertheless backed Crowley against the other concerned members.

In 1900 the London temple refused to initiate Crowley into the Order of the Ruby Rose and Golden Cross, against Mathers' specific instructions. Mathers then invited Crowley over to Paris, fired Farr and abolished the management committee which was challenging his position as leader. Mathers called on the powers of the secret chiefs to punish those opposed him. On a more practical level, Crowley was sent back to London to seize control of the order. When he broke into the Golden Dawn's headquarters in Blythe Road, Farr and her followers called the police and ejected him. He returned in full Highland garb, wearing the black mask of Osiris and brandishing a dagger. Again he was ejected.

Crowley went back to Paris, where he found Mathers shaking some dried peas in a sieve and calling on the demons Typhon-Set and Beelzebub to strike down his enemies. The malevolent spirits let him down and Mathers was expelled from the Golden Dawn. He remained in France, where he died in 1918. Yeats then took over, but could not hold the Golden Dawn together; the poet finally gave up on sorcery in 1923. One Golden Dawn spin-off – the *Stellar Matutina*, or 'Morning Star' – limped on into the 1930s.

9 ❖ The Ordo Templi Orientis

Aleister Crowley is the primary link between the Hermetic Order of the Golden Dawn and a number of other twentieth-century cults. He forged that link through a highly secretive German cult called the *Ordo Templi Orientis*.

Crowley was born in 1875 into a family of austere Plymouth Brethren. He early on rebelled against the strict and joyless sect, taking to drink and drugs, sleeping with his mother's maid and asking for the body of his still-born sister to experiment on. When he was refused the body he went to work on a live cat, taking perverse delight in testing whether it really did have nine lives. He dosed it with arsenic, chloroformed it, hanged it over a gas jet, stabbed it, drowned it, cut its throat, smashed its skull, burned it and threw it from an upstairs window. The cat did not survive. It was Crowley's own mother who first called him 'The Beast' – after the Great Beast in the biblical Book of Revelation – a name that he readily accepted.

At Trinity College, Cambridge University, Crowley changed his name from Edward Alexander to Aleister and began his lifelong study of the occult. At the age of 23 he joined the Hermetic Order of the Golden Dawn. In order to practise the magic that he learnt within the order, he rented Bokeskin House on Loch Ness, where he tried to conjure up his guardian angel. Legend has it that he summoned up a host of evil spirits instead.

Crowley's bizarre and disruptive behaviour resulted in both his and Mathers' expulsion from the order. He soon fell out with Mathers, too, over sex. A professed celibate, Mathers insisted on six months' abstinence on the part of his followers. Crowley could not manage this and initiated a magical ceremony which involved the deflowering of young girls; it resulted in the prosecution of two cult members for rape in 1901.

In 1903 he met and married the psychic medium Rose Kelly, the sister of the artist Sir Gerald Kelly. While honeymooning in Cairo in 1904, Crowley supposedly conjured up a spirit called Aiwass. Speaking for the Egyptian god Horus through Rose, Aiwass dictated Crowley's most famous book, *Liber Legis*, or *The Book of the Law*. It said that Christianity was about to be swept away to be replaced by a new religious order. Its messiah would be Crowley, naturally, and he accordingly proclaimed himself 'The Great Beast 666, Prophet of the New Aeon'. Rose became his first 'Scarlet Woman', named after the biblical consort of the Beast.

Aiwass encouraged Crowley to take all the drugs that he could lay his hands on. The message for the new age was simple: Satan was not an external force, but could be found within the heart of every man and woman. Satan was furthermore the source of unlimited power, which could be released simply by discarding all moral scruples.

In 1905 Crowley went climbing in the Himalayas. On an expedition up the world's third highest mountain, Kangchenjunga, six of the party fell down a slope. Crowley refused rescue them and four died. He also treated the porters brutally, making them walk barefoot over ice (there were persistent rumours that he'd eaten one or two). In the end he abandoned the expedition and absconded with the group's money.

'Do what thou wilt shall be the whole of the law', wrote Crowley. Sadly, it was not an original thought: it had been the motto of the co-educational Abbey of Thélème in the first book of François Rabelais' satirical classic *The History of Gargantua and Pantagruel*, which had been published in 1532.

In 1907 Crowley established his own cult, *Argentum Astrum*, or the Order of the Silver Star. On a mountain top in Morocco in 1909, with his acolyte Victor Neuburg, Crowley had a revelation that sex was linked to magic. He took as his mistress Leila Waddell, who had the 'mark of the Beast' tattooed between her breasts. By then, Rose was drinking a bottle of whisky a day, according to Crowley. They divorced, and Rose was committed to a mental institution two years later. His second wife, the Nicaraguan beauty Maria de Miramar, suffered the same fate, and a number of his other scarlet women were similarly either institutionalised, committed suicide or drank themselves to death after parting from Crowley. He apparently had an irresistible seduction technique: having filed his teeth to sharp points, vampire-style, he then sank them into the wrists of the women whom he fancied. Even when he was middle-aged, bald and bloated, he continued to attract women. In 1934 a 19-year-old girl threw herself at him in the street and insisted that he give her a baby. He obligingly took her to bed. She ended up in an asylum, too.

Neuburg became the focal point of Crowley's occult ceremonies. These usually involved sodomy in a pentagram drawn within a circle. In Paris, Crowley and Neuburg conducted a series of rituals. Worshippers danced within a pentacle painted on the floor while Neuburg had his buttocks scourged. An inverted cross was carved on his chest and then he was ritually sodomised. Blood was drunk and faeces were eaten. A large number of snakes were released, and a frog was baptised 'Jesus of Nazareth' before being crucified and stabbed. Plans were make to kidnap, rape and murder a young girl, and then to cut up her body into nine pieces which would be offered up to nine demons. It is unclear, however, whether this was actually done.

In 1912 a German Freemason, Theodore Ruess, visited Crowley in Scotland. He was the head of the secretive *Ordo Templi Orientis* (OTO), which had been founded in Germany in 1904. The cult's doctrine seems to have been a confusing mixture of oriental philosophy and European Tantrism. It claimed to possess the key to all the Masonic and Hermetic secrets. These mysteries were gradually revealed as members rose through the nine grades of the cult. Rituals involved a ceremonial garter, a dagger and a chalice, to represent symbolic sexual intercourse, and there was a strong emphasis on sexual magic.

Ruess accused Crowley of having revealed his the cult's secret rituals, but Crowley managed to convince him that he had stumbled on the rituals independently, and Ruess invited Crowley to join the *Ordo Templi Orientis*. Within five years Crowley had taken over the OTO, which increasingly became a vehicle for his Satanism. 'My master is Satan', said Crowley. 'Resist not evil.'

In order to escape the growing interest of the press and the impending bankruptcy caused by his expensive addiction to cocaine and heroin, Crowley moved to a derelict farmhouse near Celalu, in northern Sicily. He

Aleister Crowley. He provided the primary link between the Hermatic Order of the Golden Dawn and other 20th Century cults

converted it into a Satanic temple called the Abbey of Thélèma (cf Rabelais), where he kept bloodstained neckties that he claimed had belonged to Jack the Ripper. There he set up home with Leah Hirsig, a school mistress whom he had met in New York in 1918. Her friend, Ninette Shunway, acted as a nanny for their daughter, Poupée. Crowley also called Shunway his 'second concubine'.

Leah could match Crowley drug for drug and flirted with him around the edges of insanity. The floor of the central hall of the farmhouse had a circle and a pentagram painted on it. The walls were hung with obscene and blasphemous paintings; one showed the Knight Templars' goatish figure, Baphomet – a name that Crowley had taken for himself – sodomising a man. A whip, a phallus and a copy of Crowley's *Black Book of Rituals* sat on an altar, to which devotees would come from all over the world to celebrate Black Mass. Crowley would eat a communion wafer smeared with Leah's excrement. He would disembowel a live cat, collect its blood and then drink it. In one ceremony, Leah had sex with a goat whose throat was cut at the climax of the ritual; the blood was again collected and consumed.

One visitor, the American actress Jane Wolfe, found the farmhouse – or perhaps Crowley's domestic arrangements – so squalid that she lived in a tent outside. The artist's model Betty May was also appalled, but her husband, Raoul Loveday, was seduced. Already in poor health, possibly suffering from hepatitis and dysentery, Loveday collapsed and died after drinking the blood of a sacrificial cat. The British tabloids had a field day with the tales of 'drugs, magic and vile practices'.

Soon afterwards a child went missing from a nearby village. Crowley was accused of kidnapping and killing it. No charges were brought, but within a week Mussolini had ordered Crowley's expulsion from Italy. Leah followed Crowley into exile. She tolerated his new mistresses, but in 1925 he ran off with another woman. Leah continued to correspond with Crowley, but gradually sanity prevailed and in 1930 she returned to the USA and went back to school-teaching.

Crowley wrote a lurid autobiography, *Confessions*, an autobiographical novel called *The Diary of a Drug Fiend* and a number of pornographic works. He also painted, exhibiting his work in Berlin in 1930. Supported by OTO members in Germany, he produced the book *Magick in Theory and Practice* (he spelt 'magick' with a 'k' in order to distinguish his occult 'magick' from conjuring). The book was designed to be a handbook for beginners. In it, Crowley emphasised the importance of animal and possibly also human sacrifice. He concluded 'A male child of perfect innocence and high intelligence is the most satisfactory and suitable victim.' In a footnote, Crowley claimed to have performed such human sacrifices on average 150 times a year between 1912 and 1928, killing over 2,000 children. And he was unrepentant: in a court case in 1934 Crowley was asked 'Do you believe as a magician in bloody sacrifice?' He replied 'Yes.' 'You say for nearly all purposes human sacrifice is best?' 'Yes, it is', he replied.

Crowley's *Magick in Theory and Practice* remains the 'bible' of modern Satanists and has spurred on more than one would-be magician to murder a child. After its publication Crowley subsided into poverty, his impecunious state hastened by his heroin and cocaine addictions. He spent his twilight years in a private hotel called Netherwood, in Hastings. He died in Brighton, in 1947, at the age of 72. His body was cremated in a Black Mass, much to the outrage of the good people of Sussex. His ashes were sent to his successor, Karl Germer.

Germer had been arrested and interned when the Nazis had tried to stamp out OTO in Germany in 1937. In 1941 he was deported to the USA, where he set up a number of new lodges in California. One of them was the Church of Thelema, in Pasadena. It was run by Jack Parsons, who was a rocket scientist who had developed the jet-assisted take-off system during World War II. Earlier, Parsons had been a disciple of Wilfred Smith, who had held the devil-worshipping parties at Agape Lodge during the 1930s that had attracted the Hollywood crowd.

In 1946 Parsons attempted to bring down the 'Whore of Babylon' from the astral plane and make it incarnate in the womb of a woman. The experiment took place over the first three days of March. While chanting various incantations, Parsons repeatedly had sex with a willing devotee, while another OTO member, the science-fiction writer L Ron Hubbard, made copious notes. When Crowley heard about this bizarre experiment he wrote it off as being 'idiotic'. Indeed, in the event the woman did not even become pregnant. Parsons was left exhausted and Hubbard ran off with Parsons' girlfriend, as well as $10,000 of his money, and founded the Church of Scientology. Distraught, Parsons changed his name to Belarian Armiluss All Dajjaj Antichrist and then blew himself up in a chemical explosion in the basement laboratory of his home. For his part, Hubbard later claimed to have studied under Crowley.

10 ❖ Scientology

The Church of Scientology claims to have 8 million members worldwide, which makes it by far the largest of all of the non-Christian cults. It is also one of the wealthiest, most secretive and most litigious.

It was established by the science-fiction writer L Ron Hubbard, who incorporated the Church of Scientology in New Jersey in 1953. The Church of Scientology of California, which became the organisation's headquarters, was founded in Los Angeles in 1954. Its principle overseas operation was started in 1959 in Britain, at Saint Hill Manor, near East Grinstead in Sussex, but its other centres of operation have now taken the generic name Saint Hill.

Hubbard was born in 1911, in Tilden, Nebraska. His father was an officer in the US Navy. A promising student at school, Hubbard then went to George Washington University, where he studied molecular physics, but

L Ron Hubbard, scientific writer who founded the Church of Scientology

left after one term and began writing science-fiction stories.

During World War II he joined the US Navy. Scientologists say that he was a war hero, although his service record does not bear this claim out. It says that he never saw action and was invalided out of the navy with a duodenal ulcer. The Church of Scientology alleges that the authorities falsified the record because he had been involved in top-secret operations. When the Freedom of Information Act put paid to that story, the church said that enemies of Scientology had tampered with the records.

During the 1940s Hubbard was a friend of the writer A E van Vogt, who created the fictional 'Science of Nexialism' – an advanced and beneficial form of psychological conditioning. Hubbard came up with his own version of the therapy, which was published in a much-heralded, 40-page article in the magazine *Astounding Science Fiction* in April 1950. It was so well received that Hubbard dashed out the classic work *Dianetics: the Modern Science of Mental Health*. According to Hubbard, the unconscious, or 'reactive', mind stores the trauma of every unpleasant thing that has ever happened, even though the conscious mind may have forgotten them. These unconscious memories, or 'engrams', begin to be stored even before birth.

The aim of dianetics is to rid individuals of all their engrams and thus make them 'clear'. This is done by using a technique called 'auditing', whereby the auditor takes the 'pre-clear' individual back to the source of the engram. In other words, dianetics is a form of psychotherapy. Scientologists believe that engrams can be removed by this form of counselling or confession, but, of course, this takes several hundred hours of auditing, which costs thousands of pounds. Then there remain are all the engrams that individuals have accumulated in past lives to deal with. Nevertheless, once you are clear you stay clear, which gives you total recall and means that you can make mathematical calculations or solve chess problems in a matter of seconds that would otherwise have taken hours.

Hubbard's theory went down well in the therapy-crazed USA, and his book quickly became a best-seller; by 1995 Hubbard had sold over 16 million copies. Dianetics groups sprang up all over the country. Hubbard himself established the Hubbard Dianetic Research Foundation, but it quickly ran out of money. In 1952 it went bankrupt and Hubbard sold out his interest in it, which included his copyright to *Dianetics: the Modern Science of Mental Health*, to one of the backers, Don Purcell.

Hubbard next founded the Association of Scientologists and sued Purcell for using his ideas. Purcell eventually returned the rights to Hubbard's book and went to work on a similar idea to dianetics, which he called synergetics. Then Scientology became a church (although its adherents deny that it is a religion). Back in the 1940s, when Hubbard had been discussing the writer's perennial money problems with other authors, he quoted George Orwell, who said that the best way in which to make money was start a religion. Indeed, in 1955 the Church of Scientology was awarded tax-exempt status as a non-profit-making organisation, but within three years the US Internal Revenue Service (IRS) was attempting to withdraw that status.

The next 'breakthrough' in Scientology was the development of the E-meter. Like a primitive lie detector, an E-meter measures skin conductivity when the subject clutches its two probes. Its purpose, Scientologists say, is to measure engrams, and it is essential for discovering whether you are clear or not. In 1995 the latest Super 8 model cost the equivalent of £2,600. However, by the Church of Scientology's own admission, it does not work. In 1963 the US Food and Drug Administration raided the Church of Scientology in Washington, DC, and seized all of its E-meters, on the grounds that it is illegal in the USA to practise any form of medical diagnosis or therapy unless you are medically qualified. A 1969 court ruling allowed Scientologists to use E-meters only on the assumption that they were totally ineffective.

Although Scientologists deny that Scientology is a religion, many of its early adherents, including A E van Vogt and the British science-fiction writer George Hay, were put off by Hubbard's increasingly transcendental pronouncements. He probably made these because once an adherent has become clear there is nothing left for them, or the church, to do. In order to maintain the structure of the cult there must therefore be inner groups and further ladders to climb, until the clear person crosses, as Scientology puts it, the 'bridge to total freedom'.

By the time that Hubbard died there were eight new levels; there are now fifteen. Of course, these have to be kept secret because if you are not clear and have not been properly prepared by each successive stage the knowledge that is revealed could endanger you.

Level three, known as 'The Wall of Fire', for example, nearly killed Hubbard himself when he discovered it, he said. It teaches that 75 million years ago the galaxy was over-populated. The dictator Xenu persuaded billions of beings from the 75 inhabited planets of the Galactic Federation to move to Teegeeack, or the planet that we call Earth. He chained them up in volcanoes on Hawaii and bombarded them with nuclear bombs, which released the inner selves, or Theta beings, from their bodies. The disembodied Theta beings, or Thetans, were then transported to the Canary Islands, where they were frozen in alcohol, wrapped up tightly and then blasted out across the solar system. This process was naturally somewhat traumatic, so these inter-planetary cocktails are now chock-full of engrams and, of course, want to have bodies again. Millions of them cluster around every one of us, bringing with them their engrams, which are allegedly responsible for sexual perversion, religion and all the other troubles in the world.

Not surprisingly, clearing these 'Body Thetans' is a long and costly business. The auditor must take the initiate back for 75 million years in order to clear the cause of the problem.

Governments around the world soon began having problems with the Church of Scientology, especially over its claims for tax-exempt status because it was a religious organisation. In 1965 the Australian government set up a board of inquiry which still stands as the most thorough-going investigation into the cult. Its report concluded 'Scientology is evil, its techniques evil, its practice a serious threat to the community, medically, morally and socially, and its adherents sadly deluded and often mentally ill.' Furthermore, Scientology 'is a delusional belief system, based on fiction and fallacies and propagated by falsehood and deception'. The board of inquiry also dismissed the cult as the 'world's largest organisation of unqualified persons engaged in the practice of dangerous techniques which masquerade as mental therapy'.

Film star John Travolta and his wife Kelly Preston who are both members of the Church of Scientology

Scientology was banned in Australia until 1983; in the following year it was give tax-exempt status as a religion. In 1968 the Britain government banned foreign Scientologists from coming to the UK to study or work; that was ban lifted in 1980. But in a British court case in 1984 the presiding judge came to much the same conclusion as the Australian board of inquiry: 'Scientology is both immoral and socially obnoxious', he said. 'In my judgement it is corrupt, sinister and dangerous. It is based on lies and deceit and has as its real objective money and power for Mr Hubbard, his wife and those close to him at the top.'

Scientology may have made Hubbard very rich, but on a personal level things did not go too smoothly for him. In 1959 his oldest son, Ron Junior, publicly declared that his father was insane. The child of Hubbard's second marriage, his daughter Alexis, Hubbard announced, had, in fact, been fathered by Jack Parsons.

In 1966 Hubbard quit as the head of the Church of Scientology, although he kept all of his financial interests in it intact. He then started the maritime wing of Scientology, Sea Org, and went back to sea. He spent the rest of his life sailing around the world, conveniently remaining off-shore for tax purposes. His three sea-going vessels were crewed by an elite band of Scientologists called 'messengers', who were largely teenage girls. They did everything for him and were subjected to stringent punishments for even the most minor infraction.

On shore, Scientology's discipline was similarly draconian. Auditing had to be done in precisely the way that Hubbard had specified; not even the slightest deviation was permitted. One former Scientologist claimed that adherents were expected to exhibit the mentality of soldier ants. In 1966 Hubbard declared that critics of Scientology should be investigated and undermined; any tactic was fair game when used against Scientology's opponents, who could be 'tricked, sued or lied to or destroyed'. Dirty tricks were used to blacken the name of individuals who opposed them.

The church set up an intelligence unit called the 'Guardian's Office' with which to infiltrate any organisation which was deemed threatening to Scientology. Top of the list was the IRS. During the early 1970s cult members established that the tax authorities were launching a major investigation of the church. In a covert operation, they therefore stole hundreds of relevant documents from the IRS offices in Los Angeles. The US government responded by sending in the FBI. Nine senior Scientologists, including Hubbard's third wife, Mary Sue, were arrested; she eventually served a year in prison after a number of appeals failed.

Hubbard suffered another personal tragedy when his second son, Quentin, committed suicide. He was gay, and the church banned homosexuality. In 1978 Hubbard was convicted of fraud in Paris and sentenced *in absentia* to four years in prison. During the late 1970s Hubbard had a series of heart attacks and a young acolyte named David Miscavige began taking over the organisation, expelling all those who stood in his way. By 1982 he was in full control of the church.

By this time Hubbard was living such a reclusive life that few people know for certain when he died. Some say that it was as early as 1983, although his demise was not announced until 1986.

The controversy over Scientology continues. There can be little doubt that it funds a number of worthwhile drug-rehabilitation, environmental and human-rights programmes. However, disaffected members and those forced out by Miscavige's *Putsch* claim that it is rigid and authoritarian, although when they say so in print they have a writ slapped on them.

In 1985 both France and Denmark revoked its tax-exempt status on the grounds that the Church of Scientology was a profit-making organisation. On the other hand, its tax exemption was restored in the USA in 1993. In Germany, the church's status is still in dispute, with leading adherents of the organisation, such as *Pulp Fiction* star John Travolta, having appealed to the US Congress to put pressure on the German authorities to recognise the civil liberties of its followers.

11 ❖ The Church of Satan

Satanism is as old as Christianity itself, and grew up alongside it as Christianity's mirror image. The depiction of Satan – a goat-like figure with horns and a tail – is widespread among the world's religions. The Mexican god of hell, Mictantecauli, could be a photofit, for example, and the ancient Egyptian gods Apepi and Tiawath are similar; in Teutonic myth Loki, the god of fire, is the personification of evil.

The Christian concept of the devil had its roots in Jewish tradition. The word 'Satan' comes from Hebrew and means an opponent or enemy, so there are thus numerous 'satans'. Only in the biblical Book of Job is Satan represented as a single character. He appears with the son of God, standing before the throne of Jehovah, and although he is God's opponent, in the cruel test that Job is subjected to Satan in no sense personifies evil.

Satan's status changed when the Jews were living in exile among the Babylonians, who had a pantheon of evil spirits. The children of Israel also seem to have adopted the Greeks' child-god, Astaroth, and the Persian Asmodeus, the lieutenant of the prince of evil, Ahriman. By the time when the New Testament was written Satan had become established as a demonic figure in his own right: indeed, the Gospel of to St Matthew refers to him as the 'prince of demons'. In his letter to the Ephesians, St Paul writes of Satan ruling over the evil beings in the lower heavens and tempting the good into wickedness. In the Christian mind, the devil seems subsequently to have become personified by the image of the Greek god Dionysus, who was a horned god, half man, half goat.

This horned goat was mentioned during the Roman Catholic Church's persecution of the Knights Templar and the Cathars. Worship of the goatish creature also featured in a trial held in Toulouse, in 1335, when 63 men and women were tried for witchcraft and sorcery. One of the defendants,

Catherine Delort, admitted to killing two of her aunts, and said that children were killed and eaten at the cult's Sabbats. Another of the accused defended these actions by saying that although God was the king of the heavens, Satan was the master of the world. The Sabbats, or ceremonies, took place on a large area of flat, high ground, with a wood or grove at one end. An altar was built from stones. On it stood the cult's image of Satan: a goat-like creature with a human body, horns and an erect penis. The worshippers carried torches that had been lit from a flame that burned between the horns of the idol. The priestess was a young girl, who prayed to the 'Lord Satan' to save her from treachery and violence and then kissed the idol. In some accounts she kissed it on the rump, in others on its erect phallus.

Hallucinogenic herbs mixed with alcohol were then taken, and the naked priestess would lie across the altar. A male worshipper would then take over, playing the part of the devil. A version of the Christian creed, substituting the word Satan for Christ, was recited. Then the body of the priestess was mutilated and burned. An orgy followed, often involving children and generally employing sodomy rather than vaginal intercourse. Some of these ceremonies were presided over by rogue priests, in the Cathar tradition. Black turnips were substituted for bread in the blasphemous communions and water replaced the wine, while urine was sprinkled over the congregation instead of holy water. Children were sometimes sacrificed.

The legendary French knight Gilles de Rais followed in this Satanic tradition. Born in 1404, he was the bodyguard and confidant of Joan of Arc. After she was burnt to death – a punishment in which de Rais took great pleasure, some say – he retired to his estates in Brittany. There he squandered his fortune on art and maintaining a lavish court. When his family obtained a decree from the king of France to prevent him from selling off or mortgaging any more of his inheritance, he turned to alchemy and the occult. He gathered a group of Satanists around him and started practising ritual magic in the cellars of his *château* at Tiffauges.

De Rais' servant, Poitou, was sent out to procure children – usually boys aged between six and twelve. The children were tortured and sexually abused; then they were killed, often at their abusers' point of orgasm. Once dead, their mutilated bodies would be sexually abused again before ritually burnt. When de Rais was arrested, he confessed, under threat of torture, that he and his followers had murdered over 800 children in the name of Satan.

In 1633 the French priest Urbain Grandier, a well-known womaniser and deflowerer of virgins, was accused of seducing nuns into adopting devil worship. Along with the nuns from his local convent, he had organised orgies in his church to honour the Persian god Asmodeus. His home was searched by the authorities and a pact that he had signed with the devil was found; it was written backwards, in Latin, and was signed in Grandier's blood.

At around the same time there was an outbreak of Satanism at the Monastère de Saint-Louise de Louvier in Paris. Father David, the confessor there, encouraged the nuns to go about their devotions in the nude. They took communion while stripped to the waist and practised lesbianism in the chapel. When Father David died, his place was taken by Father Mathurin Picard, who introduced the Black Mass and incited the nuns to have sexual intercourse with a devil figure – a priest dressed as an animal, reading from a 'book of blasphemies'. Communion wafers would be stuck to the penis of the priest before he penetrated the nun. A new-born baby was crucified and two men who had come along to watch a Black Mass were murdered when they tried to leave. And when the nuns gave birth, their babies were killed, cooked and eaten.

Another Satanic cult was discovered in Paris in 1673. The investigation began when two priests told the Paris police commissioner, Nicholas de la Reynie, that they had heard a string of disturbing confessions from wealthy men and women. A number of them had admitted to murdering their respective husbands or wives. The priests would not break the sanctity of the confessional and give their names, but de la Reynie nevertheless decided to investigate the matter.

The mid-seventeenth century was known in France as the 'age of arsenic'. Arsenic was widely available at that time because it was used as an ingredient in the facial cosmetics that were then all the rage. Murder by means of poisoning was also fashionable, especially among the upper classes. At first de la Reynie thought that he was after a gang of crooks which was were selling 'succession powders' to the aristocracy. Succession powders were so called because they disposed of an unwanted spouse or relative and thereby facilitated the succession of the poisoner to the deceased's property and titles.

Suspicion fell on a fortune-teller named Marie Bosse. De la Reynie sent an undercover policewoman to consult the clairvoyant on the best way in which to get rid of her troublesome husband. Madame Bosse sold her some arsenic and was consequently arrested, along with her husband, her two sons and another fortune-teller named La Vigourex, who admitted sleeping with all the members of the Bosse family. A huge cache of poison was found in the Bosses' home. Facing torture, La Vigourex and the Bosse family provided a list of their clients, which included a number of prominent members of King Louis XIV's court.

Plainly this was a very delicate matter politically, but de la Reynie explained to the king that although an investigation might embarrass a number of important courtiers Paris was in the grip of an epidemic of poisoning and Louis might find himself the next victim. Louis was persuaded to set up a commission of inquiry. Officially known as the *La Commission de l'Arsenal* (the 'arsenal commission'), it was also called by who appeared before it *L'Affaire de la Chambre Ardente* (the 'affair of the burning room') because de la Reynie, with theatrical flare, conducted the investigation in a room that was draped in black and lit solely by candlelight. In *La Chambre Ardente*, Marie Bosse and La Vigourex admitted that they were part of a devil-worshipping cult headed by one La Voisin, whose real name was Catherine Deshayes.

Madame Deshayes was the wife of a failed haberdasher, who had set up in business making skin-cleansing treatments which contained a lot of arsenic. Her experiments led her to learn about chemistry and to develop preparations which, she claimed, promoted 'inner cleanliness'. As a sideline, Madame Deshayes worked as an astrologer. Her clients were rich and aristocratic. In order to lend weight to her predictions she developed a network of informants throughout French society. These were exclusively women, and many, including La Voisin and La Vigourex, adopted pseudonyms. As an astrologer, La Voisin would predict that a woman's husband, say, was going to die suddenly. If the woman seemed pleased at the prospect, La Voisin would then supply her with some poison with which to hasten the event.

Her business was so lucrative that La Voisin could afford to pay 30,000 *livres* for a secluded house in a rundown area of Paris. It was protected by a high wall and was hidden by trees. Madame Deshayes lived there with her husband, now a successful jeweller; her 21-year-old daughter, Marie-Marguerite Mont Voisin; and their lodger, Nicholas Levassuer – an executioner by trade.

De la Reynie put the house under surveillance. One of his agents, working undercover in a bar, overheard one of Deshayes' assistants drunkenly describing acts of devil worship. The police then arrested two people who had attended meetings at Deshayes' house. Under interrogation, they said that Deshayes and a 66-year-old priest, L'Abbé Guibourg, had regularly conducted Black masses there. During the service, a naked woman would act as an altar table; she would lie in front of the altar with her legs splayed. The abbé, wearing an alb with black phalluses embroidered on it, would rest the chalice and wafers that had been stolen from a local church on her stomach. Intoning passages taken from the Catholic Mass, with the words 'infernal Lord Satan' substituted for 'God' and 'Christ', he would press the wafer against the breasts and vulva of the woman. A child would next urinate in the chalice and the contents would be sprinkled over the worshippers. Then the wafer was inserted into the woman's vagina, while the abbé chanted 'Lord Satan sayeth' "in rioting and drunkenness I rise again. You shall fulfil the lusts of the flesh. The works of the flesh are manifest – they are drunkenness, revelling, immodesty, fornication, luxury and witchcraft. My flesh is meat indeed"'. An orgy of indiscriminate sex followed.

The police raided Deshayes' house. In a pavilion in the garden they found a room that had been draped in black and had an altar in it. The candles on the altar were said to have been made from fat that had been rendered down from human flesh.

Under interrogation, Deshayes' daughter, Marie-Marguerite, told the police that animals had been sacrificed and their blood drunk. Then she admitted that there had been human sacrifices, too. During the sacrificial ceremony, she said, the abbé had intoned 'Astaroth, Asmodeus, prince of friendship, I beg you to accept the sacrifice of this child which we now offer you'. Then Guibourg held the infant up by its feet and slit its throat; the blood spurted into the chalice that had been placed on the belly of the naked woman. The abbé next smeared the blood onto both his penis and the vagina of the woman and had sex with her.

One of the children that had been murdered during these sacrifices had been Deshayes' own goddaughter, Françoise Filastre. Others had been supplied either by the cult's inner circle of devotees or by a compliant midwife. Madame Deshayes also had another sideline, as an abortionist, and often provided living foetuses that had been ripped from the wombs of her unsuspecting clients. The victims' entrails were retained for occult use after their deaths and the rest of their bodies were burnt in a stove.

It turned out that one of the devil worshippers was none other than the marquise de Montespan, Françoise-Arthenais de Mortmat, who had been the king's mistress for 12 years. Fearing that she was losing the king's favour to a younger rival, the duchesse de Fontages, she attended three of the 'love masses' in order to try to win back his attention by acting as the nude human altar table. Given the sensitivity of her position, much of her evidence had to be hushed up.

Deshayes and Guibourg were nevertheless arrested. They confessed to murdering hundreds of children over a career in Satanism that spanned 13 years. Some 150 courtiers were arrested for poisoning and sentenced variously to death, slavery in the French galleys and banishment. Madame Deshayes herself was burnt at the stake in 1680. However, the marquise de Montespan returned briefly to the king's favour.

There were sporadic reports of similar practices in Britain. In 1541 the English parliament outlawed witchcraft and Satanism. In 1562 such activities became capital offences. And in 1563 'witchcraft, sorcery and necromancy' were also outlawed in Scotland.

The seventeenth century saw the rise of the witch-finder, and over 30,000 people were put to death for devil worship. Nevertheless, in 1662 a young, attractive redhead named Isobel Gowdie made an astonishing confession to the elders of her local kirk in Lochloy, near Auldearne in Morayshire. Bored by her marriage to a dull farmer, Gowdie admitted to having sex with the devil. She had been initiated into Satanism at a Sabbat in Auldearne Church on one night 15 years earlier. A large, black, hairy figure had read a diabolical liturgy from a black book; she had been required to renounce Christ; then the 'devil' had sucked blood from her shoulder. A few nights later she had attended a meeting in which the devil had had sex with her and 12 other women. At later meetings, two children were sacrificed in the devil's name and their bodies and blood were used in Satanic rites.

There were similar instances of such confessions in England's North American colonies. In 1648, in New England, for example, Mary Johnson admitted to consorting with the devil and murdering a child.

During the eighteenth century Britain was scandalised by Satanic activities amongst the aristocracy. They occurred at Sir Francis Dashwood's infamous Hell-Fire Club, which he had established in 1721 while still in his teens. Although he remained a committed Christian throughout his life, Dashwood claimed to have used the Black Mass with which to evoke the devil in the form of either a black cat or a goat-like figure. Despite his condemnation by King George I, Dashwood continued his practices. In 1728 he set off to 'fornicate his way across Europe'. In Rome, he attended the ceremony recalling the scourging of Christ that was held in the Sistine Chapel on Good Friday. During the ceremony, Dashwood pulled out a real whip from under his coat, cried 'Il Diavolo' ('the devil') and lashed the congregation viciously. He was ejected from the chapel and subsequently expelled from Italy.

Dashwood's Hell-Fire Club was by no means the only Satanic organisation to exist in eighteenth-century England. Young bucks amused themselves at the Banditti, the Blasters and the Sons of Midnight, clubs which emulated the French obsession with devil worship and debauchery. There were also at least three Hell-Fire clubs in London and three more in Scotland. They all offered their members excessive quantities of alcohol, drugs and sex. Dashwood's club was undoubtedly the most exclusive, however. Members included Frederick, Prince of Wales; the earl of Bute, who went on to become a prime minister; the earl of Sandwich; the MP John Wilkes; the poet Charles Churchill; the novelist Lawrence Sterne; the satirist George Selwyn; at least one Oxford professor; and the archbishop of Canterbury's son, Thomas Potter. Dashwood himself rose to become chancellor of the Exchequer in Bute's government.

Meetings were initially held in the George and Vulture pub, in George Yard, in London. A naked girl, spread-eagled on the bar-room table, was used as an altar. A communion wafer was pushed up her vagina and the sacrificial wine was drunk from her navel; when the Black Mass was over there was an orgy.

When Dashwood married, in 1745, his Hell-Fire Club curtailed its activities, but in 1753 it started up again, this time at Medmenham Abbey, near West Wycombe in Buckinghamshire. A complete Satanic temple was excavated in the chalk caves there. Members were now called 'monks' and wore red habits. The cave walls were hung with inverted crosses and pagan idols. One resembled a bird, with its head turned around so that its phallus-shaped beak protruded from its back; women would ride this, in preparation for the mass orgies that would follow. Monks also had individual cells in which they could perform private rituals. Prostitutes dressed as nuns were shipped in from London for rites and orgies. Virgins were much in demand and counterfeiting virginity was consequently a growth industry at the time, although some of the women used were mere girls.

There are some indications that the rites performed in the Hell-Fire Club's caves may have included sacrifices, possibly human. But all of the clubs records were burnt by Paul Whitehead, the man who actually ran the club, shortly before he died in 1774. Dashwood paraded the Buckinghamshire militia for Whitehead's funeral and his heart was placed in a mausoleum built over the caves; the heart was said to have been 'as black in death as in life'.

Satanism went underground after the death of Dashwood in 1781, but two books published in France during the 1890s by Karl Huysman, a veteran of the French *Sûreté* (France's CID), claimed that devil worship was rife from Paris to Hong Kong.

There were furthermore theories that Jack the Ripper's murders were the work of a Satanist. One suspect was the newspaper reporter Roslyn

D'Onston; a failed doctor and drug addict, he was said to have killed the women in order to give his career a fillip. In 1890 he became involved with Mabel Collins, the editor of *Lucifer*, the Theosophical Society's magazine. He later went into business with Baroness Vittoria Cremers, who revealed during the 1920s that she had found neckties caked with dried blood in D'Onston's room and said that he had told her that they had belonged to Jack the Ripper. These eventually found their way into the hands of Aleister Crowley, who claimed that D'Onston was indeed the Ripper and that he had performed his ritual murders in an attempt to become invisible.

During much of the first half of the twentieth century there was enough tangible evil in the world to make Satanism somewhat surplus to people's requirements. But it made something of a comeback during the 1960s. Throughout the British Isles there were reports of graves being disturbed and magical symbols being painted on the walls of churches. In Ayrshire, Scotland, in 1964, a minister reported finding a partially burnt Bible, an inverted cross and a smashed chalice in a disused, seventeenth-century church. And in the small town of Helikon, in Switzerland, a group calling itself the 'Seekers of Mercy' was broken up after a young girl in its care died in mysterious circumstances. An investigation revealed that the cult's 'church' boasted black candles and a fully equipped torture chamber. The dead girl had been sexually assaulted and brutally whipped while tied to an inverted cross.

Then, on 30 April 1966 – *Walpurgisnacht* (the German for 'Walpurga's Night', on which a witches' Sabbat was traditionally held in the Harz Mountains) – the First Church of Satan was established in San Francisco. Its founder was the former circus artist and animal trainer Anton Szandor LaVey. During the early 1960s he had quit the circus in order to work as a conjurer and hypnotist. His interest in magic slowly grew and he set up a circle of students to study the black arts. His Satanic beliefs were very much in the Crowley mould: 'There is a demon inside man and it must be exercised not exorcised – channelled into ritual hatred', he said.

LaVey claimed that Satanic ages lasted for 1,458 years. The last one, when God was all-powerful and Satan was cast down, had started in AD 508, he said. Consequently, the new Satanic age, when Satan would be omnipotent, began in 1966. LaVey accordingly proclaimed 1966 'Year One, *Anno Satanas*'.

LaVey reflected the mood of the time. He claimed that Christianity had brought restraint, mortification, self-denial, discipline and conformity. Instead, he believed, Satanism offered indulgence, vitality and gratification. Sins, he argued, were really virtues when they brought physical and emotional pleasure. Within five years he could boast 10,000 disciples world-wide. His 'church' was furthermore recognised as a legitimate religion and as a result received tax-free status. LaVey also produced two books, *The Satanic Bible* and *The Satanic Rituals*; these works have been cited at almost as many murder trials as Crowley's *Magick In Theory and Practice*.

The First Church of Satan attracted a lot of devotees in California because of LaVey's unashamed showmanship. He called himself the 'black pope', dressed entirely in black, shaved his head and grew a goatee beard. His home in San Francisco was in the middle of a block with empty lots on either side; the only things that grew in the barren garden were weeds. The curtains were black and were never opened. A human skeleton hung at the end of the hallway. The living room was full of stuffed animals, including a wolf and a raven. His wife claimed to be a fully fledged witch, and her hair fell a full 3 feet (91cm) below her shoulders.

LaVey would use a pantomime-devil suit for his ceremonies, complete with a horn and tail, and he would be greeted with the cry 'Hail, Satan'. His congregation would also be masked and robed in theatrical style. There was the obligatory nudity and a naked woman draped across the altar was, of course, *de rigueur*. LaVey took Satanism to the people and choreographed show-stopping Satanic extravaganzas using topless dancers from seedy San Francisco bars. One of them, Susan Atkins, played a blood-sucking vampire in LaVey's 'Witches' Sabbath', a Satanic review performed at Gigi's night-club in North Beach. Atkins would later go on to become a leading member of Charles Manson's 'Family'.

The 'black pope' revelled in his celebrity and boasted Sammy Davis Junior and the veteran actor Keenan Wynn among his followers. Another member of his congregation was Jayne Mansfield, but her lawyer, Sam Brody, was very much against her involvement in the cult, fearing that it would harm her public image. On 29 July 1970 Mansfield and Brody were driving in San Francisco when a truck crashed into their car, killing them both and decapitating Mansfield. LaVey claimed to have had prior knowledge of the accident: he said that he had put a curse on Brody and had warned Mansfield not to travel in a car with him. This statement was dismissed by many as being merely tacky opportunism, but it nevertheless helped to bring LaVey and the First Church of Satan to the public's attention.

LaVey was employed as an adviser on the film *Rosemary's Baby*, in which he also had a walk-on part as the devil himself. He was the technical director of the movie *The Devil's Rain*, starring John Travolta, too. His perceived sell-out to the world of show business alienated some of his more committed followers, and when he started selling posts in the higher echelons of the 'church' to his Hollywood friends his followers became irrevocably divided. US Army officer Michael Aquino led one break-away group and founded the Temple of Set, which was also recognised as a legitimate religion by the IRS. The Temple of Set claims that it aims to teach 'responsible and ethical knowledge of the Black Arts' and intends to become the 'pre-eminent repository of the wisdom of the "left-hand path"'.

Aquino claimed to be a follower of the ancient Egyptian god Set, not of Satan. He, too, published a book, *The Book of the Coming Forth by Night*, which again propounded the Crowleyan view that Satan was within humans and must be released. Despite the more secretive and intellectual approach of his Satanic 'church', Aquino, like LaVey, indulged in theatricality and modelled himself on Damien Thorn, the primary character in the *Omen* films.

Although it is easy to dismiss him as a harmless crank, Aquino had top-security clearance from the US Army and served on the World Affairs Council, as well as working for NATO. His dual life became a worry to the authorities when it was rumoured that he had recruited at least 12 members of US Army Intelligence into the Temple of Set. A police report noted that Aquino had worked in the US Army's psychological-warfare department, and when the army subsequently tried to dismiss him because of his involvement in Satanism he sued it for discrimination, arguing that his right to freedom of religion was guaranteed by the First Amendment to the Constitution. He won the case. He was later promoted to the rank of lieutenant colonel, though his increasingly fascist leanings were even disturbing members of his own Satanic organisation.

Among the other spin-off cults that were created by the collapse of the First Church of Satan were included the Temple of Baal, which claims in its advertising material to be a 'spiritual organisation dedicated to dominance, conquest, murder and slavery'. Another, the Warlords of Satan, is said to crave 'nothing less than to turn human beings into prey'.

In 1970, the 18-year-old Patricia Hall – also known as Inca Angelique – was arrested, along with three male drifters, for the rape and cat-o'-nine-tails' flogging of a teenage girl in a wax museum's hall of mirrors on Bourbon Street in New Orleans. She threatened to turn the arresting officers into frogs and claimed to have been 'baptised' by LaVey in San Francisco, although LaVey denied all knowledge of her. She was later extradited to Florida, where she was convicted of stabbing a 66-year-old man.

Throughout the 1970s and 1980s in the USA there were a series of murders committed by confused young men, usually under the influence of drugs, who claimed Satanism as their inspiration. Many of them said that their interest in the occult had been sparked by reading LaVey's *The Satanic Bible*.

In Britain, Satanism did not die out with Crowley. In 1995 the self-styled Satanist John Kilminster appeared in court charged with drug possession. His trial and exposure were embarrassing to Kilminster because he had been trying to keep his worship of Lucifer and his orgiastic rituals secret from his wife.

A furniture-maker, chess champion and pillar of the local Conservative association in Northampton, Kilminster had founded the English Church of Satan by putting an advertisement in the local paper. The cult's first meeting was held in a nearby Little Chef fast-food restaurant. Kilminster provided his new recruits with a do-it-yourself werewolf kit, among other things.

The membership largely comprised middle-aged men who were interested in the possibility of enjoying free sex (fortunately for them, a number of women signed up, too). Rituals were held in Kilminster's workshop, which had been transformed by black drapes, black candles, burning incense and pentagrams. Kilminster would lie in a coffin while the other Satanists pranced around naked under their black cloaks awaiting his resurrection. The evening would end with a 'celebration of lust'.

In court, the bald, bearded Kilminster admitted to having sex with two cult members. He had also pursued one former cult member, with whom he was besotted. Her cult name was Shiva, and she claimed that Kilminster had spiked her drink with methadone in order to make her more receptive to his advances. Other cult members were given harmless aphrodisiacs.

12 ✦ The Process Church of the Final Judgement

The Process Church of the Final Judgement was the brainchild of Robert Sylvester DeGrimston Moore (known as DeGrimston), who was born in Shanghai, China, in 1935. He was educated at Winchester public school and studied architecture at Regent Street Polytechnic in London. While a student, he became a Scientologist, and by 1962 DeGrimston had become a senior member and high-ranking officer of the Church of Scientology in the UK. Just as L Ron Hubbard had claimed to have had studied under Aleister Crowley personally, so DeGrimston claimed to have been taught by Hubbard.

DeGrimston met Mary Anne MacLean at the Scientologists' London headquarters in Fitzroy Street. She was born in Glasgow in 1931, had spent time in a reform school and had been briefly engaged to the boxer Sugar Ray Robinson. But when she met DeGrimston she was working as a night-club hostess on the fringes of the social circle that included Christine Keeler and Mandy Rice Davis. Indeed, one of her boyfriends was the society osteopath Dr Stephen Ward, who was the only person to stand trial as a result of the Profumo scandal. Among Ward's many interests was a deep and enduring fascination with the occult.

DeGrimston and MacLean set up an informal group which practised what it called 'compulsion therapy'. This attempted to rid participants of all manner of compulsive behaviour by examining the complex reasons behind it. By 1963 the group's ideas had begun to deviate from those of Scientology, so DeGrimston, MacLean and their followers left the Scientologists and set up on their own, establishing the Process Church of the Final Judgement, whose members believed, like the Cathars, in both God and Lucifer.

The Process Church preached a particularly broad interpretation of the concept of free will. The Jews, they argued, for example, had elected to be exterminated in the Nazi gas chambers during the Holocaust and people who had been born with disabilities had chosen this course in a past life. These weird, ultra-libertarian ideas struck a chord in the London of the 1960s and beatniks and bikers flocked to join the new religion. The Process Church, however, put most of its efforts into recruiting wealthy and well-connected people who would supply it with funds and introduce its philosophy to the highest levels of society.

By 1966 the Process Church had enough money to lease a huge London mansion in Balfour Place, Mayfair, and DeGrimston, MacLean and 25 other cult members moved in, each bringing an Alsatian dog. A few months later, 18 members of the Process Church went on a six-week-long holiday in the Bahamas. They then travelled to Mexico, where DeGrimston leased a large piece of land at Xtul, a beach area on the Yucatán Peninsula. There members began practising the sex-and-Satanism rites that had been perfected by Crowley.

Back in London, DeGrimston was determined to bring his new theology to a wider audience. He therefore threw the mansion at Balfour Place open to the public, opened an occult bookshop and began publishing a magazine that expounded his philosophy. He tried to recruit members of the new, young, pop glitterati – among them the Beatles and the Rolling Stones – with some success: Marianne Faithfull posed, clutching a rose and pretending to be dead, on the front cover of the first issue of *Process* magazine.

DeGrimston also began to write books explaining the Process Church's creed in more detail. His first book, *As It Is*, was published in 1967. In it, DeGrimston laid out a clear, if perverse, philosophical line. According to him, Christ had said 'Love thine enemy'. Christ's enemy was Satan, so Christ should love Satan, and anyone who followed Christ should therefore love Satan, too. This love would eventually break down the schism between Christ and Satan, representing good and evil. On the Day of Judgement, DeGrimston claimed, Christ and Satan would be reconciled; Christ would do the judging and Satan would carry out Christ's judgements. Anyone who understood this simple truth should help to bring about this reconciliation between Christ and Satan and thereby hasten the Day of Judgement. Naturally, DeGrimston knew how do this: in his second book, *Jehovah on War*, he wrote simply 'Thou shalt kill'.

DeGrimston believed that a spree of motiveless killing would herald the Final Judgement. After all, the biblical Book of Revelations said that the Battle of Armageddon would precede the Day of Judgement; what was the battle if not gratuitous killing? DeGrimston did not think that the human sacrifices that Crowley claimed to have made were enough and instead preached that life should be one long, murderous ritual.

In the summer of 1967 the cult moved to San Francisco and established itself in the epicentre of the hippie counter-culture, the Haight-Ashbury area. Its headquarters were at 407 Cole Street; just two blocks down the street, at number 636, lived an ex-convict and drifter named Charles Manson.

The US wing of the Process Church later moved to South Cochrane Street, in Los Angeles, where Hell's Angels and drug addicts from Sunset Strip, as well as minor pop singers and movie actors, became willing converts. The cult tried to link itself with the First Church of Satan, but Anton LaVey dismissed DeGrimston and his followers as 'kooks'.

During the late 1960s, when people were wearing clothes in every colour of the rainbow, the Process Church's members stood out with their black suits, black pullovers and black capes. The Satanic 'Goat of Mendes' was embroidered in red on the back of their capes. They also wore silver crucifixes around their necks, often inverted in the Satanic manner. Another symbol of the Process Church was four 'P's joined together at the foot like the arms of a swastika.

The Process Church was divided into three factions, which, DeGrimston said, would be reunited on the Day of Judgement. New members were free to choose which path they would follow. One group followed Christ; its members were straight-laced and puritanical. The second followed Lucifer, and its initiates enjoyed sex, drugs and rock 'n' roll, as well as all the other pleasures of the flesh. The third group followed Satan; it, too, was puritanical, but also believed in blood sacrifice and violence.

Process magazine gave equal space to the three factions. Issue four, for example, was devoted to sex. In it, the Christian faction argued that sex was a defilement: it was degrading and humiliating to the participants. Worse still, the coupling of two human beings excluded God. The followers of Lucifer, on the other hand, called for cult members to wash away 'all pointless guilt, all worthless fear, all futile shame . . . all embarrassment and the crippling bonds of self-restraint'. For their part, the Satanists described naked women lying on mortuary slabs – 'You feel the atmosphere of death as you stroke the woman and then lie upon her'. 'Priests in midnight garb, the congregation, men and women, unclothed except for blood-red masks upon their faces stand silent for the presence of their Lord and Master Satan', they wrote. 'A naked girl, fair-haired and in the very prime of youth, lies like a human sacrifice upon the altar.' The Satanist faction furthermore urged its recruits to 'sink down in the decadence of excessive self-indulgence. Let no so-called sin, perversion or depravity escape your searching senses; partake of them all of them to overflowing . . . There is nothing else now, with the end of man so near. There is no dialectic but death.'

Even though the Process Church seemed to treat its three factions even-handedly, the whole of DeGrimston's own philosophy was skewed towards the Satanic. On the cover of the 'Sex' issue of *Process* magazine, for instance, a naked girl was pictured spread-eagled on an altar; she was surrounded by hooded worshippers and above her was placed an inverted cross.

The fifth issue of *Process* magazine was the 'Fear' issue. In it, DeGrimston told cult members that 'by seeking out fear in living experience, we become fear itself'. No doubt these words were taken to heart by Manson, who, by this time, had joined the Process Church.

Whichever faction the recruits joined, they were all expected to spend some time in Satanic worship. After all, blood rituals and sacrifices were a good way in which the cult could maintain a hold over its members. The Process Church was highly structured: it had six levels – acolyte, initiate, messenger, prophet, priest and master. DeGrimston referred to the cult as 'The Family' and members were assigned temple names; there were brothers, sisters and fathers, but, strangely enough, no mothers.

The sixth issue of *Process* magazine was the 'Death' issue. Manson, who had just formed his own 'Family', contributed an article to it. His piece was rambling and incoherent and revealed Manson's growing obsession with death. There can be little doubt that the teachings of DeGrimston helped him along his path to mass murder.

During his time in California, DeGrimston published his third work of cult philosophy, *Satan on War*. In it, he wrote 'Release the fiend that lies dormant within you, for he is strong and ruthless and his power is far beyond the bounds of human frailty.' These words could have been written for Manson.

Soon afterwards, the Process Church broke up, largely because many of the original members from London had gone to the USA on 90-day tourist visas which they had long outstayed. Some went back to England, others went underground. New branches of the Process Church were set up in Chicago, Dallas, New Orleans, Toronto and Cambridge, Massachusetts. DeGrimston and MacLean headed for New York and established a branch of the cult on Corelia Street, in the fashionable Greenwich Village. But the Boston branch was by far the most successful. It recruited through a soup kitchen that it ran for the homeless; several members of rock bands joined it and it had its own show on a local radio station.

Although the Process Church pulled out of California, many of its followers did not. A large number of dead dogs was found in the area around Santa Cruz, just south of San Francisco. Most were Alsatians which had been beheaded, mutilated, skinned and often drained of their blood. By the early 1970s District Attorney Peter Chang was describing Santa Cruz as the 'murder capital of the world'.

Twenty-two-year-old Stanley Dean Baker, a lumberjack from Wyoming, was stopped by the California Highway Patrol near the Big Sur on suspicion of being a hit-and-run driver. When the registration plates of the vehicle failed to check out, the officers searched Baker and his companion, Harry A Stoop. In Baker's pocket they found a well-thumbed copy of LaVey's *Satanic Bible*, as well as a finger. When the patrolman asked him to explain himself, Baker said, with masterly understatement, 'I have a problem. I am a cannibal'.

The car, as it turned out, belonged to James Schlosser. Schlosser was a social worker from Montana who had picked up Baker while he was hitch-hiking outside Livingston, Montana. That night they camped on Yellow river, at the foot of a hill called, appropriately enough, Devil's Slide. There was a thunderstorm. Awoken by the lightning, Baker said that he was overwhelmed by a cannibalistic compulsion which had gripped him since he had received electrical burns in a car accident when he was a teenager. He killed the sleeping Schlosser, cut out his heart and ate it in ritual fashion. Then he stole Schlosser's car and took one of his fingers with him in case he became peckish later.

When Baker was strip-searched, it was discovered that his body was covered in occult tattoos. Baker claimed to be a practising Satanist and a member of a blood-drinking cult in Wyoming which was an off-shoot of the Process Church. They sacrificed dogs during their ceremonies and then drank their blood. The group, he said, had a movable, carved, wooden altar, a special sacrificial knife with six blades and a portable crematorium with which to dispose of any unwanted remains. (This statement was confirmed by another member of the cult.) The cult called itself the Four P Movement – or Four Pi for short – an obvious reference to the symbol of the Process Church. Four Pi's leader, Baker said, was a wealthy doctor or business executive who lived in Los Angeles; he was known as the 'grand chingon' but his description fitted neither DeGrimston nor Manson, both of whom had left LA by that time.

During his trial, Baker was linked to the murder of 40-year-old Robert Salem, an internationally known lamp designer in San Francisco. The victim's throat had been slashed and his ears cut off. His killers had written 'Satan Saves' on the wall of his apartment; next to this was a crude drawing of a crucified man, along with the word 'Zodiac'. On Salem's stomach was carved the circle and crosswire that later became the symbol of the 'Zodiac killer', a serial murderer who may have been responsible for as many as 40 murders in the Bay area during the 1970s. He was never caught.

Although Baker was not charged with the murder of Salem, he was sentenced to life imprisonment for the killing of Schlosser. At Deer Lodge Prison, he would crouch in his cell and howl like a werewolf. He was subsequently transferred to a maximum-security prison in Illinois, where he became a model prisoner. In 1976 he applied to join the First Church of Satan, but was refused admission.

13 ❖ Death cults

The most famous killer cult in history is the Assassins, which was founded by Hasan-e Sabbah, who died in 1124, in Daylam, in what is now Iran. He was the leader of the Nizari Isma'ilites, a religio-political Islamic sect which existed from the eleventh to the thirteenth century. In its early years it regarded murdering its enemies a religious duty.

The Arabic name means 'hashish-smoker', referring to the Assassins' alleged habit of taking hashish in order to induce ecstatic visions of paradise before setting out to face martyrdom. (The actual existence of this practice is doubtful: the stories that were told by Marco Polo and other travellers about the gardens of paradise into which the drugged devotees were thus introduced in order to receive a foretaste of eternal bliss are not confirmed by any known Isma'ilite source.)

In 1094, along with some Persian allies, Hasan-e Sabbah seized the hill fortress of Alamut, in Daylam. Opposing the growing empire of the Seljuq Turks, he established a loose, but cohesive, state, which he defended by sending Assassins into enemy camps and cities with orders to murder the generals and statesmen who opposed him. His deadly tactics were not confined to his enemies, however: when one of his sons was accused of murder and another of drunkenness he had them both executed.

The cult's most prominent follower was Rashid ad-Din as-Sinan, who died in 1192. He was leader of the Syrian branch of the Assassins at the time of the Third Crusade and operated independently of the headquarters of the cult in Alamut. His own base was a fortress at Masyaf, in northern Syria, and he was known to Westerners as the 'old man of the mountain'. Feared for his practice of sending his followers to murder his enemies, he made several attempts on the life of the Ayyubid leader, Saladin, who opposed the Isma'ili Shi'i sect.

The Assassins' power was ended when the Mongols invaded Persia. One by one their castles fell, until Alamut was over-run in 1256. The Syrian fortresses were gradually subjugated by the Mamaluk sultan, Baybars I, who installed Mamaluk governors. Now considered a minor heresy, cult followers are still found in Iran and Central Asia. The largest group is in India and Pakistan; its members are known as Khojas and they owe allegiance to the Aga Khan.

The Thuggee

The British Raj stamped out the murderous cult of Kali in India. Kali is the Hindu goddess of destruction and bloodshed. She is the fierce, terrifying incarnation of Devi, the supreme goddess. While Devi's other faces are tranquil and calm, Kali is depicted as a hideous, black-faced hag, smeared with blood, with her teeth bared and a protruding tongue. She has four hands, which respectively hold a sword, a shield, the severed hand of a giant and a noose. And she is always depicted naked, except for a necklace of skulls and a belt of severed hands. She is often shown dancing with the dead body of her lover, Shiva.

Kali is said to have developed her taste for blood when she tried to kill the demon Raktavija. The problem with trying to kill Raktavija was that every time a drop of his blood touched the earth a thousand new demons sprang up. But Kali had a plan and stabbed Raktavija with a spear and drank his blood before it could touch the ground.

Like Satan in the West, Kali is associated with the goat and demands blood sacrifices. At her temple at Bindhachal, near Mirzapur on the Ganges river, some 700 miles (1,127km) from Calcutta, goats were sacrificed day and night so that rivers of blood cascaded down the steps of the temple. Supplicants from all over India would make an annual pilgrimage there and would flagellate themselves into a state of ecstasy. But Kali's terrible influence spread far beyond the confines of the temple to her followers, the Thuggee, or Thugs, a secret society of stranglers who terrorised travellers in northern India for hundreds of years.

The Thuggee had their own hierarchy, rites and traditions, but their principal activity was strangling travellers and stealing their possessions. The Thuggee did not consider themselves thieves: each murder was carried out according to a rigid ritual and the victim was a sacrifice to Kali. Strangulation was regarded as a holy act because they believed that Kali herself had strangled another demon, Rukt Bij-dana, at the dawn of the world. As she did so, two men were formed from the sweat of her brow and they – and their sons and their son's sons – were then sent out in the world to strangle people.

The Thuggee enjoyed the protection of the ruling rajahs and rich men, both Muslim and Hindu. The lower castes were too terrified to complain about them because they could all too easily become their victims themselves. The Thuggee worked in bands, and at the end of the rainy season each year they would make a pilgrimage to Bindhachal and hand over a share of their loot to the priests of Kali. In return, they would be told in which area they were to work during the following year, what fees would be expected of them and which rituals they would have to perform. Then they would be given the blessing of Kali to protect them and would be sent on their murderous way.

The Thuggee worked in absolute secrecy. They would seek out a group of travellers, preferably of their own caste, befriend them and then join their caravan. When the omens were right, they would strangle their new friends. In order to do this, the Thuggee would use a *rumal*, a yellow handkerchief with a silver *rupee* tied in the middle as a garrotte. The killer would shove his knee deep into the victim's back to hasten his death. The body was then ritually mutilated with a series of gashes and was finally buried or thrown down a well. Any of the victim's possessions that had no cash value were burnt. The rest, along with any attractive children, was taken as the Thuggee moved swiftly on, leaving no trace except for a secret sign that could be read by other Thuggee.

The profits that they raised by selling the stolen goods was not their primary motive for the killings, the Thuggee maintained. They considered themselves to be honourable and honest and would never stoop to common thieving. The killing was done for Kali. Any material benefit that accrued to the murderer was due to the munificence of Kali. She had been bountiful enough to provide the Thuggee with a living so that he could continue the sacred slaughter.

The son of a Thuggee would follow his father into the craft. He would begin as a scout and then become a grave-digger. After that, he graduated to become an assistant strangler and finally a strangler himself. A boy's first murder would be celebrated as a rite of passage, like puberty or circumcision. There would be elaborate ceremonials involving the *kussee*, or sacred pick-axe that every band of Thuggee carried. The *kussee* was said to be a tooth from the mouth of Kali and without it no murder could be sanctified.

The Thuggee had a secret language, as well as other rites and rituals that surrounded their murders. There were special, sacred groves in which their murders were carried out and where they would bury their victims in a circular pit, with the corpses packed tightly around a central core of earth. This arrangement prevented jackals from digging up the bodies and the murders thus being discovered. After each murder, the Thuggee would consume a lump of consecrated yellow sugar – or *goor* – which they believed sanctified them. Once a man had tasted the *goor*, they said, he would become a Thuggee, no matter how rich or squeamish he was.

When the British first came to India they tolerated the Thuggee: their actions were a local custom and should be respected, the old India hands said. The Indians themselves rarely complained about the Thuggee because they were far too frightened: the Thuggee permeated all levels of society and news of any protest would be bound to reach them. If any Thuggee was prosecuted he would almost always be acquitted because the local judges were too intimidated to punish them. The Thuggee could strike in any place, at any time and no one felt safe from the wrath of Kali. The Thuggee furthermore boasted that they had a mystical partnership with the tiger. 'Those who escaped the tiger fell into the hands of the Thugs', said one Thuggee. 'And those who escaped the Thugs were devoured by tigers.'

It is estimated that the Thuggee killed up to 40,000 people a year. At some times of the year the chances of completing a journey safely were just one in three. In 1830 one gang murdered 108 people in only 3 months and an individual Thuggee boasted more than 1,000 victims. Thuggee gangs themselves had up to 300 members.

In 1802 the British Army celebrated the signing of the Treaty of Amiens with a parade, led by a military band, outside the Temple of Kali. In 1827 three Thuggee turned informers and four others were consequently charged with murder. But a British circuit judge dismissed the case and charged the informers with giving false evidence. They were found guilty and sentenced to five days' riding backwards on donkeys around the city of Jubbulpore, followed by five years in jail.

This tolerant British attitude towards the Thuggee ended in 1830, when Lord William Bentinck was appointed India's governor-general. Fired with reforming zeal, he was determined to put an end to what he called the 'most dreadful and extraordinary secret society in the history of the human race'. He made Captain William Sleeman 'superintendent for the suppression of Thugs' and gave him 50 mounted irregulars and 40 sepoy infantrymen with which to perform the task. Sleeman established his headquarters in Saugor, where he mounted an intelligence operation with which to build up a complete picture of the history, rituals, customs and practices of the Thuggee. He traced their activities on a map that was 10 feet (3m) square, the most detailed map of India made at that time.

Sleeman was ruthless. Convicted Thuggee were branded with the words 'Convicted Thug' on the shoulder, and 'Thug' was tattooed on their eyelids; then they were hanged. Those who were willing to provide information about other Thuggee were spared, but not freed: Sleeman argued that 'like tigers, their thirst for blood would never be appeased'. His methods were extremely effective. Many were increasingly prepared to speak out and thereby more and more information on the Thuggee was yielded. Sleeman found Thuggee everywhere: they worked as senior aides to Indian rajahs and as the trusted servants of British officials. Many served in the Indian Army and several worked for British Intelligence.

The exposed Thuggee expressed no remorse for what they had done: killing brought them a sense of elation, rather than guilt, and they were proud to have followed in the footsteps of their fathers and grandfathers. One man, who had personally killed 931 times, explained to Sleeman the joy of outsmarting the travellers who were constantly on their guard against Thuggee. Befriending and killing the witless victim was an exquisite pleasure, the man said. When Sleeman accused him of thieving, he was shocked. 'Thieving? Never', he said. 'If a bankers' treasure were before me and entrusted to my care, though in hunger and dying, I would spurn to steal. But let a banker go on a journey and I would certainly murder him.'

Soon even the Thuggee realised that their goddess, Kali, was losing the battle with the Christian God of Sleeman and Bentinck. They blamed themselves: Kali, they said, had withdrawn her protection from them because they were unworthy of it. 'We have sadly neglected her worship', they said. They were also overwhelmed by the power of the British. A Thuggee told Sleeman 'Before the sound of your drums, sorcerers, witches and demons take flight. How can the Thuggee stand?'

Sleeman went on to track down the patrons and bankers who had backed the Thuggee – the 'capitalists of murder', he called them. Some did not require much persuading that investing in the Thuggee was not a very safe bet anymore, especially when more solid investment opportunities presented themselves. One banker in Omrautee, for example, withdrew his funds from the Thuggee and invested them in the East India Company, which, at the time, had just secured a monopoly of the opium trade in China.

By 1841 the Thuggee had been almost completely stamped out. Several thousand had been tried and hundreds hanged. The rest were either imprisoned or transported to penal settlements on the Andaman Islands. The less blood-thirsty were held in Jubbulpore and were taught weaving, carpet-making, carpentry and bricklaying. A walled village was later built near the jail, where their wives and families lived. Up until the end of the nineteenth century foreign visitors would come and peer over the wall at what Sleeman hoped were the last members of this murderous cult.

However, in 1970 a bus driver and his father were accused of sacrificing a ten-year-old boy to Kali. Villagers claimed that they had felt giddy after eating a sacred chapatti that the accused had distributed after they had worshipped the goddess.

Nazism

Nazism could itself be described as a killer cult; and it certainly had links with a number of German cults which took many of their ideas from the Rosicrucians and Theosophy.

During the 1870s a mystic called Guido von List had a huge cult following in Germany. He worshipped the pagan god of war, Woden. One of the symbols that he used in his ceremonies was the hooked cross, an ancient symbol of good fortune known as the swastika. His cult spawned the Thule Society, which restricted its membership to high-ranking Germany Army officers and the professional classes.

Adolf Hitler, leader of the Nazi Party

One of von List's most dedicated disciples was a failed Cistercian monk called Adolf Lanz, who changed his name to Dr Jorg Lanz von Liebenfelds. Lanz founded the New Order of the Templars at the ramshackle Werfenstein Castle on the banks of the Danube. On the flagpole of the castle he flew a flag with a swastika on it. One of his most fanatical followers was the young Adolf Hitler, who was an avid reader of Lanz's cult magazine, which was mouthpiece for his brand of occult and racial mysticism.

When the Nazi Party was in its infancy, Hitler decided that it should have a symbol to rival the Communist Party's hammer and sickle. Another occultist, Friedrich Kohn, came up with a suggestion. (Kohn belonged to the German Order, which believed that there was a world-wide Jewish conspiracy for global domination, underpinned by occult practices, and that the only way in which to fight it was for Nordic Freemasonry to respond in kind.) He suggested a black swastika – symbolising the triumph of the Aryan will – on a white disc, representing racial purity; with a red background symbolising blood. Hitler agreed, but in what has been interpreted by some as an indication of a black magic, he turned the swastika back to front. This reversed swastika became the emblem of the Nazi Party.

Another influential believer in the occult in Hitler's Third Reich was Karl Haushofer. Born in 1869, in Bavaria, Haushofer came from a military family. After graduating from Munich University he joined the German Army. During the early years of the twentieth century he became interested in mysticism and travelled to India and the Far East. He became convinced that the Indo-Germanic people had originated in Central Asia and that it was they who gave nobility and greatness to the world. In Japan he also joined a secret Buddhist cult. During World War I it was said that his ability to predict where shells would fall was uncanny, and he was promoted to the rank of general.

After the war Haushofer returned to Munich University, where he began teaching his own theory of the 'science of geo-politics'. This was thinly disguised nationalistic propaganda. He promoted the idea that it was the destiny of the German people to rule Europe and Asia. The heartland of Central Asia, he said, was, of course, the Indo-Germanic people's ancient homeland and it must therefore be recovered from the Slavic peoples who occupied it. It would become the centre of unassailable world power. He published a journal called the *Geo-political Review*, in which he expounded his views on Aryan superiority. Haushofer also said that on his travels he had discovered a race of supermen who lived in a vast cavern beneath the Himalayas at a place called Agharti. (Similar ideas had been put forward by the Rosicrucians and Theosophists.)

One of Haushofer's students was Rudolf Hess, who became his assistant before being appointed Hitler's deputy in the Nazi Party. When Hess and Hitler were jailed for their failed *Putsch* against the Bavarian government, Haushofer visited Hess in prison and there met Hitler. He began visiting Hitler daily, and Hitler incorporated many of Haushofer's ideas into his book, *Mein Kampf* ('My Struggle'). Hess later said that Haushofer was the secret 'master magician' behind the Reich; his concept of 'cones of power' was used in the staging of the Nuremberg rallies and he also brought lamas from Tibet, as well as members of the Green Dragon Society from Japan, to Germany in order to give the Nazi war effort mystical backing.

Heinrich Himmler, the head of the SS, was another believer in the occult. Members of the SS practised occult rituals and worshipped the Nordic god Woden in ceremonies held at the castle at Wewelsburg, in north-western Germany, where Himmler had built a temple known as the 'Hall of the Dead' (after Valhalla).

During World War II such harmless practices as astrology and palmistry were banned in all German-occupied countries. Even occult organisations like the Thule Society and the German Order, which had backed Hitler from the outset, were outlawed. Occult practice was confined to those at the top of the Nazi Party.

Whatever help the occult may have lent Hitler, his experiment in evil failed. But even in defeat Hitler hung on to his beliefs and delayed his suicide until the pagan festival of *Walpurgisnacht*, killing himself on 30 April 1945.

14 ❖ The Manson Family and the Son of Sam

Charles Manson's murderous ideas were derived directly from the Process Church, while his chief lieutenant and hitwoman, Susan Atkins, was a Satanist who had connections to Anton LaVey and his First Church of Satan.

Manson was born 'no-name Maddox' in Cincinnati, Ohio, the illegitimate son of a teenage prostitute. His mother, Kathleen Maddox, could not remember whether she had given birth on 11 or 12 November 1934, so she plumped for 11 November. But giving her child a first name was just too much effort, so he was registered with no name. She was just 16 when Manson was born, and had run away from her home in Ashland, Kentucky, to escape her Bible-thumping mother. Manson's father was a drugstore cowboy who called himself Colonel Scott; he had left long before the child's birth. But one William Manson married Kathleen briefly and gave her child his surname. Manson also acquired a first name at around this time. But the marriage did not last. Kathleen was furthermore not maternal and regularly abandoned her child. By time that he was six she realised that she could not support her son, even on the profits of prostitution. So she left him with her mother while she and her brother, Luther, robbed a petrol station. They were caught and jailed for five years.

Manson stayed with his strict grandparents for a few weeks before being farmed out to his mother's sister, Joanne, in McMechen, West Virginia. When Kathleen was paroled she came back for the boy. Manson was ecstatic. They began living a shiftless existence together, roaming the Midwest. Kathleen was always on the fringes of crime and prostitution and Manson never knew whether she was coming home or had been arrested. He feared that he might be farmed out again at any moment.

Then the inevitable happened: Kathleen met a man who wanted her but not her child. So she made her son a ward of court and he was sent to the Gibault Home for Boys in Terre Haute, Indiana. His mother visited him there often and promised that he would be back with her soon, but gradually they lost contact with each other. He was later sent to Boys' Town, Nebraska, the orphans' home made famous by the 1932 Spencer Tracy film of the same name, but Manson was soon kicked out on account of his surly manner and constant thieving.

Still in his teens, Manson became a drifter and was arrested for stealing food. He was sent to Indiana Boys' School, from which he escaped 18 times. In 1951 he was again arrested for theft, in Beaver City, Utah, and served four years in a federal reformatory. The reformatory was a great improvement over children's homes, Manson thought: the harsh, often sadistic, regimes of the orphanages had taught him how to survive, but at the reformatory he found that he had graduated to a university of petty crime.

In 1954 he was released into the custody of his aunt, Joanne, in McMechen. There he met a miner's daughter named Rosalie Jean Willis; they married in 1955. But he was soon arrested for taking a stolen car over the state line into California and was sentenced to three years in Terminal Island Federal Prison in San Pedro, near Los Angeles. Shortly afterwards his wife gave birth to a son. She then divorced Manson and disappeared from his life, taking Charlie Junior with her.

In jail, Manson took an intensive, but informal, course on how to become a pimp. Paroled in 1958, he started pursuing his new career in Hollywood. His first attempt was a disaster, however, because he fell in love with his main woman, who promptly dropped him. He did little better in his subsequent attempts and was repeatedly arrested under the terms of the Mann Act for transporting women across state lines for immoral purposes.

Manson decided that he may have more success by forging cheques. He didn't. He was caught passing a stolen cheque for $38 and absconded to Mexico. When the police caught up with him he was sentenced to ten years in the federal penitentiary on MacNeil Island in Washington State.

Being small, just 5 feet 2 inches (1.6m), Manson had a hard time in prison and was repeatedly raped by other prisoners. Many of his assailants were black, and this left him with a life-long racial chip on his shoulder.

Manson was introduced to Scientology in jail. He claimed to be a 'clear', but there is very little evidence that he took Scientology seriously. What attracted him was the power that Scientology's ideas gave him over other people. Jail had already taught him to be shifty, cunning and manipulative and the techniques of Scientology were the perfect extension of these qualities. He was therefore well prepared for the outside world when he was released on 21 March 1967.

He had gone to jail during the 1950s, when the world had been conservative and dull. When he came out a new generation was turning on, tuning in and dropping out. The 32-year-old Manson headed for the epicentre of the 'happening' counter-culture, the Haight-Ashbury district of San Francisco. He had already heard what was going on in the outside world from the men who came into jail, but he could still hardly believe his eyes.

> Pretty little girls were running around every place with no panties and bra and asking for love. "Grass and hallucinatory drugs were being handed to you on the streets. It was a different world than I had ever been in and one that I believed was too good to be true. It was a convict's dream and after being locked up for seven solid years I didn't run from it. I joined it and the generation that lived in it.

One of Manson's first experiences on the outside was attending a Grateful Dead concert, where he dropped a tab of acid. People remember him dancing like a man possessed, then suddenly falling into a trance and curling up in the foetal position. When he left jail he had just $30. In order to make a living he bought a guitar and began busking; he soon became something of a star on the streets of Haight-Ashbury. Students also flocked to hear him on the campus of the University of California at Berkeley, another centre of counter-culture. Young people were turning against the establishment, and Manson, the institutionalised social reject, became the flavour of the month.

Manson quickly discovered that the manipulative techniques that he had learnt in jail also worked on the long-haired flower children who inhabited southern California. His hypnotic stare, unconventional lifestyle and the strange, meaningless phrases that sprang to his lips made him the perfect hippie guru. Along with the Scientological babble that he had picked up in jail, he supplemented his new-age line with the rhetoric of the Process Church. Although men were attracted to him Manson expended most of his energy on recruiting young, middle-class, hippie women who had dropped out in accordance with the current fashion.

His first female follower was Mary Bruner, a librarian. She was a slim, flat-chested redhead and not very pretty, but she was naïve and impressionable – very much Manson's type. Soon he had picked up another woman, called Darlene, and then discovered something new: by sleeping with Mary and Darlene on a strict rota he found that he could control them both. He had discovered the power of sex.

Charles Manson who began the hippie cult "The Family"

When the Process Church moved to Los Angeles Mary bought a VW camper van and with Manson's parole officer's approval they headed south, down the West coast. On the way, Manson and Bruner sampled communal living – and loving – in the hippie communes that were being established throughout California. They eventually reached Los Angeles, where Manson intended to establish himself as a rock superstar.

On Venice Beach, in LA, he met another slim redhead, Lynette 'Squeaky' Fromme. She had just had a row with her father and was emotionally vulnerable. Manson brought her back to Mary and then had sex with her. The three of them subsequently became the nucleus of 'The Family', Manson's hippie cult. A loose collection of hangers-on formed around this central core. Among them was a harem of young women who were all around ten years younger than Manson. They were each promised a baby in return for their devotion to Manson. There was also a number of docile young males who did anything that Manson told them to do.

At any one time the Family numbered around 30 or 35. Manson controlled them by means of acid – LSD – and sex. Every woman who joined the Family was initiated by Manson, who gave her a tab of acid and had sex with her for a few hours. He liked to keep the women naked, or at least topless, and choreographed complex orgies in which Manson would control who did what and with whom.

An early recruit was Patricia Krenwinkel. A former girl scout, she came from an ordinary, middle-class family. Her expensive education had earned her a good job as a legal clerk at a big insurance company in Los Angeles.

She met Manson on Manhattan Beach when she was 21 and abandoned everything to be with him: she ditched her car and walked out of her job without even bothering to pick up her last pay cheque. Another, Leslie Van Houten was just 19 when she dropped out of school. She lived on the streets in a perpetual acid trip until she met Manson. Twenty-year-old Linda Kasabian left her husband and two children and stole $5,000 from a friend in order to join the Family in a haze of LSD. Another redhead, Diane Lake, linked up with the Family after her own parents had dropped out to join the Hog Farm commune. And Ruth Ann Moorehouse, a preacher's daughter, married a hapless bus driver so that she could leave her parents' home and be with the Family.

The woman who brought Satanism into the Family was Susan Atkins, whose real name was Sadie Mae Gutz. At the age of 21 she was working as a topless dancer and a bar-room hustler. Then she became involved with LaVey's First Church of Satan. She later became Manson's closest aide and used the Family's acid-fuelled orgies in which to plant Satanic ideas into his followers' receptive minds.

One of the few men in the commune was the 23-year-old former high-school football star from Farmersville, Texas, Charles 'Tex' Watson. He had once been an honours student, but had become a mindless automaton in Manson's hands. Another college drop-out, Bruce Davis, joined them. So did Bobby Beausoleil, a former guitarist with the Digger band Orkustra and a protégé of the underground film-maker Kenneth Anger (a follower of Crowley, and also one of LaVey's magic circle). Beausoleil had played Lucifer in Anger's film *Invocation of My Demon Brother* and had taken part in a Black Mass performed on stage at the premier. Beausoleil spoiled the occasion, however, by stealing some of Anger's camera equipment and Anger had a locket made with a picture of Beausoleil on one side and a depiction of a toad on the other; the inscription read 'Bobby Beausoleil – who was turned into a toad by Kenneth Anger'. Two years later Beausoleil would be arrested for the Manson murders, while Anger went on to write the best-selling exposé *Hollywood Babylon*.

The Family hung around the fringes of the movie community. Consisting as it did of three women to every man, it was welcome at any party. They would often sit in a circle and take acid, thereby instigating a group trip. A Family member, Paul Wilkins, later remembered that Manson was always the one who handed out the tabs, making a habit of taking less than everybody else in order to remain in control.

Dennis Wilson, a member of the 1960s' Californian band the Beach Boys, was particularly fascinated by Manson and his lifestyle. The Family freeloaded on Wilson's generosity unmercifully and he put its members up, fed them and clothed them from his own wardrobe.

The Family quickly grew, to the point at which the camper van could not longer contain all of them, so they moved out to a huddle of shacks around Topanga Canyon. Almost every young, hippie drifter on the West coast passed in and out of the Family at one time, including Joan 'Juanitta' Wildebush, Juan Flynn, Cathy Gillies, Brook Poston, Sandra Good, T J 'The Terrible' Walleman and Steve 'Clem' Grogan. But Kitty Lutesinger, Cathy 'Gypsy' Share and Stephanie Scram became more or less permanent members. There were junior Family members, too: Atkins gave birth to a son, imaginatively named Zezozoe C Zadfrack, while Bruner had a boy called Valentine Michael, after the protagonist in Robert Heinlein's cult 1960s' science-fiction classic work *Stranger in a Strange Land*.

By and large, the female members of the Family were middle-class drop-outs. Atkins was the only one with a criminal record. The others brought with them money, cars and their fathers' credit cards, which provided everything that the Family needed in order to survive. They formed the secret core of the Family. If they were to be accepted, they had to meet Manson's hypnotic gaze and perform seemingly impossible tasks. They were collectively taught to think of themselves as an elite and the outside world as hostile, threatening and beneath their contempt. With their personal means of support having been surrendered to Manson, they were completely under his control. Those who did not do what they were told were threatened with expulsion and occasionally death.

Manson stayed close to the Process Church during his time in Los Angeles. When it courted pop stars, like John Phillips, of the Mamas and the Papas, so did Manson. He certainly saw himself as part of the Satanist wing of the Process Church. For example, Manson traded the VW camper van for a school bus, which he had painted black. It was adorned with the image of the Goat of Mendes/Baphomet, which was painted by Beausoleil. The words 'Holywood [sic] Film Production Company' were painted on the side in an attempt to avoid any trouble with the police.

When the Process Church broke up, Manson and the Family headed for the Mojave Desert. Through contacts in San Diego, they got permission to stay on the Spahn Ranch, an old movie set where westerns were shot. It belonged to the 80-year-old George Spahn, who was virtually blind. In return for being allowed to stay there, the women cooked and cleaned for him – and, according to some, provided him with sexual favours. Fromme later told prosecuting attorney Vincent Bugliosi that she was in love with Spahn and would have married him if he had asked her.

True to its counter-cultural image, the Family fed itself with food that had been thrown out by supermarkets, thereby supposedly demonstrating how wicked and wasteful the capitalist world was. (The effect was somewhat marred, however, by the fact that they picked up the discarded food in a Rolls-Royce.) The cult freed itself from other constraints of conventional society by hustling dope, 'borrowing' credit cards and 'liberating' automobiles and other valuables. Gillies rented the Family's second home, the Baker Ranch, using Wilson's collection of gold records as a deposit.

Surrounded by adoring sycophants, the drug-addled Manson began developing a self-serving philosophy fuelled by Atkins' Satanic studies and his own brushes with Scientology and the Process Church. Atkins managed to convince him that his own name, Manson, was significant: he was supposedly Man-son, the Son of Man, or Christ. According to her twisted logic, this meant that he was also the devil. Manson began to see himself as the Gnostic deity Abraxas – a rooster-headed god with a serpent's feet, in whom light and darkness, good and evil, were supposed to be unified and transcendent. He believed himself to be both Christ and Satan. Naturally, in Manson's opinion, an apocalypse was at hand, which, to Manson, meant a war between black and white people.

When the Beatles' *White* album came out, Manson believed that it was a message directed at him and the Family. 'Sexy Sadie', he claimed, was Atkins, whose real name was Sadie. 'Piggies' sneered at the police and the establishment, and the word soon became part of the Family's everyday vocabulary. 'Blackbird' was a call for black people to revolt. 'Revolution 9' meant Chapter Nine of the biblical Book of Revelations (although he had been illiterate until his early 20s, Manson had been brought up with a thorough knowledge of the Bible). Chapter Nine of the Book of Revelations talks of the coming of the Apocalypse and of the Exterminating Angel, another persona that Manson adopted. One verse in Chapter Nine reads 'Neither repent they of their murders, nor of their sorceries, nor of their fornications, nor of their thefts.' Manson was completely unaware that a helter-skelter is a British fairground ride and interpreted the track 'Helter Skelter' as heralding what he saw as an inevitable race war. Black people would rise up and wipe out the 'piggies' – the forces of law and order, those in authority, the rich and famous and those whom Manson called 'movie people', the very people with whom he had partied with in Los Angeles, but who had inexplicably passed over his cinematographical potential.

Throughout this imminent cataclysm Manson and the Family would wait in safety in the desert. Once black people were in charge he believed that they would find themselves incapable of intelligent rule (because they were inferior beings in his view). They would therefore naturally turn to him and ask him to take over as world leader. Like Asahara, Manson believed that the attainment of this apocalyptic scenario needed a helping hand and tried to recruit biker gangs, such as the Straight Satans, later, also turning to violence himself.

In the meantime, Manson thought that he should try to emulate his heroes, the Beatles, and broadcast his message to the world through the medium of music. He started writing songs and took one of his compositions to the successful West-coast musician Gary Hinman. It was then that Manson learned that Hinman had recently inherited $20,000. He therefore sent Bruner, Atkins and Beausoleil to Hinman's house on Old Topanga Canyon Road to steal the money and murder Hinman for refusing to help Manson's song a number-one hit.

The three Family members did as they were told and went to the house. Beausoleil talked with Hinman for about two hours before losing his patience and pulling out the Family's gun, a 9mm Radom pistol. He handed it to Atkins and began searching the house. With Beausoleil out of the room, Hinman attempted to escape and Atkins tried to stop him. The gun went off and the bullet ricocheted around the kitchen before embedding itself under the sink. Hearing the shot, Beausoleil ran back, grabbed the pistol and beat Hinman around the head with it. Once Hinman had been was subdued they called Manson, who drove over to the house. There Manson took a sword and cut Hinman's ear. He told Beausoleil to find the money and the women to clean up Hinman's wound before bringing him to the ranch. Manson then left.

Bruner stitched up Hinman's ear with dental floss, bandaged his other wounds and gave him something to drink. After tying Hinman up on the hearth rug, Beausoleil and Atkins ransacked the house. They could not find any money but instead discovered two pink slips – the ownership documents for two cars. Under threat of death, Hinman signed them over to the Family.

Hinman made another escape attempt at dawn the next morning, reaching the window and screaming for help. Beausoleil panicked. He grabbed a knife and stabbed Hinman twice in the chest, then leaving to bleed to death. Atkins dabbled her fingers in his blood and wrote 'political piggies' on the wall, also drawing a cat's paw in a crude imitation of the logo of the militant black-separatist movement the Black Panthers. The three of them bundled up the blood-stained bandages and clothes and tried to wipe off their fingerprints from everything they had touched during their stay in Hinman's house. Then they left, locking the door behind them. Once outside they began to worry that Hinman was not actually dead, so they climbed back in through a window and smothered him for good measure. Next they hot-wired Hinman's VW van and drove to the Topanga Kitchen, where they celebrated their deeds with coffee and cherry cake. Afterwards they returned to the Spahn Ranch to tell Manson what they had done.

Hinman's body was discovered by friends on 31 July 1969, four days after he had been murdered. The Los Angeles Sheriff's Office – which deals with crime outside the metropolitan area – was called in. Sergeant Paul Whiteley and Deputy Charles Guenther were assigned to the case. The investigation started easily enough: the killers had not done a very good job of cleaning up and they found Beausoleil's fingerprints in Hinman's house. On 6 August they picked up Beausoleil and discovered the knife that had killed Hinman, as well as a T-shirt drenched with Hinman's blood, in Beausoleil's car. He was tried, convicted of murder and sent to jail without implicating Atkins, Bruner or Manson.

Manson now he began to plan new acts of violence. He also tried to have his song recorded by Terry Melcher, the son of Doris Day, to whom Wilson had introduced him. Melcher was a big player in the music industry, but failed to see the potential of Manson's material.

By now Manson was becoming angry and formed his followers into a death squad. Its members were dressed in black and were trained in breaking into and entering abandoned buildings; these exercises were known as 'creepy crawlies'. As part of their training, Manson told them that they were to kill anyone who stood in their way.

On 8 August 1969 Manson's death squad was dispatched to reconnoitre Melcher's remote home on Cielo Drive, in Benedict Canyon in the Hollywood Hills. Melcher had actually moved, but this did not matter to Manson because the people who were observed going in and out of the house were 'movie types' and their slaughter would act as a warning to others. He therefore sent Watson, Atkins, Krenwinkel and Kasabian to the house armed with a .22 Bluntline Special revolver, a knife and a length of rope.

The house at the end of Cielo Drive was indeed occupied by 'movie types'. The film director Roman Polanski lived there, but was currently away shooting a film in London. His wife, the movie star Sharon Tate, who was eight months pregnant, was at home, however. The coffee heiress Abigail Folger and her boyfriend, the Polish writer Voytek Frykowski, were visiting, as was Tate's friend, the celebrity hairdresser Jay Sebring.

Manson's death squad parked its white-and-yellow Ford outside 10050

Cielo Drive and Watson shinned up a telegraph pole and cut the phone lines. Then Watson, Atkins and Krenwinkel pushed open the wrought-iron gates; Kasabian lost her nerve at the last moment and stayed outside. As the other three went in, a white, two-seater Nash Ambassador came down the driveway. It was driven by the 18-year-old Steven Parent, who had been visiting the caretaker. Brandishing the .22, Watson leapt in front of the car's headlight beams and ordered the driver to stop. He then thrust the gun into the car window. While Parent begged for his life Watson pumped four bullets into his chest.

Atkins and Krenwinkel scouted around the house, but could not find a way in, so Watson began cutting his way through a screen on the window of an empty room at the front. Once inside the house, Manson's followers found Frykowski asleep on the couch. He awoke to find a .22 being brandished in his face and asked them what they wanted. 'I am the devil', said Watson. 'I am here to do the devil's business. Give me your money.'

Watson told Atkins to get some towels with which to tie up Frykowski. On her way back from the bathroom she saw Tate and the other guests talking in the bedroom. She reported this to Watson, who ordered her to go and get them. Atkins told Tate and the others that the house was being robbed, but that no harm would come to them. While she was tying them up, Sebring broke free and made a lunge for the gun. Watson shot him in the armpit and then stabbed him four times.

Fearing that they were all going to be killed, Frykowski attacked Watson, who beat him to the ground with the pistol butt, hitting him so hard that the pistol's walnut grip broke in two. Frykowski staggered to the door, screaming for help. Then, in a frenzy, the women stabbed Frykowski to death; 51 stab wounds were later found on his body. Frykowski's gallant stand put some fight into the others. Folger made a break for it, but Krenwinkel caught up with her halfway across the lawn. She was knocked to the ground and Watson then stabbed her to death. Tate begged for her life and for that of her unborn child. Despite being a mother herself, Atkins showed no mercy: while Krenwinkel held Tate down, Atkins stabbed her 16 times. Tate's mutilated body was then tied to Sebring's corpse. Watson next went around kicking and stabbing the lifeless bodies. The killers spread an American flag across the couch and wrote the word 'pig' in Tate's blood on the front door. They changed their bloody clothes, collected their weapons and made their way back to the Spahn Ranch, disposing of the incriminating evidence on the way.

'I felt so elated', said Atkins. 'Tired, but at peace with the world. I knew this was just the beginning of helter skelter. Now the world would listen.'

Later that night, Manson and another member of the Family returned to Cielo Drive to look for Atkins' knife and to tidy up. They first wiped Parent's car clean of fingerprints, then the house, using the towel that had been used to tie up Frykowski. They left it draped over Sebring's face.

Back at the Spahn Ranch, Manson got high on marijuana and read the reports of the murders in the newspapers as if they were film reviews. In celebration of this great victory, as he regarded it, he had an orgy with his female followers.

Two days later, it was clear that the slaughter at Benedict Canyon had still not sparked helter skelter and the apocalypse. So on 10 August Watson, Kasabian, Krenwinkel and Atkins set out again. This time Manson accompanied them, Van Houten and Grogan coming along for the ride, too. Manson randomly selected a house in the Silver Lake area of Los Angeles; the address was 3301 Waverley Drive. He took his sword and gun, walked up the drive to the long, low house and broke in. The house belonged to the 44-year-old grocery-store-owner Leno LaBianca and his 38-year-old wife, Rosemary, who ran a fashionable dress shop. They awoke to find Manson holding a gun to their faces. He tied them up and told them that they would not be harmed: he only intended to rob them, he said. He took LaBianca's wallet and then went outside to the car where the rest were waiting. Manson next sent Watson, Van Houten and Krenwinkel back into the house. He told them that he was going to break into the house next door and murder the occupants, but instead he drove home.

Once in the LaBianca house, Watson went to work. He dragged Mr LaBianca into the living room and stabbed him four times with a kitchen knife, which he left sticking out of his throat. Using his own knife, Watson then stabbed LaBianca another eight times in the stomach, leaving him to bleed to death with a pillow over his face. Watson and Krenwinkel next stabbed the helpless Mrs LaBianca 41 times while chanting a murderous mantra. They wanted Van Houten to join in and she reluctantly stabbed Mrs LaBianca 16 times in the buttocks, but she was already dead. Watson carved the word 'war' on Mr LaBianca's abdomen before Krenwinkel stabbed both bodies with a carving fork, leaving it embedded in Mr LaBianca's stomach. They then tied a lamp flex around his neck and put a pillowcase over his face. Using their victims' blood, they wrote revolutionary slogans on the walls – 'death to pigs' and 'rise' in the living room, as well as 'healter [sic] skelter' on the refrigerator door. Then the three killers took a shower together. Finally, they had something to eat and went home.

When Sergeant Whiteley and Deputy Guenther – the men from the LA Sheriff's Office who had arrested Beausoleil – read about the Tate murders, they saw similarities with the Hinman case, particularly with regard to the slogans that had been written on the walls in blood. They knew that Beausoleil could not have been directly involved because he was in custody at the time. But they had always suspected that he had not acted alone and they knew that he had hung out with a weird bunch of hippies at the Spahn Ranch. Anyone who had participated with Beausoleil in the Hinman murder would clearly be a prime suspect for the Tate killings. Whiteley called Sergeant Jesse Buckles, who was a member of the team handling the Tate case at the Los Angeles Police Department (LAPD), and told him of his suspicions. But Buckles pooh-poohed the idea and did not even report it to his superior officer: there was no need to, in his opinion, because the LAPD believed that it already had its man.

The Tate murders had been discovered the next morning by Winifred Chapman, the housekeeper who lived out. The young caretaker, William Garretson, who lived in the guesthouse in the back garden, immediately fell under suspicion. He claimed to have slept through everything, but the LAPD did not believe him and put him under pressure to change his story. When reports of the LaBianca murders came in, however, Garretson had to be released because he could clearly not have killed Mr and Mrs LaBianca while he was in custody.

By this time, the whole of Los Angeles was in a state of panic. Poolsides emptied, gun sales soared and security firms were inundated with work. The pressure was on the LAPD to make a quick arrest.

With no record of Whiteley's tip, the LAPD's most promising lead was narcotics: it was well known that Sebring had supplied his clients with marijuana and other drugs. A Polish friend of Frykowski told the LAPD that Frykowski had been setting himself up as a drug dealer, too. However, the Tate case was furthermore clearly linked to the LaBianca murders, which were also under investigation by the LAPD. The LaBiancas were a respectable, middle-aged couple who had no connection with drugs. Yet LaBianca had been a keen gambler and a racehorse-owner; could he have had Mafia connections? This line of inquiry also led nowhere.

It was not until 15 October, over two months after the Tate murders, that one member of the LaBianca team at the LAPD thought of checking to see if any similar cases had been handled by the Los Angeles Sheriff's Office. Unlike Sergeant Buckles and the Tate team, the LaBianca investigators were immediately interested in the Hinman case. In the meantime, Whiteley and Guenther had not been idle: on 16 August the LA Sheriff's Office had raided the Spahn Ranch looking for stolen cars and credit cards. The raid made it clear to the killers that their murderous actions had not set off helter skelter, the great revolutionary race war, as they had expected, but had instead provoked a police crackdown. With Manson's predictions thus having been discredited, the cult began to break up. 'When they catch me, it's going to be like feeding me to the lions', said Manson, exhibiting considerable insight for once. 'They're going to put me far away because I have no family, no one that will help me.'

Some of the Family fled to the Barker Ranch, but that, too, was raided on 12 October by the local Inyo County Police, which was looking for stolen cars and illegal firearms. Twenty-four Family members were arrested, including Manson himself. It took three days to search the huge ranch properly. When the police approached a dry gully on the outskirts of the ranch, Lutesinger, who was five months pregnant with Beausoleil's child, and Scram stumbled out. They were exhausted and frightened and begged for police protection.

As several of the Family members gave the Spahn Ranch as their address, the Inyo County Police phoned the LA Sheriff's Office, in whose area of jurisdiction it was. Whiteley and Guenther had been looking for Lutesinger, whom, because she was Beausoleil's girlfriend, they wanted to interview in connection with the Hinman killing. They therefore drove to Inyo County to see her. Lutesinger was eager to help. She told them that she had heard Manson order Beausoleil and Atkins to go to Hinman's house and extort money from him. This evidence tied Manson to the Hinman case. She also said that she had heard other Family members talking about a man being grabbed by the hair and stabbed in the legs. This man was not Hinman, who had suffered no wounds to his legs, but it could have been Frykowski.

Atkins had long been gone: she had taken off on her own and had turned to prostitution in order to support herself. By the time that Lutesinger was being questioned, however, Atkins was already in custody. When she was interviewed, Atkins admitted to being at Hinman's house when he was murdered. She was booked on suspicion of murder.

The LAPD already had one of the Tate murder weapons in its possession. The .22 Bluntline Special had been thrown out of their car by the killers on their way back from the LaBianca murders and had been found on a Los Angeles hillside by ten-year-old Stephen Weiss. But the police had just tagged it and then filed it away in a Manila envelope and its significance was only recognised after Weiss' father had read a description of the gun used in the Tate killings in the *Los Angeles Times* and had alerted the LAPD. Meanwhile, the LaBianca team's intelligence-gathering unit was set on gleaning any information that it could find on the Manson cult. It even pulled in Danny de Carlo and Al Springer, of the Straight Satan biker gang, for questioning, who provided it with a lot of hearsay and circumstantial evidence linking Manson to the murders. And Melcher told the police that Manson had visited 10050 Cielo Drive when he had lived there. The net was closing in on Manson.

Atkins could not keep her mouth shut in jail and began bragging to her cellmate, Ronnie Howard, as well as another prisoner, Virginia Graham, about the killings. She also said that she planned to do unspeakable things to Elizabeth Taylor, Richard Burton, Frank Sinatra, Tom Jones and Steve McQueen when she was released. Howard and Graham became increasingly frightened and reported what she had said to the authorities. Atkins' so-called 'hit list' was released to the papers and a number of the celebrities named consequently left town. In the light of her jail-cell confession Atkins could hardly deny her involvement in the murders and on 5 December 1969 she testified to a Grand Jury, describing what had really happened at 10050 Cielo Drive on the night of 8 August. And she blamed Manson.

The Manson trial began on 15 June 1970. It lasted for nine-and-a-half months, making it the longest murder trial in the USA at that time. The transcript ran to over 8 million words. Throughout the entire trial, the jury – seven men and five women – was sequestered, being kept *incommunicado* in a hotel and supervised by bailiffs for 225 days. There had been a vast amount of evidence to gather and a huge number of witnesses to locate and interview. Watson had gone home to Texas and fought extradition, while Manson himself had his own line in delaying techniques. First he said that he wanted to defend himself. When his request was denied, he rejected each of the attorneys that the court provided, one after another. In the end, Manson was defended by Irving Kanarek, who was himself a master of delaying tactics: his notorious obstructionism had once stretched out a simple case of theft until it took up two years of the court's time.

The defence began by challenging the right of the judge, William Keene, to preside over the case. It won and Keene was replaced by Judge Charles Older. When the trial was almost over, the newly elected president, Richard Nixon, made a potentially disastrous error by declaring Manson guilty and thereby going against the presumption of innocence until guilt had been declared. This would normally have resulted in the proceedings being declared a mistrial and the whole process having to begin all over again, but as the jury was sequestered it was assumed that the jurors had not heard the president's remark and the trial therefore went ahead.

The Manson trial was unique: never in the history of US jurisprudence had a defendant been charged with mass murder by proxy. After all,

Manson had not actually killed anyone with his own hand, nor had he been present when the killings were carried out. Manson's strategy was to continue maintaining absolute control over his followers and, through them, their attorneys. His female followers were still largely under his thrall. Atkins, for example, who had promised to turn state's evidence and testify against Manson, retracted her earlier statements and faced the charges beside him. Both inside the court and out, Manson's women pledged to follow him to the end.

On 24 July Manson appeared in court with a cross carved into his forehead; he had cut it himself with a hacksaw blade. He said nothing, but issued a press statement. 'I have Xed myself from your society', it said. A few days later, his co-defendants presented themselves in court with the same mark on their foreheads. By the end of the week the Family women who were camped outside the court building were sporting a similar symbol. Manson's 'X' was later transmuted into a swastika.

When Manson turned his back on the judge, so did his followers. He later caused an uproar by hurling himself at the bench, screaming at the judge that he should have his head cut off. Prosecution attorneys were given bodyguards and walkie-talkies for the duration of the trial. Family members made no direct attack on them, but they did attempt a raid on a gun store, which failed. They were apprehended in a bullet-riddled van after a shoot-out with the police. Their plan had been to use the stolen guns to hijack a plane and demand Manson's release.

During its investigations the LAPD had spotted the connection between Manson's Family and the Process Church. One former member of the Process Church, who was a suspect in two motorcycle-related murders, told them that Manson had used typical Process Church tactics, but that he had lost patience with anyone whom he could not indoctrinate, whom he had dubbed the so-called 'grey forces' – black people and members of the wealthy establishment.

Two members of the Process Church – calling themselves Brother John and Brother Matthew – turned up unannounced to see Deputy District Attorney Vincent Bugliosi during the course of the investigation. They claimed to have been sent by officials at the Process Church's national headquarters in Cambridge, Massachusetts, and delivered a stack of Process Church literature that officially denied that Manson had had anything to do with DeGrimston and the church. But Bugliosi subsequently discovered that the two men had also visited Manson in jail.

During his interrogation of Manson, Bugliosi asked whether he knew Robert DeGrimston or Robert Moore – Moore being DeGrimston's surname. 'You're looking at him', Manson said. 'Moore and I are one and the same.' Bugliosi later drew parallels between the teachings of Manson and those of the Process Church, particularly their joint view that it was their duty to help to instigate an imminent and violent Armageddon. They also both cultivated connections with motorcycle gangs in order to promote this goal. In fact, the only difference that Bugliosi could identify between them was that Manson had replaced the Process Church's three great gods – Christ, Lucifer and Satan – with the traditional Catharite duality of God and Satan, both combined within one man: himself.

Manson's strategy of letting his acolytes take the rap failed. Kasabian took the stand as a witness for the prosecution. She said that she loved Manson and then told the court everything that she knew about the murders. She had been outside 10050 Cielo Drive during the Tate killings and she had heard other Family members talk about the murder of the LaBiancas. More damningly, she addressed Manson from the stand, saying 'I am not like you, Charlie, I can't kill anyone'.

Manson's defence had tried to portray Watson as the evil genius behind the murders. But when he finally arrived from the Texas jail in which he had been held during his lengthy extradition battle the jury saw a good-looking, clean-cut, square-jawed, all-American boy – nobody's image of an evil genius. Watson told the court 'Charlie called me over behind a car. He said for me to take the gun and the knife and go up to where Terry Melcher used to live. He said to kill everyone in the house as gruesomely as possible.'

In what amounted to a threat, Manson told the jury 'You say there are just a few in my Family. There are many, many more, coming in the same direction. They are running in the streets, and they are coming right at you'. Then he taunted the jury with a chilling half-truth: 'I've killed no one', he said. 'I've ordered no one to be killed. These children who come to you with their knives, they're your children. I didn't teach them – you did.'

But no one was fooled: everyone knew who was really responsible. Manson, Beausoleil, Atkins, Krenwinkel, Van Houten and Grogan were all sentenced to death in the gas chamber. Manson was not even afraid: 'My faith in me is stronger than all your armies, government, gas chambers or anything you may want to do to me,' he said.

In some ways he was right. Before the sentences could be carried out the death penalty was abolished in California. Manson and his followers had their sentences commuted to life imprisonment and are now eligible for parole. So far, only Grogan has been granted it.

The former Family member Lynette Fromme made a half-hearted attempt to get Manson released from prison. In 1975 she pulled a gun on President Gerald Ford, but she did not pull the trigger and succeeded only in putting Manson's name back into the headlines again.

Manson constantly asks for parole. He does it but because it gains him publicity, not because he thinks that he has a chance of getting out. He revels in his image as Satan incarnate and boasts that he has been responsible for 35 other murders.

Stephen Kay, a Los Angeles Country district attorney who worked as Bugliosi's assistant during the trial, keeps his eye on Manson's parole hearings and attends them in order to oppose Manson's potential release. At a parole hearing in 1981 Manson said that Kay would be murdered in the car park when he left, but he was present, alive and well, at the next parole-board hearing. In the following year, 1982, Manson was transferred to a maximum-security block at Vacaville Prison after the authorities had learned that he was planning an escape by means of a hot-air balloon. A ballooning catalogue, a rope, a hacksaw and a container of flammable liquid were found in the jail.

At one parole-board hearing Manson was asked why he had unravelled his socks and had then used the yarn to make woollen scorpions. He rose from his seat and said, quite seriously, 'From the world of darkness I did loose demons and devils in the power of scorpions to torment'. Parole was refused. In 1986 Manson's latest parole request was opposed by California's governor, George Deukmejian. In response, Manson read out a 20-page-long, hand-written statement, which was described by those who heard it as 'bizarre and rambling'. Three years later he refused to appear before the parole board while wearing manacles. They made him look dangerous, he said.

In 1992 Manson's parole hearing was held within hours of the first execution to be carried out in California for nearly two decades (however, Manson's death sentence cannot be reinstated). Manson did not do his chances of getting parole much good when he told the parole board "There's no one as bad as me. I am everywhere. I am down in San Diego Zoo. I am in your children. They've tried to kill me 30 or 40 times in prison. They've poured fire over me. They haven't found anyone badder than me because there is no one as bad as me – and that's a fact'. It is also a fact that Manson has had to be excluded from taking exercise in the prison's exercise yard because of the threats on his person made by other prisoners, who are, presumably, badder.

Manson will never be allowed out of prison, but his female followers do stand a chance of being released. Atkins, Van Houten and Krenwinkel have all got skilful lawyers who are working on legal loopholes. Atkins has become a born-again Christian; like Van Houten, she is now a model prisoner. Van Houten herself has earned degrees in literature and psychology since she has been in prison. She also argues that she did not actually kill anyone, but only stabbed Mrs LaBianca after she was already dead. Even Bugliosi concedes that the women will be released eventually.

Watson's chances of release are less good. He found God in prison and became an assistant pastor at the California Men's Colony at San Luis Obispo. When he appointed another Family member, Bruce Davis, as his deputy, however, Kay suspected that he was trying to build a power base in jail.

At the time of the trial Manson's connections with the Process Church became quite well known, and the church suffered something of a backlash as a result. Its members discarded their distinctive black attire and wore grey leisure suits instead, while DeGrimston disappeared. In an effort to save the Process Church in the USA, Mary MacLean changed its name, closed the Lucifer and Satan wings and then dropped out of sight herself. According to the retired Captain Dale Griffis, of the Tiffin, Ohio, Police Department, she changed her name to Circe and opened an occult shop in Toledo, Ohio. She bought a tract of real estate that was adjacent to a location that was said to be the site of Satanic rituals involving human sacrifice. In 1985 law-enforcement officers dug up the site, but although some ritualistic paraphernalia was found there was no evidence of any human remains. However, the occult shop in Toledo closed soon afterwards and Circe mysteriously vanished.

Meanwhile, a number of other members of the Process Church returned to England. By 1988 they were proselytising their murderous creed as if they had never been away.

The Son of Sam

There are links between the Manson Family, the Process Church and another famous killer: the 'Son of Sam', who terrorised New York between 1976 and 1977. The murderer had been given the nickname by the newspapers after he sent a note to the police saying that he had been ordered to kill by his father Sam, who was a vampire.

In a letter to *Daily News* columnist Jimmy Breslin, he identified himself as 'Sam's creation'. When the *Daily News* published the letter it withheld the postscript, which read

> HERE ARE SOME NAMES TO HELP YOU ALONG. FORWARD THEM TO THE IN-
> SPECTOR FOR USE BY THE NCIC: 'THE DUKE OF DEATH', 'THE WICKED KING
> OF WICKER', 'THE TWENTY-TWO DISCIPLES OF HELL', JOHN 'WHEATIES' –

RAPIST AND SUFFOCATER OF YOUNG GIRLS. PS: J B PLEASE INFORM ALL THE
DETECTIVES WORKING ON THE SLAYINGS TO REMAIN.

The police said that they did not want this section of the letter released because they did not want the public to know about the NCIC – the National
Crime and Information Center. But perhaps the real reason for its omis-
sions was the Satanic undertones contained in the list of names that were
given. The 'Wicked King of Wicker' was presumably the king of 'Wicca' (a
witchcraft cult). And the 'Twenty-two Disciples of Hell' certainly sounded
like a Satanic organisation. Then there was John 'Wheaties', who was supposed to be the 'rapist and suffocater of young girls'; 'Wheaties' had quo-
tation marks around it, as if it were a nickname, but the police investigations
led nowhere.

One of the problems with capturing the Son of Sam was that although
the killer always used the same gun – a .44 – his description varied wildly.
But in August 1977 David Berkowitz was arrested. He pleaded guilty to all
of the Son of Sam murders and was sentenced to 365 years in prison. And
that seemed to be the end of that.

However, not everyone was satisfied. The investigative reporter
Maury Terry spotted a number of inconsistencies in Berkowitz's story. A
number of the descriptions given of the Son of Sam did not match
Berkowitz, neither with regard to in height nor to hair colour, although
they were consistent with each other. Furthermore, Berkowitz could not
have acted alone in one of the killings if all of the witnesses were telling the
truth. Terry interviewed them again and was convinced that they were.

Terry was fascinated by the name 'Son of Sam'. Berkowitz's real father
was named Tony; he had a stepfather, but his name was Nathan. There was
only one Sam connected with the case: Sam Carr, a neighbour of Berkowitz's
in the Bronx, who suspected Berkowitz of being responsible for a long campaign of harassment. Carr's house had been petrol-bombed; shots had been
fired through a window and Carr's dog had been shot. Berkowitz had complained to other neighbours that Carr was spying on him. Strangely enough,
although Carr's house was visible from Berkowitz's sixth-floor apartment,
both said that they had never met, despite Berkowitz's claims that he had received his murderous instructions from Carr's dog.

Carr had two estranged sons, John and Michael. He also had a daughter named Wheat, and John Carr was nicknamed 'Wheaties'. Terry remembered the John 'Wheaties' who was allegedly the 'rapist and suffocater of
young girls' in the Breslin letter. Descriptions of John Carr also matched
those given by the Son of Sam witnesses that did not fit Berkowitz.

Terry was also interested in Berkowitz's apparent obsession with dogs. He discovered that in Walden, New York, about an hour's drive from Berkowitz's home, the skinned bodies of 85 Dobermans and Alsatians had been found during the year of the Son of Sam killings. More dead dogs had been found in a wooded area of Untermeyer Park, nearby in Yonkers; a local teenager said that devil worshippers held ceremonies there. Could Berkowitz have been involved in a Satanic cult? The police, however, dismissed the idea.

In October 1978, when Terry eventually traced John Carr, it was too late to question him about any of this: he had been shot dead in the small town of Minot, North Dakota. His body had been found in the bedroom of his girlfriend, Linda O'Connor, with a bullet through the roof of his mouth and a rifle lying beside his corpse. The coroner's verdict was suicide, but the police believed that he had been murdered.

John Carr had been born in Yonkers, New York, on 12 October 1946 (he shared his birthday with Aleister Crowley). After leaving his Catholic school, Carr joined the US Air Force (USAF). He was stationed in Korea and served for 12 years. In 1972 he returned to the USA and was stationed in Minot, North Dakota. He was discharged from the USAF in 1976, allegedly for drug addiction. During 1976 and 1977 he went to hospital three times, having taken overdoses, and had a reputation as a drug dealer and heavy drinker. He was in New York at around the time of five of the eight Son of Sam attacks, including those whose witnesses had given descriptions that matched his.

In late January 1978 Carr again drove the 1,500 miles (2,414km) from Minot to New York, saying that he was going to stay in the city for a long time. But within two weeks he had called his girlfriend and had told her that the police were after him. On 14 February he flew back to Minot. He rented a post-office box, opened a bank account and inquired about the continued payment of a disability allowance that he received for a service injury – hardly the actions of a man contemplating suicide. Two days later he was dead.

Mysteriously, the letters 'S.S.N.Y.C.' were scrawled in blood on the skirting board by Carr's body. A man who has blown off the top of his head with a rifle's bullet seldom has time to write messages in his own blood. Terry deduced that Carr had been beaten to the ground by his assailants before his killer – or killers – had gone to search for his gun with which to kill him, leaving him time to write the message. The letters 'S.S.N.Y.C.', Terry concluded, stood for 'Son of Sam, New York City'. Carr furthermore had the figures '666' written in blood on his hand (666 is the number of the

Beast in the biblical Book of Revelations and was used as a Satanic pseudonym by Crowley). The police in Minot had also discovered that Carr was connected with a number of local occult groups, while his girlfriend said that when Carr had seen the news of Berkowitz's arrest for the Son of Sam shootings on TV he had said 'Oh, shit'.

Up to this point Terry had been dismissed as a conspiracy theorist. But John Santucci, the district attorney of the Queens district, began to believe that there was something to Terry's investigation and re-opened the case. It was soon discovered that far from being the classic, psychotic loner Berkowitz had a wide circle of friends. Chief among them was John 'Wheaties' Carr's brother, Michael. In 1975, the year before the killings started, Michael, a drug addict who hung around Berkowitz's apartment block, invited Berkowitz to a party. The guests included John Carr and other members of the Twenty-two Disciples of Hell, the Satanic group to which Berkowitz had allegedly referred in the Breslin letter. In due course Berkowitz moved to Yonkers, to within 600 feet (183m) of the home of Sam Carr, where Michael Carr then lived.

Since then, Michael Carr had moved out, and by the time that he could be traced he, too, was dead. In the early hours of 4 October 1979 his car had collided with a street lamp as he drove towards Manhattan at a speed of 75mph (121kmh). There were no skid marks, and his sister, Wheat, who worked for the Yonkers Police Department, was convinced that he had either been forced off the road or that one of his tyres had been shot out.

None of the other members of the Twenty-two Disciples of Hell was found, but the postman who used to deliver Berkowitz's letters in Yonkers killed himself. His name was Andrew Dupay, and he was a young married man. During the month before Berkowitz was arrested he was noticeably worried. Then, on 20 September 1977, five weeks after Berkowitz's arrest, he and his wife were bathing their two baby daughters when Dupay excused himself, went down to the basement of his home and blew off his head with a shotgun. A neighbour reported that Dupay had told him that he had learned something on his rounds that had frightened him. One of Terry's informants said that Dupay knew both Carr and Berkowitz and had killed himself because threats had been made against his family.

On 7 January 1978 the body of Mary Hirschmann was found in a vacant lot in Queens; she had been strangled and stabbed. Her husband's bullet-riddled corpse had been discovered the day before in the East Fishkill district of north Yonkers. He had mystical figures tattooed on his body.

On 16 December 1979 the abstract painter Howard Green and his girl-friend, Carol Marron, were found beaten to death in New Jersey, across the

Hudson river from New York. It was discovered that their apartment on DeKalb Avenue in Brooklyn was filled with Satanic paraphernalia and that Caroll had been making inquiries about joining Crowley's OTO.

The most unexpected witness in Santucci's new investigation was Berkowitz himself. In February 1979 he had called a press conference and had then announced that the story about Sam Carr's dog had been concocted in the hope of an insanity plea, but the court-appointed psychiatrists had declared him to be sane. Now, a year after having been incarcerated in Attica Correctional Facility, he confessed that he had lied. In prison, he had become prolific letter-writer and his letters revealed that even before his arrest he had staged his apartment to look like that of a lunatic.

In a letter to a priest in California, he wrote

> I really don't know how to begin this letter, but at one time I was a member of an occult group. Being sworn to secrecy or face death, I cannot reveal the name of the group, nor do I wish to. The group contained a mixture of Satanic practices which included the teachings of Aleister Crowley and Eliphas Lévi. It was (and still is) blood-orientated, and I am certain you know what I mean. The Coven's doctrines are a blend of ancient Druidism, the teachings of the Secret Order of the Golden Dawn, Black Magick, and a host of other unlawful and obnoxious practices. These people will stop at nothing, including murder. They have no fear of man-made laws or the Ten Commandments.

Berkowitz made other disturbing references in his letters. Shortly after the Son of Sam shootings had begun, he wrote, he had applied for a job in a dog pound. The pay was not good, but Berkowitz said that 'there was another way in which I was getting paid. Someone needed dogs. I guess you understand what I'm trying to say'. Terry's investigation had again proved that Berkowitz was telling the truth.

Then Berkowitz dropped a bombshell. He ripped out a chapter from a standard work on Satanism and witchcraft, claiming that it referred to the Satanic practices employed by Charles Manson and his Family. He wrote in the margin 'Call Santa Clara's Sheriff's office. Please ask the sheriffs what happened to Arlis Perry'. He went on to say that Perry had been 'hunted, stalked and slain. Followed to California, Stanford Univ'.

Stanford University is in Santa Clara County. A 19-year-old student called Arlis Perry had been horribly murdered in the church at the university at midnight on October 1974; she had only been a California for a few weeks. Her body was naked from the waist down. Her legs were spread and a 30-inch (76cm-) candle had been rammed into her vagina. Her arms were crossed over her chest and another candle had been placed between her breasts. Her jeans lay inverted over her legs. She had been beaten, strangled and stabbed behind the ear with an ice pick.

Little of this information was made public until 1988, but Berkowitz nevertheless knew many of the details of the murder that had been withheld by the police. He even cut out a picture from a newspaper that he said resembled Perry. The photograph of Perry that had appeared in the newspapers was taken from her high-school yearbook, but Berkowitz had singled out a photograph that looked much more like Perry on the night of her death. At the very least, Berkowitz had seen a picture of the murder, Terry maintained. He claimed that it was performed by a group of Satanists in California that was linked with Manson. Berkowitz said that Perry had once been a member of the group and had tried to leave.

Terry noted that some of the Son of Sam killings were performed with ruthless efficiency; others were inept and bungling. He concluded that Berkowitz had committed only three of the Son of Sam murders. His victims had either been women who had known about the Twenty-two Disciplines of Hell or who had offended its members. Terry believes that the other murders were committed by John Carr and a female member of the Twenty-two Disciples who had disguised herself with a balaclava. He also thinks that at least two of the killings were filmed.

On 10 July 1979 Berkowitz was slashed with a razor by another inmate in his maximum-security block; the cut needed 56 stitches and nearly killed him. He would not reveal who had attacked him, although he later said that it had been an attempt by a Satanic cult to make him observe his vow of silence. Terry claimed that the cult was a 'Process offshoot with OTO crossover' and even named its leader: Roy Alexander Radin, a tycoon who had made his money in show business. He moved to California in 1982, but by the time that Terry had tracked him down it was yet again too late. Radin had been murdered on Friday, 13 May 1983. His body was found dumped in Death Valley – Manson's old stamping ground; a defaced Bible was discovered nearby. Could Radin have been the 'grand chingon' of the Four P movement who had been described by the Satanic cannibal Stanley Dean Baker?

Although Radin and the Carr brothers were dead, and Berkowitz was locked up in prison, Terry believed that the other members of the Twenty-two Disciples of Hell were still at large and active. 'I am convinced', said Terry.

The evidence is quite clear that organised Satanic groups – be they genuine Process, official OTO or subgroups resulting from internal schisms – exist and carry out illegal rituals. It is beyond doubt that some of these involve murder. And this isn't just an American problem. The whole thing started up again in Britain [with] Aleister Crowley and he exported it to the United States. This is a multinational problem and England isn't exempt.

15 ❖ Christian cults

In 1517 Martin Luther put the cat among the pigeons when he nailed his famous 95 theses to the door of the church in Wittenberg. After the Protestant movement that he thereby initiated had broken with the Roman Catholic Church, established Western Christianity smashed into pieces, the larger pieces making up the various Protestant churches and the smaller shards the tiny cults that inhabited the religious fringes.

John Knox founded Presbyterianism in Scotland in 1560 and self-governing Congregationalist churches began to take root and spread in England during the reign of Elizabeth I. The Anabaptists, who believe in adult baptism for their believers, were also established during the sixteenth century and were hated by the other Protestant churches, as well as the Roman Catholics. Burning heretics is now thought of as the Roman Catholic Inquisition's domain, but it was also practised by Protestants. John Calvin, for example, had the Spanish scholar Michael Servetus burnt at the stake in 1553, in Geneva, for being both an Anabaptist and a Unitarian, despite the fact that he had a letter of safe conduct.

The first Baptist Church was founded in 1611. And in 1650 an itinerant apprentice shoemaker established the Religious Society of Friends, whose members quickly became known as the Quakers because, they quaked in the presence of God at their meetings. The Quakers rejected all orthodox Christian trappings, including baptism, the Eucharist, the creed and priests; instead, they worshipped mainly in silence. Largely free from any theological doctrines, they believed that the Holy Spirit lived within the human soul and accordingly they sought to find it there. However, when they did speak out, they scared their Puritan neighbours with their practice of *glossolalia*, or speaking in tongues. They made themselves even more unpopular in Cromwell's Puritan England by refusing to recognise either the authority of magistrates or that of the established Church of England.

Like the Pilgrim Fathers, who were Congregationalists, the Quakers looked to America for religious freedom. However, while Congregationalist state of Massachusetts reluctantly tolerated Baptists and Episcopalians, it imprisoned and flogged Quakers. And in 1659 three Quakers were executed for their beliefs, or lack of them. The Quaker William Penn established the state of Pennsylvania as a haven for Quakers, but it was also tolerant of other religions.

The Amish

Another cult which sought refuge in Pennsylvania was the Amish. More accurately called the Amish Mennonites, they are a breakaway group from the Mennonites, a radical, Anabaptist sect that was formed during the sixteenth century by the Dutch priest Menno Simmons. The Mennonites themselves were a spin-off from the non-conformist Swiss Brethren, a group that had been established in 1525, whereupon it immediately found itself being persecuted in Switzerland and southern Germany. The Mennonites then spread across Europe as far as Russia, and also travelled to America. As pacifists, they found themselves being charged with treason for helping destitute British soldiers during the War of Independence. Those who fought in the American Civil War were excommunicated by their church.

The Amish were established in Europe by the elder Jakob Ammann between 1693 and 1697. Ammann believed that any Mennonite who uttered a falsehood should be excommunicated and that any excommunicated Mennonite should be avoided and shunned. He also introduced footwashing to church services and established the standard Amish style of dress. Men wear broad-brimmed hats and beards, which they do not trim, but no moustaches. Their clothes are plain and home-made and are fastened with hooks and eyes rather than with new-fangled buttons or zips. Women wear bonnets, long, full dresses with capes over their shoulders, shawls and black shoes and stockings; no jewellery of any kind is tolerated. This severe form of dress is supposed to have been sanctioned by the Bible, but is, in fact, just a continuation of seventeenth-century rural costume.

In Europe, the Amish gradually merged back into the Mennonite congregation, but in the USA, especially in Pennsylvania, they remain distinct. They shun electric lights and telephones and drive horses and buggies rather than cars. They refuse to use modern agricultural machinery, and although they send their children to elementary school many Amish prefer to go to jail rather than let them attend high school.

Another Mennonite spin-off, not unlike the Amish, is the Hutterites. They are followers of Jakob Hutter, who was burnt to death as a heretic in

Members of the Amish Mennomite group. They are easily identified by their distinctive appearance

1536. He believed in the community of goods that was practised by the early Church. The Hutterites were persecuted to extinction in Europe, but survive in the USA and Canada, even though they were also punished in the USA on account of their pacifism and communal lifestyle. Hutterites live on huge, collective farms and have an extraordinarily high birth rate. In some places, local laws have been enacted in order to try to stop the uncontrolled growth of Hutterite colonies.

Unitarianism

Unitarianism is essentially a throwback to Arianism and rejects the deity of Christ. It was initially called Socinianism, after Laelius Socinus (1525–62), an Italian who travelled around Europe expounding his views, and his nephew Fautus, (1539–1604), who took the Unitarian word to Transylvania, in modern Romania, and Poland. The name 'Unitarian' was first used in 1600 to distinguish it from the Christian mainstream and most other Christian sects who are Trinitarian, believing as they do in the divinity of the trinity of God the Father, God the Son and God the Holy Ghost.

After the Catholics expelled the Unitarians from Poland they moved to Germany and Holland. Unitarianism fared poorly in England to start with. When the Act of Uniformity of 1662 imposed strictures on who could preach and what they were allowed to say, few of the dissenters were Unitarians. But as seventeenth-century theologians tried to grapple with the advances of science, Unitarianism seemed a promising way forward. The 1689 Act of Toleration accepted the Congregationalists, Presbyterians, Baptists and Quakers, but not the Catholics or Unitarians. Throughout the eighteenth century the Unitarians were regarded as a radical cult of dangerous free-thinkers. But Unitarianism began to take hold in America, however, especially around Boston, and it came to be seen as the thinking man's religion. Ralph Waldo Emerson embraced the faith, along with five US presidents, Thomas Jefferson and John Quincy Adams among them. Intellectuals in England also turned to Unitarianism and its followers included Charles Dickens, Josiah Wedgwood, Mary Wollstonecraft and Elizabeth Gaskell.

The Swedenborgians

The Swedenborgians are the followers of Emanuel Swedenborg (1688–1772). A Swedish nobleman and the son of a Lutheran bishop, Swedenborg received a vision that told him that the Second Coming had occurred in 1757 and he wrote numerous books in Latin about it.

His followers set up Swedenborgian societies. Two of the most prominent – the Church of New Jerusalem and the New Church – take their names from the titles of his books. The Anglican priest John Clowes, rector of St John's, Manchester, was the first person to translate Swedenborg's books into English, thereby establishing Swedenborgianism in the north-west of England. The Methodist minister Robert Hindmarch founded the New Jerusalem Church in 1787.

The Swedenborg Society was established in London in 1810 to translate and publish Swedenborg's books. It has a library and a bookshop and organises lectures. Those who have been influenced by the works of Swedenborg include John Wesley, William Blake, Robert Browning, W B Yeats, Immanuel Kant and Goethe.

The Mormons

The Church of Jesus Christ of the Latter-day Saints, whose followers are popularly known as Mormons, was founded in 1830 by Joseph F Smith. Smith was the son of a farming family living in the so-called 'burned-over' district of New York State (it was said to have been 'burned over' because so many evangelists had set fire to people's hearts there during the early nineteenth century). By the age of 14 the young Joseph Smith had been exposed to so much religion that he had become deeply confused, so he asked God whether he should become a Quaker or an Episcopalian, a Baptist or a Methodist, a Congregationalist or a Unitarian. Which was the one, true faith?

According to Mormon legend, God and Jesus both appeared to him in a vision and told him that he should join none of these sects. Three years later he had another vision: this time an angel called Moroni told him that there were some golden plates buried in a nearby hillside. Four years later

**A member of the Church
of Jesus Christ of the
Latter-Day Saints, whose
followers are popularly
known as Mormons**

he dug them up. There was a form of writing on them which Smith called
'reformed Egyptian hieroglyphics'. However, by wearing a huge pair of
eyepieces called Urim and Thummin he was able to decipher them.

Smith then set to work. He sat behind a curtain and dictated his
English translation of the text on the plates. When the translation was complete, Moroni returned and took the plates away. Next, in 1830, Smith's
neighbour, Martin Harris, mortgaged his farm in order to fund the publication of Smith's *Book of Mormon: Another Testament of Jesus Christ*.

The *Book of Mormon* tells of the emigration to America of three of the
lost tribes of Israel. The prophet Mormon, who had written their story
down on the plates, and his son, Moroni, were the last of one of the tribes
who had been visited by Jesus after his resurrection. Smith said that citi-
zens of the United States must now prepare for the new Jerusalem in the
New World: Christ was coming to rule over the USA for a thousand years.

There are problems with the legend, however. Some contemporaries
described Smith as a 'notorious liar' and he had certainly once been arrested for fraudulently claiming that he had a special eyepiece that could
find buried treasure. Furthermore, no one had ever heard of 'reformed
Egyptian hieroglyphics'. Smith claimed that Professor Charles Anthon, of
New York City, had confirmed that his translation was accurate. However,
as the *Book of Mormon* says that no one had ever seen this language before
how could anyone have judged how accurate the translation was?
Professor Anthon himself stated that the 'hieroglyphics' that he had seen
were a transparent hoax, consisting of letters from various alphabets that
had been jumbled up. Smith's translation also contains passages that have

been directly lifted from the King James version of the Bible, as well as a Methodist tract called the *Westminster Confession of Faith*.

If having a new book of the Bible was not enough, John the Baptist now appeared to both Smith and the school teacher Oliver Cowdery, who had transcribed Smith's dictation, and conferred the Aaronic priesthood on them. The apostles John, James and Peter also appeared in order to ordain them into the Melchizedek order. Thus qualified, Smith, Cowdery and four others set up the Church of Jesus Christ of the Latter-day Saints.

The church grew quickly, attracting converts from the Campbellite movement of Primitive fundamentalist Christians. Smith used his swelling congregation as a political power base, which led to violent conflict with his non-Mormon neighbours. In 1839 the church, now 10,000 strong, moved to Kirkwood, Ohio, where Smith established its first temple. Then it moved on to Missouri and Nauvoo, in Illinois. There its membership continued to grow, augmented by some 5,000 converts who had come from England.

The non-Mormon residents of Nauvoo were not happy about this take-over of their town, particularly when Smith became the mayor, the commanding officer of the local militia and the editor of the local newspaper. There was also dissent within the church itself. Many former Campbellites were concerned about the increasingly elaborate rituals that Smith was introducing. Others had doubts when Smith started practising polygamy (it was said that he had up to 80 wives). Smith justified his multiple marriages by claiming that Christ had had three wives – Mary of Bethany, Mary Magdalene and Martha. Abraham, Isaac, David and other Old Testament figures had had lots of wives too, he added.

Some dissenters left the church and set up their own, rival newspaper, whereupon Smith ordered the paper to be burnt and the printing presses smashed. In the resulting furore, Smith and his brother, Hyrum, were jailed. The jail was then stormed by an angry mob, which shot and killed Smith and his brother.

With its founder dead, a power struggle now developed within the church. Brigham Young, a polygamist, took over. and the church subsequently spit into two. Young's wing trekked through Nebraska and Iowa to what is now the state of Utah. There he and his followers set up their own territorial government and judicial system. The church sent out missionaries and some 100,000 converts poured into Utah, mainly from Britain and Scandinavia.

However, the authority of the federal government slowly began encroaching on the autonomy of the church. In 1862 the US Congress passed the Anti-bigamy Act, which outlawed polygamy, with the result that polygamous Mormons were arrested and fined. The Edmunds-Tucker Act of 1887 dissolved the church as a legal entity and confiscated over $50,000-worth of its property. The church now realised that it would face total destruction if it did not give way over polygamy and in 1890 it officially suspended the practice, although many Mormons continue to have many wives privately, even today.

The Mormons who remained in Illinois, including Smith's wife, Emma, formed the Reorganized Church of Jesus Christ and the Latter-day Saints under Smith's son, Joseph III (his father's father had also been called Joseph). The church is today based at Kirkwood, Ohio, and its members do not practise polygamy.

The Church of Christ (Temple Lot) has its headquarters at Temple Lot, in Independence, Missouri, which Smith once said would be the site of the 'New Zion' when Christ returns. These Mormons are against polygamy, too.

There are a number of other fundamentalist Mormon off-shoots around Colorado City, Arizona. As well as practising polygamy, they also seem to enjoy murdering the heads of rival sects.

The Plymouth Brethren
The Plymouth Brethren were established in Dublin in 1827, but took their name after a crucial meeting held in Plymouth in 1830. Their most effective evangelist, the former Episcopalian curate John Nelson Darby, who spread the cult to France, Germany, Switzerland, America and Australia, also published many of the brethren's early tracts in Plymouth. A fundamentalist Protestant cult, it has no rituals, no set prayers and its followers feel no need for a priest. The brethren believe in the imminent return of Christ and that they will form part of an elite which will be saved on the Day of Judgement.

In 1848 the brethren split into two groups – an open order and a closed one; members of the closed order have no association with anyone from outside the order. An even more severe off-shoot is the Exclusive Brethren, whose members ban televisions and radios from their homes. Their children are not allowed participate in sports or any type of social activity at school.

The Seventh-day Adventists
The Seventh-day Adventists constitute another apocalyptic cult. They have their roots in the Shakers, a group officially known as the United Society of Believers in Christ's Second Coming, who believed that Christ would reappear during the 1760s. The Shakers were the first Adventists. When Jesus did not return to Earth after all, a German Lutheran minister named J G

Bengel worked out that Christ would instead appear in 1836. The former US Army officer William Miller disagreed. From his studies of the biblical Book of Daniel and the Book of Revelations he computed that the Second Coming would occur on 21 March 1843. Miller attracted thousands of followers, but had to revise his figure when Christ again failed to return. Perhaps unsurprisingly, he subsequently discovered that he had been a year out because he had made a simple error of arithmetic. Between the years 1 BC and AD 1 there was no year 0, so consequently Jesus would reappear on Earth on 21 March 1844. Membership of his Church of God again swelled and Miller soon boasted 100,000 followers. Many of them sold all their worldly goods and waited for Christ all the night of 20 March 1844 in the open. But, once again, Christ did not materialise. His non-appearance was known as the 'Great Disappointment'. Miller himself was so disappointed that he died four years later.

The day after the Great Disappointment, however, one Hiram Edson had a vision, which revealed to him that Miller had indeed got the date right, but that his interpretation of events was wrong. In fact, 21 March 1844 was the day on which God had started 'cleansing the heavenly sanctuary' and sorting out the sheep from the goats in preparation for the Day of Judgement. How long this would take, no one knew. Then God would send Christ back to Earth to separate the righteous from the wicked. In the meantime, Edson was told, those Adventists who had died would be put into a suspended state of 'conditional immortality' until it was decided on the Day of Judgement whether they would either be extinguished with the wicked or would live forever on Earth under Christ's millennial reign.

By December 1844, Ellen G White was also having visions, although some cynics put these down to her fragile mental condition and her harsh upbringing. Her visions largely concurred with those of Edson, but were regarded as carrying more weight. She was married to a prominent Adventist minister and soon began publishing books extolling healthy living and discouraging the consumption of meat and intoxicants. Virtuous living, she said, would bring the Day of Judgement closer. In 1860 her followers became the Seventh-day Adventists when they decided that God would be encouraged to hasten the Day of Judgement if the Sabbath was celebrated on the seventh day of the week – that is, on Saturday, as decreed in the Bible, rather than on the first day, Sunday.

The Brothers of Christ

In 1832 the English doctor John Thomas was in the process emigrating to the USA when his ship was wrecked. Fearing imminent death, he vowed that if his life was saved he would devote it to religion. Initially a Congregationalist, when Thomas arrived intact in Brooklyn, New York, he joined the Campbellite Disciples of Christ. But after an intensive study of the Bible he founded the Brothers of Christ, or Christadelphians, in 1848, a movement which aimed to return to the original New Testament beliefs. In his work *The Hope of Israel*, Thomas explained that the 'Latter Day', which heralded Christ's return, had already begun. Thomas returned to Britain to preach his gospel, where the cult flourished.

Christian Science

Christian Science was founded by the redoubtable Mary Baker Eddy. Born in 1821, she was a sickly child and remained ill until well into her 20s. Her first husband died of yellow fever soon after they married; her second husband introduced her to the hypnotist and faith-healer Phineas P Quimby, who cured her of what she believed was a crippling spinal disease.

She began lecturing on his methods. Then, a month after Quimby died in 1866, she slipped on some ice and hurt herself. While she was convalescing she read the Bible and came across a passage in the Gospel of St Matthew in which Christ healed a man who was sick of the palsy. After reading this she said 'The healing Truth dawned on my sense and the result was that I rose, dressed myself and ever after was in better health than I had before enjoyed'. She then sat down to study the Bible for more hints on health. By 1870 she had started lecturing on the subject and in 1875 published the book *Science and Health with a Key to the Scriptures*. Critics say that it borrows heavily from Quimby's work.

With the encouragement of her third husband, she established the Church of Christ, Scientist in Boston, Massachusetts, in 1879. She also opened the Massachusetts Metaphysical College in Boston, where she ran courses for which she charged hefty fees. The church nevertheless grew quickly.

Eddy accepted no deviation from the truth as she saw it. She allowed no churches in which an individual pastor might give an independent view. Instead, she instituted Christian Science reading rooms in which her works would be read, along with the Bible, which she considered to be apocryphal. There was no Holy Communion in Christian Science because Mrs Eddy did not believe that God had been made flesh. Members were denied the comfort of tobacco and alcohol; strict adherents even forswore tea and coffee. But Christian Scientists are more famous today for rejecting all forms of medical treatment, including blood transfusions, on the grounds that God alone will provide salvation from sickness. Disease is regarded as a mere 'error', since God intended humankind to be healthy and happy.

Mary Baker Eddy, founder of the Christian Science cult

Christian Scientists are also required to buy the *Christian Science Monitor* every day, along with the weekly *Christian Science Sentinel*, the monthly *Christian Science Journal* and the *Christian Science Quarterly*. Not surprisingly, when she died in 1910 Mary Baker Eddy left $3 million.

The Jehovah's Witnesses

The Jehovah's Witnesses are members of another of the millennial cults that sprang up during the nineteenth century, although the name 'Jehovah's Witness' was not introduced until 1931. The name is significant, however, because Witnesses claim that Christ proclaimed the new relationship between humankind and God by saying the word 'Jehovah' out loud (for Jews, it is prohibited to pronounce the name of God). Yet many authorities say that the Hebrew name for God, *Yahweh*, was not rendered as 'Jehovah' until the twelfth century AD and others that it was instituted as late as 1520.

The Jehovah's Witnesses were founded by Charles Taze Russell, who had left formal education at the age of 11. Brought up as a Congregationalist, he joined the Seventh-day Adventists before coming under influence of Jonas Wendel, who believed that the Second Coming would occur in 1874. When nothing happened in that year, Russell claimed that Christ had indeed returned, but as an invisible presence. He first expounded this view in the booklet *The Object and Manner of the Lord's Return* in 1877, but in later editions pushed the initial publication date back to 1873, claiming that he had known about Wendel's mistake in advance.

He also said that believers would be 'called away bodily' in 1878. When nothing occurred in that year either, he explained that he had meant that believers would go directly to paradise from 1878 onwards, rather than waiting in the grave for the Second Coming like those who had been buried before that year.

Russell had already started publishing *Zion's Watch Tower and Herald of Christ's Presence* in 1871. In 1881 he established the Watch Tower Bible and Tract Society, which is still the publisher of *Watchtower* and *Awake*, the two magazines that are sold door to door by believers. Over the next three decades Russell wrote six volumes of *Studies in the Scriptures*. Although he maintained that the Bible was the fount of all truth, unassisted study was no use, he said. Even if a student did not study the Bible at all, but instead only read *Studies in the Scriptures*, they would still attain enlightenment within two years.

Jehovah's Witnesses have conveniently forgotten some of Russell's other claims, however. In 1911, for example, he sold 'Miracle Wheat' through the pages of the *Watchtower* at 60 times the price of ordinary wheat. He said that he had produced a similarly inflated yield, although it was shown in court to be slightly less fertile than unmiraculous wheat. He also swore under oath that he understood Greek, but it was proved in court that he did not even know the Greek alphabet. And a messy divorce revealed him to have been a rather less moral man than his followers would have wished.

Russell claimed that the end of the world would occur in 1914. This prediction was based on the dimensions of the Great Pyramid at Giza, which were not precisely known at the time. As 1914 approached, Jehovah's Witnesses postponed the end of the world to 1915 and then 1916. The end has also been expected in 1920, 1925, 1940, 1975 and 1984.

Because the world was about to end, Russell thought that there was little point in appointing a successor, so when he died in 1916 it was inevitable that infighting should have begun. The cult was eventually taken over by the New York attorney Joseph Rutherford, who called himself 'The Judge'. He was almost immediately arrested and sentenced to 25 years' imprisonment for opposing the USA's involvement in World War I. Jehovah's Witnesses are pacifists, not because they are against killing, but because they do not think that they should take up arms on the behalf of Earthly governments. After all, Russell had preached that they would fight at Armageddon, in which everyone would be wiped out except for his followers – 144,000 places in paradise had been set aside for them.

The precise limit that Russell had put on the capacity of heaven began to cause problems during the 1930s, when the cumulative total of the cult's following began to approach that figure. Rutherford, who wrote a seventh volume of *Studies in the Scriptures*, announced that once heaven was full new Witnesses would populate the freshly cleansed Earth. Rutherford also made another great leap forward in theological doctrine: from his luxury home in San Diego he pronounced that Christ had not died on the cross at all, but rather at the stake. The word for stake, he claimed, had been mistranslated.

When Rutherford died in 1942 he was succeed by Nathan Homer Knorr, who commissioned a new translation of the Bible – the New World Translation – in which to incorporate these new doctrinal departures. He was also responsible for the cult's systematic, door-to-door sales pitch. Even though its repeated prophecies regarding the imminent end of the world have been proved wrong and have lost the cult followers, the Witnesses' publications continue to offer 'evidence' that the Earth is experiencing its final hours.

The Worldwide Church of God

The Worldwide Church of God was founded by the former advertising executive and failed businessman Herbert W Armstrong. After a dispute with his wife he began studying the Bible and made a detailed investigation into the history of Christianity.

He concluded that the Church had gone wrong in around AD 70. The Sabbath, he claimed, should be celebrated on Saturday, not Sunday, and he furthermore stated that any church worth its salt should call itself the Church of God. Armstrong then discovered that there was a Seventh-day Adventist church in Stanberry, Missouri, which was indeed called the Church of God. He accordingly moved to Stanberry and in 1934 began producing the magazine *Plain Truth* – originally 250 copies of a Mimeographed sheet – and broadcasting a show called *The World Tomorrow* on the local, 100-watt radio station. From these humble beginnings a multi-billion-dollar operation has developed, which today publishes a glossy *Plain Truth* and broadcasts world-wide as the Radio Church of God.

16 ❖ The Moonies

The followers of Sun Myung Moon's Unification Church – who are more commonly known as the Moonies – are best known for their mass weddings. In 1992 Moon earned a place in the *Guinness Book of Records* by marrying 20,825 couples simultaneously, in the Olympic Stadium in Seoul, South

Korea; another 9,800 couples around the world participated in the ceremony by means of satellite link. These mass weddings are a regular practice within the cult. The marriage partners are selected more or less at whim by Moon. The couples have often never met each other and frequently do not even speak the same language. The only criterion necessary to qualify them for marriage is that they must have been a member of the sect for seven years, during which time they are supposed to have been celibate.

Sun Myung Moon was born Yong Myung Moon in 1920, in Chongju-gun in northern Korea. He later changed the name Yong, which means dragon, to Sun. His name now literally means 'Sun Shining Moon'.

When he was ten, Moon's family converted from Buddhism to Christianity. He was then brought up a Presbyterian. On Easter Sunday in 1936 he claims to have met Christ on a Korean mountainside. It was then that Moon says that he received the first of a series of divine revelations spelling out his special mission on Earth. Christ apparently told Moon that he must carry out Christ's unfinished task on Earth and complete humankind's salvation. Moon began his work by producing his own version of the Bible, entitled *Divine Principle*.

Moon spent World War II in Japan, where he studied electrical engineering. In 1945 he returned to Korea, married and then left his pregnant wife in Seoul while he went north to preach. In 1948 he was arrested and imprisoned for inciting social disorder; critics claim that this involved 'ritual sex', although his followers say that he was imprisoned for his religion beliefs. He was released when UN troops pushed the communists back to the Chinese border in 1950. The improbable story told is that he cycled the 600 miles (966km) to Pusan, in South Korea, carrying a fellow prisoner on his back.

In 1957 he established the Unification Church. God, he claimed, was now discarding Christianity and all the Christians in the world would be absorbed into his new movement. They must develop a unified front in order to defeat communism. Moon sometimes claims to be God incarnate, who has come to 'conquer and subjugate the world'. At other times he claims to be a pure man and says that having sex with him will therefore purify body and soul in a process known as 'blood cleansing'. To start with, the marriages of other members of the cult were proclaimed invalid until the woman had slept with Moon. As the cult grew, that dictate proved to be impractical. Instead, Moon arranged his disciples' weddings, and after the mass-wedding ceremonies the newly weds are supposed to abstain from sex for 40 days while the wife sleeps with Moon metaphysically, on the level of the unconscious. After that anything goes.

According to the *Divine Principle*, Eve was seduced by Satan and passed on this impurity to Adam and her children. Christ's mission was to marry an ideal woman, whom he would have to perfect further by sleeping with her. Unfortunately, he was crucified before he could fulfil his task of creating the 'perfect family'. It is now up to Moon to take over where Christ left off and create the perfect, God-centred familial community, from which will spring the God-centred nation and ultimately the God-centred world.

Moon is probably not the ideal candidate for this task, as he has been divorced twice. But in 1960 he married the 33-year-old Hak Jan Han, who bore him 12 children. She became 'heavenly mother' to Moon's 'father'. Moonies pray in front of the couple's picture, addressing them as their 'true parents'. Followers are expected to sever their ties with their real families and sleep in communal dormitories until they marry. They live austere lives, working for long hours and eating simple food; tobacco and alcohol are banned.

In Moon's vision, money is the route to global dominance. The more money that his followers bring into the cult – through work, donations or selling items on the street – the more God-centred they are said to be. Moon had close ties to the dictator Park Chung Hee, who seized power in South Korea in a military coup in 1961. This connection helped Moon to win lucrative National Defence contracts for weapon parts manufactured in Moonie factories. Moon also imports honey from China and sells it world-wide. Other factories produce machinery, air rifles, stone handicrafts and ginseng tea. Moon's business interests are run by a series of companies, but Moon is chairman of the board of each of them and exercises complete control over their

left **Members of the Moonie cult who entered into *The Guinness Book of Records* when 20,825 couples were simultaniously married**

right **Sun Myung Moon, founder of The Moonies**

operations. In 1975 the export of ginseng tea along brought in $10 million.

From Korea, the Unification Church spread to Japan, where it won a sizeable following, and then to the USA, Britain and the rest of Europe. During the 1980s the Moonies penetrated mainland China, and in 1990 President Gorbachev allowed them to recruit in the Soviet Union. They now claim a largely youthful membership of between 2 and 3 million world-wide.

In 1972 Moon decided to transfer the base of his operations to the USA. He moved into a multi-million-dollar estate in Westchester County, where he moors two yachts for his family's use. He invested $20 million in ventures in California and New York, spending $5 million on the New Yorker Hotel, which he turned into a hostel for his followers. During the Watergate Affair he held prayer meetings for President Nixon and also bought the *Washington Times*, a rival to the *Washington Post*, the newspaper that was credited with bringing Nixon down.

As a recognised religion, the Unification Church enjoys tax-free status in the USA (which is fortunate, as his Japanese flock alone contributed some $746 million between 1975 and 1985). However, the operation of a number of his front organisations – such as the Collegiate Association for Research Principles and the Confederation of Associations for the Unity of Societies in America – caused the authorities concern during the 1980s. In 1981 Moon brought an unsuccessful libel suit again the *Daily Mail* in Britain, which cost him £750,000. And in 1984 Moon was fined $250,000 and sentenced to 18 months' imprisonment in the USA for tax evasion; the Unification Church then spent $5 million on public relations in an effort to restore his good name.

Curiously, despite his long stay in the USA and his world-wide following, Moon has never learnt English. He addresses his followers in Korean and his words of wisdom are then translated by Colonel Bo Hi Pak, the one-time assistant military attaché at the South Korean Embassy in Washington, DC.

17 ✦ 'Jesus freaks'

Back in the late 1960s and early 1970s everybody was freaking out. Usually this involved loud rock music and hallucinogenic drugs, but some charismatic evangelical Christian preachers realised that young people could be encouraged to freak out on Jesus as well. One of the most effective was David Berg. At first sight he appeared uninspiring: a former Methodist minister, by the late 1960s he was middle-aged, pot-bellied and balding. He had been dragging his family around the American Midwest for some years, preaching the gospel of the Lord to no great effect. In 1968 he arrived in California, when the hippie movement was in full swing.

The generation of drop-outs who congregated on the beaches of California were drawn to a club that Berg called 'Teens for Christ'. There they heard the homespun philosophy of the self-styled 'Moses', or 'Father' David, which delivered traditional evangelical teaching dressed up in the language of sex, drugs and rock 'n' roll. Berg's wife, Jane, or 'mother', dished out peanut-butter sandwiches. Many of Berg's young recruits had abandoned their families and jobs and were attracted by the free food, as well as Berg's anti-establishment view of the meaning of life.

It was a journalist who dubbed Berg's followers the 'Children of God'. Berg seized upon the title and became a tele-evangelist, appealing particularly to the young. And when Jeremy Spencer, a guitarist with the band Fleetwood Mac, quit the group mid-tour and joined the Children of God the movement acquired a new cachet.

Berg originally extolled the joys of celibacy, but when an attractive young female recruit named Karen 'Maria' Zerby joined the cult Berg proclaimed the joys of free love instead. He declared that Karen/Maria was his second wife, although his first, Jane, stayed on with the cult. He also 'shared' the wives of other cult members. Berg preached that because God is love anything goes sexually – including incest, homosexuality and paedophilia. However, when allegations of the sexual abuse of the cults' children surfaced in the press Berg back-pedalled on paedophilia, declaring it to be an excommunicatable offence. Homosexuality was also later banned because of the biblical injunctions against it.

Recruits had to give up that everything they owned to the cult. They were warned of the forthcoming apocalypse and were told that if they left the Children of God they would forfeit any hope of salvation. Children of God were expected to sever all ties with their friends and families outside the cult, and as a result FREECOG was set up in 1972 to help parents to re-claim their children from Berg's clutches. FREECOG was the first of the modern anti-cult organisation whose aim is to kidnap cult members and then subject them to intensive, anti-brainwashing techniques. The cult was now also under investigation by the US authorities, so Berg decamped to England and set up his new headquarters in Bromley, Kent.

The Children of God (COG) cult spread widely throughout the world, but Berg feared that it was moving beyond his control: leaders in individ-ual countries were taking too much authority for themselves. In 1978 he therefore dismissed over 300 of them – including his own daughter and her husband, who were COG leaders in South America – along with 2,600 members, a third of the cult's world membership at the time. Those that re-mained were invited to join Berg's new brainchild, the Family of Love, which, chillingly, began calling itself the 'Family'.

In order to boost its membership, Berg introduced what he called 'Flirty Fishing', or 'FFing'. His second wife, Karen/Maria, had been taking other men to bed and thereby successfully converting them for years. Christ was a fisher of men and, Berg said that in order to fish you needed bait. So he sent out young, attractive, female cult members – both married and single – to pick up men in bars and clubs. Once bedded, they would be lured into the fold. During the 1980s the fear of AIDS put a stop to FFing. It is not known how effective a recruiting method it was; some say that it brought more women into the cult than men.

Sexual freedom has since been confined to those within the cult and is not extended to new recruits until they have completed a six-month pro-bationary period. Children of God live a communal life, supported by do-nations and the sales of their posters, music cassettes and videos. A cult member sometimes takes an ordinary job if more income is needed.

By and large, the Family of Love does not look after its members well. Police inquiries established that of the 1,000 members recruited in the south of England at least 116 had died over a 10-year period. When prosecutions of the cult began in 1994 Berg mysteriously disappeared. Cult members say that he died, but many believe that he went into hiding in Europe.

In 1995, in the British High Court, Lord Justice Ward declared that Berg was sexually depraved and that the rights of the children within the cult had been violated. However, Ward ruled that a 28-year-old member could keep her 3-year-old son – over the protests of the child's grandmother – provided that she renounce Berg's teachings. The cult's spokeswoman proclaimed that the verdict was a vindication of the cult.

The Jesus Army

Another group of 'Jesus freaks' which took root in Britain was the Jesus Army. This was established in 1967, when the Baptist minister Noel Stanton and some members of his church in Bugbrooke, Northampton, started speaking in tongues. They began healing people and preaching the gospel in the new hippie jargon of the 'Jesus revolution'.

Soon his church was too small for its growing congregation, so Stanton appealed for donations and bought buildings with them in which to house his followers. His congregation became a community, which was supported by the produce of the New Creation Farm. Communal houses spread across the UK. The Jesus Army also owns health-food shops, building and plumbing operations, as well as a clothes shop. Members are ferried around in brightly painted 'battle busses' and wear camouflage jackets, combat gear and army boots.

The Jesus Army's philosophy is straightforward evangelical Christianity. But Stanton preaches it using theatrical displays. He condemns sports, drinking and 'worldly music', and even takes a hammer to guitars, videos and music cassettes.

Within the communal houses everything is shared, including money and clothes. TVs and radios are banned, along with most newspapers. Only religious music is played. The Jesus Army does not celebrate such Christian festivals as Christmas, on the grounds that they have their origins in paganism. Sex is actively discouraged and even long-married couples are required to sleep in separate beds. Romantic liaisons between members require the permission of the leadership. And traditional gender roles are strictly observed.

Recruits are required to hand over everything that they own to the army. But this strategy is not the rip-off method used by other cults in order to prevent defection, which leaves those who are contemplating quitting to face a life of poverty. The Jesus Army says that it keeps members' money in a separate trust fund; later, if they decide to leave the church, it is returned to them, sometimes with interest.

18 ❖ Voodoo

Voodoo has had a bad press and is now associated in the popular mind with blood rituals, decapitated chickens, drug-induced trances, dolls with pins stuck into them, and, worst of all, zombies. In fact, Voodoo is a mixture of a number of religions native to west Africa that were brought to the Caribbean by slaves. It main features are ancestor worship and animism. Unlike Christians, instead of venerating one God in heaven, followers of Voodoo believe that spirits are present everywhere in nature.

The most widespread form of Voodoo originated in Haiti during the colonisation of Hispaniola (the island that later became Haiti and the Dominican Republic) and was practised by the African slaves that were brought there. The name 'Voodoo' derives from the word *vodun*, meaning 'god', or' spirit', in the language of the Fon people of Benin. Other elements of Voodoo come from the Yoruba and Kongo peoples. The French in particular tried to suppress Voodoo, but runaway slaves – known as *maroons* – who set up a resistance movement in the interior embraced it. And during the first slave rebellion in 1758 the *maroon* leaders wrote the Voodoo Declaration of Independence, in which slaves were encouraged to avenge themselves on their white masters. They did this in 1802, under the leadership of Toussaint-L'Ouverture. Although he was captured and burnt at the stake in France, his legacy was an independent Haiti, in which 80 per cent of the population are followers of Voodoo.

According to believers, the universe was created by a great snake called Damballah, whose 7,000 coils made up the hills and the valleys, and who put the stars in the skies. When he shed his skin waters flowed over the Earth. When the sun shone on the water it created a rainbow called Ayido-Wedo, who was so beautiful that Damballah married her.

Busy with his heavenly duties, Damballah left the Earth to be tended by spirits, or *loas*. There are hundreds of these spirits, each of which has several names. There are in two types of *loas*. *Rada loas* are the good ones. During their rituals, the faithful build large fires and wear white; an iron bar is stuck in a fire to symbolise the *loa* Ogoun. *Petro loas* are the bad lot. They are evoked by the sacrifice of a chicken or a black goat and are propitiated by means of all sorts of fetishes, such as skulls, dogs' bones and chickens' feathers; live snakes are also used. The most famous of the *petro loas* is Baron

Samedi, 'Lord of the Graveyard', and – in Hollywood movies, at least – the leader of the zombies. His symbols are the coffin and the penis.

Priests called *hougans*, or *manbos*, intercede with the *loas*. The most important part of the intercession ritual is to summon the *loa* of the crossroads, Legba. Legba is the only *loa* who can give permission for the others to leave the spiritual world and enter the material one. Once Legba has been summoned, the *hougan* prepares the metaphysical gate by sprinkling water and waving a sacred sword towards the four cardinal points. The *hougan* then draws a design, or *vever*, on the floor with flour. The design chosen is the symbol of the *loa* whom he wants to summon and each *loa* has its own design. He then strikes the *vever* with his *asson*, a sacred rattle. This opens the spiritual gateway and the *loa* whom he has called duly arrives. It is then rewarded with its favourite food and drink, which are laid out on the *vever*. Some *petro loas*, however, require a blood sacrifice, and the congregation have to drink the blood of the animals that are slaughtered. It is said that humans are sacrificed and their flesh consumed by members of some secret sects.

Hougans also perform exorcisms and healing rituals. In Voodoo belief disease is caused by bad spirits, who must be removed using spells, drumming, dancing and herbal medicines. An animal, usually a black cockerel, has to be sacrificed and its blood must be applied to the affected part while the animal is still alive. The spirit is then drawn out into the bird, which is thrown into the fire which consumes the spirit.

Voodoo's most famous character is the zombie – the living dead. In fact, the zombie of popular belief is largely the creation of Hollywood. In Haiti, the zombie is more of a manifestation of the Christian idea of purgatory, in that it exists in an in-between state, to which those who have done wrong in life are consigned. However, Voodoo priests *can* create real zombies, but not through sorcery. Instead they inject their victims with a nerve-paralysing toxin culled from the flesh of a Caribbean fish, which plunges victims into a catatonic state for several days before they revive with a mild case of amnesia. There is a superstition that robbing human beings of their free will in this way makes the perfect slave.

Voodoo claims some 40 million followers world-wide. Other forms evolved in further Caribbean islands. In the English-speaking Caribbean areas the darker side of Voodoo has manifested itself as *obeah*, a kind of black magic.

In Cuba Voodoo has assumed a Catholic face in the form of Santeria, which means the 'Path of the Saints'. The saints of the Roman Catholic Church are regarded as manifestations of the *orishas*, the gods of the Yoruba tribe. Adopting Santeria was one way slaves in which could continue worshipping their old, African deities without falling foul of their Catholic masters. The practice still flourishes in the officially atheist Cuba and also among Cuban exiles in the United States.

Followers of Santeria believe that there is one god, called Olorun and sometimes Olodumare, the fount of the universe's spiritual energy of *ashe*. Olorun communicates to humankind via the *orishas*, who again represent the animistic spirits of nature. Believers communicate with them through prayer, ritual and sacrifice. The animal sacrificed is treated with great respect and its death is a symbol that one day all humans will die.

The priests, or *santeros*, have to learn all the songs, rituals and folklore of Santeria. They must dress entirely in white for a year, not touch or be touched by anyone and not look in a mirror or go out at night. This abstinence gives them great power and they can hold ceremonies with which to bestow money and power on others. Their influence is not always benign, however. When General Manuel Noriega was overthrown in Panama in 1990, for example, a Santeria altar was found in his office which was adorned with the effigies of US President Ronald Reagan and Vice-President George Bush, who had been cursed. As Noriega is now serving a long sentence in a federal penitentiary for drug smuggling one supposes that it did not work.

A darker incarnation of Santeria is Abaqua, which involves human sacrifice. In 1978 a play call *Abaqua* was produced in Havana purporting to show some of cult's rituals. Within a fortnight all the cast members had been tracked down and killed.

In Mexico there is another black-magic version of Santeria called Palo Mayombe, which has been responsible for a number of murders.

19 ❖ The new pagans

When the United Kingdom was formed by the Act of Union between England and Scotland in 1707, the non-English inhabitants of the British Isles sought to define their separate identity within the new state. It was then that the Scottish, Irish, Welsh and Cornish people – although very different – assumed a common Celtic heritage.

It was said that the Celts, an Indo-European tribe, had migrated westwards to the British Isles between the fifth and first centuries BC. There is no historical evidence for this migration, however. Although the Romans said that they had found Celts when they arrived in the British Isles they used the name 'Celt' was a catch-all term for any northern European person who was not a Roman.

Julius Caesar also mentioned that there were Druids in Britain, as in Gaul. Druids were judges and kings rather than priests. What little is known of the ancient Druids comes from Caesar and other Roman sources, which are antagonistic to them and likely to be inaccurate. Caesar particularly dwelt on the Druidic practice of human sacrifice, in which victims were burnt alive in a huge, wicker effigy. This claim may well have been propaganda.

However, modern Druidism was conjured from these slender historical beginnings. It began in 1717, when John Tolland founded the Ancient Order of Druids; in 1726 he published the largely specious *History of the Druids*.

In 1792 the Welsh stonemason Edward Williams, who liked to style himself 'Iolo Morganwg', began performing what he said were 'ancient' Druidic ceremonies on Primrose Hill in London. The Ancient Order of Druids still holds ceremonies there, as well as on Tower Hill (on the roof of a McDonald's restaurant) on the equinoxes. Williams also established the Eisteddfod in 1819, but it is hard to say how deeply these events are rooted in Druidic tradition as Williams appears to have originated many 'early' Welsh documents himself.

The ceremony that takes place at Stonehenge on the summer solstice has even more tenuous connections with the Druids. Stonehenge, in Wiltshire, was first linked to the Celts by the diarist John Aubrey during the 1690s. However, the structure has nothing to do with any people who might have come to the British Isles after the fifth century BC because it dates from the Bronze Age, which ended 500 years earlier. Nevertheless, in 1908 the then chief Druid, George Watson McGregor, campaigned for the right to worship at the stones.

Druidism also comprises numerous varieties. Fifteen different groups came together to form the Council of British Druid Orders in 1989. These include the Ancient Druid Order, which was founded in 1964 and has subsequently spawned the Order of Bards, Ovates and Druids. The British Druid Order was founded in 1979, while the Secular Order of Druids was established 1986 to further that most ancient of Celtic philosophies – environmentalism. One of the most popular cults is the Druid Clan of Dana, which is based at Clonegal Castle in Eire. It is one of three branches of the Fellowship of Isis, which was founded in 1976 by the Reverend Lawrence Durdin-Robertson, who, apparently, can trace the Robertson line back via the Celts to ancient Egypt.

There are Cornish Druids, Breton Druids and Scottish Druids, the latter in the form of the College of Druidism in Edinburgh. The Insular Order of Druidism, which is based in Portsmouth, is on the Wiccan wing of Druidism. Then there is King Arthur Pendragon's Loyal Arthurian Warband, which campaigns against nuclear weapons and the Criminal Justice Act, neither of which were pressing concerns of the pre-Christian inhabitants of the British Isles.

Wicca

Another form of paganism is the 'Old Religion' – witchcraft, which is today more fashionably called as 'Wicca'. This can certainly trace its roots back to the 1950s.

There may have been an ancient European cult which practised magic. But witchcraft, in the form that has been known for the last five centuries, was the invention of two Dominicans named Jacob Sprenger and Heinrich Kramer, who were sent to Germany by the Roman Catholic Inquisition during the fifteenth century to root out heresy. In 1486 they wrote *Malleus Maleficarum* ('The Hammer of Witchcraft'), which described the vile and diabolical practices that they came across. They justified their torture, mutilation and killing of large numbers of women as being necessary for stamping out witchcraft and denied that they were doing this for their own, kinky pleasure.

In *The Witch-Cult in Western Europe*, published in 1921, and *The God of the Witches*, published in 1931, Dr Margaret Murray claimed that the worship of a female deity, which she associated with the Roman goddess Diana, 'appears to have been the ancient religion of Western Europe'. Her work borrows heavily from *Aradia, or the Gospel of Witches*, published in 1899 by the American humorist Charles Leland. Murray's theories have since been comprehensively disproved, but her books still sell well in the USA.

The founder of Wicca was the retired civil servant Gerald Gardner. He was a Rosicrucian and was initiated into Aleister Crowley's *Ordo Templi Orientis* before discovering a witches' coven in the south of England in 1939. Apparently, they let him join (which was lucky for him as he was a keen naturist). He was also into flagellation, an enthusiasm which came over strongly in his hand-written *Book of Shadows*, in which he 'recreated' the traditional rituals of witchcraft, augmented by elements borrowed from Freemasonry, Crowleyism and his own sexual predilections. These practices remain the basis of modern witchcraft, although much of the heavy S & M requirements have since been dropped.

Robert Graves gave modern witchcraft another fillip with the 1946 publication of *The White Goddess*, his study of the moon goddess in different cultures. Then, in 1951, came the British Fraudulent Mediums Act, which effectively repealed all remaining witchcraft acts and allowed individuals to indulge in any cult practices that they fancied, provided that their activities harmed no one. And in 1954 Gardner published *Witchcraft Today*. In the end, however, Gardner tired of Wicca and joined the Order of Bards, Ovates and Druids, the brainchild of his friend, Ross Nichols.

When Gardner died, Alex Sanders and his wife, Maxine, became Wiccanism's pre-eminent figures and popularised their trendy version of witchcraft during the 1960s. After the couple's separation in 1973, Maxine Sanders took over the movement.

Many Dianic cults only allow women members. Those who do not often insist that their male initiates are 'new men' – 'caring, loving and supportive'. This requirement is interesting, because Sprenger and Kramer revealed their fear of women in *Malleus Maleficarum* by claiming that witches emasculated men (which was the pair's justification for killing them). According to Sprenger and Kramer, witches always seemed to deposit the severed organs in birds' nests, and men had to go to considerable lengths in climbing trees to get their penises back.

Many Wiccan groups adhere to the 'Charge of the Goddess', a rather flowery statement of their common beliefs. It was written by Gardner and Doreen Valiente, although some of it was lifted from Leland's *Aradia* – so it has a pedigree of a hundred years. It evokes the 'Great Mother' and links her to Artemis, Athene, Aphrodite, Diana, Isis and other ancient goddesses.

There is an even older tradition of Wicca that traces its history back to 1965, or 1271, according to its adherents. Called the Association of Cymmry Wicca, it is based on the Church of Y Tylwyth Teg in the US state of Georgia. Its leader is one Rhuddlwm ap Gawr, who met Sarah Llewellyn in 1965.

She claimed that in 1271 Sarah's distinguished forebear, Prince Llewellyn, commanded his trusted scribes to write down what was left of the family's mystical knowledge. His Druidic bard complied in a volume called *The Thirteen Treasures*, which also included elements derived from other pagan groups, as well as the Knights Templar.

For 700 years, the Llewellyn family kept its knowledge secret, but when Sarah met Gawr she immediately revealed all. He then set up Y Tylwyth Teg – which has tax-free, religious status – and the Association of Cymmry Wicca. The cult's secluded mountain base, which is located somewhere in northern Georgia, is called 'Camelot-in-the-Woods', and its spiritual training college, the Bangor Institute, teaches natural healing, spiritual consciousness and many other New Age interests. By the mid-1990s it claimed a total of 15,433 followers throughout the world, which means that Llewellyn's secret knowledge is not so secret any more.

20 ❖ Eastern promise

During the 1960s all things Eastern became trendy, especially the serene form of the Maharishi Mahesh Yogi. Born Mahesh Srivastava in Jabalpur, he claims to have learnt the basics of his technique, transcendental meditation (TM), from spiritual masters in the Himalayas, who made him a *yogi* (a master of yoga). He then took it upon himself to spread its benefits to the world.

In 1957 he embarked a tour of southern India and established a series of spiritual-development centres there (this marked the beginning of his Spiritual Regeneration movement). Indian pundits gave him the title *Maharishi* (the Hindu for 'spiritual teacher'). In 1960 the Maharishi went to the USA, where he refined his techniques and coined the term 'transcendental meditation'. His most inspired move was to secularise TM, stripping it of all religious rites and mysticism, which brought it down to the level of Western psychology. Marijuana and LSD were then beginning to become popular, and the Maharishi marketed TM as an alternative, safe means of expanding the human consciousness.

The Beatles and the actress Mia Farrow accepted the Maharishi as their guru. They followed him to India and stayed at the Rishikesh Ashram, but became disillusioned when they discovered that the Maharishi had not entirely rid himself of earthly desires – not when it came to Mia Farrow, at least. Their disillusionment did little to dent his world-wide reputation, however.

In 1975 he established the Maharishi European Research University in Switzerland to conduct research into human consciousness. US universities began including TM in their courses. It was also practised in jails, factories, farms and offices. Many athletes, in particular, said that they found the technique useful. In some European countries, as well as in the Soviet Union, the basics were taught in schools and soon the Maharishi had become one of the richest men in the world.

He controlled more than 4,000 TM centres in 150 countries, employing over 25,000 teachers. He set up more universities, libraries and presses, whose equipment alone was worth billions. His personal wealth includes

left **Maharishi Mahesh Yogi, guru to among others, The Beatles and Mia Farrow**

right **Followers of Krishna Consciousness who can easily be identified by their shaved heads and saffron robes**

a large fleet of aeroplanes, helicopters, luxury cars and ships. His British headquarters, Mentmore Tower in Buckinghamshire, was bought from the queen for £250 million.

In 1984 Ferdinand Marcos, then the president of the Philippines, paid vast sums for the services of TM consultants to prevent him from losing control of the country. They failed. And in 1988 the Soviet authorities gave him permission to build a huge, domed city in Armenia, after the state had been devastated by an earthquake.

All sorts of claims have been made for TM. The Maharishi says that its purpose is 'to spontaneously unfold the full potential of the individual and thereby to unfold the full potential of every nation'. Furthermore, 'it is a very cosmic design for a global upsurge of orderliness to take the whole human race with all its divergent qualities and values in the direction of happiness and fulfilment'. I leave it to the reader to decide whether the sum total of human happiness and fulfilment has increased a lot over the past 40 years.

Krishna Consciousness

Following in the footsteps of transcendental meditation was Krishna Consciousness, the brainchild of Srila Prabhupada. Like many Indian *swamis* (religious teachers), this was only one of the many names that he used during his lifetime.

Born in 1896, Prabhupada was brought up at 151 Harrison Road, Calcutta, where both his father and mother worshipped the Hindu god Krishna; they were strict vegetarians and even abjured tea and coffee. Prabhupada emulated them and dedicated himself to Krishna from the age of six. He would eat nothing until he had had a bath and had worshipped Krishna. At night, before going to bed, he would recite religious verses and chant Krishna's name while counting on his rosary before going to bed.

His mother wanted him to go to England to study to become a lawyer, but his father was afraid that the young Prabhupada would be seduced by Western ways and would start wearing Western clothes, eating meat and chasing women. So Prabhupada stayed in India and spent most of his life working in a chemical plant in Calcutta. In his spare time he devoted himself to religion. During the 1920s there was a revival of the Krishna Consciousness movement in India. Swept along by it, Prabhupada took as his *swami* Sri Bhaktisddhanta Sarawati, who told him to 'print books' and 'carry Krishna Consciousness to the West'. Prabhupada subsequently spent his time translating sacred Hindu texts and writing in English on Hindu thought.

His first vehicle for promoting Krishna Consciousness was an English-language magazine called *Back to the Godhead*, which he wrote and published himself. He then left his wife and in 1959 became a *sanyassi* (a religious ascetic who relinquishes material things in order to pursue his faith).

In 1965 Prabhupada sailed to the USA with a bag full of religious books. In New York, his lectures attracted a small following. Within a year he had initiated 11 disciples into his order of Krishna Consciousness; they vowed to abstain from alcohol, tobacco, drugs, meat, tea, coffee and sex outside marriage. Prabhupada was an uncompromising *guru*. Disciplines had to renounce all earthly values in order to follow the spiritual path. Soon his shaven-headed followers, wearing orange, Indian robes, became a regular sight on US streets, dancing and chanting *Hare Krishna* ('Lord Krishna'). After establishing the International Society for Krishna Consciousness (ISKCON), in 1968 he based ISKCON's headquarters at an English country house – bought at a knockdown price from the former Beatle George Harrison – near Watford in Hertfordshire. By the time of his death, in 1977, more than 200 Krishna Consciousness centres had sprung up around the world.

Before Prabhupada died, he had set up the International Governing Body Commission to run the Hare Krishna movement, comprising 29 of his young followers. However, none of them had the slightest idea of how to run the multi-million-dollar empire that the *swami* had bequeathed them. Eleven of them staged a *Putsch*, on the unsubstantiated grounds that Prabhupada had authorised their succession on his deathbed. Their leader was Keith Ham, who had taken the name Kirtanananda and subsequently ran his operation from the New Vrindavan, a temple that he had his followers build for him in West Virginia. A British breakaway group was controlled by James Immel, who was known as Jayatritha.

Without Prabhupada's restraining hand, his disciplines began expanding their Krishna consciousness with LSD. In 1987 Immel was beheaded by his follower John Tiernan, or Navanita Cora, who was probably tripping at the time. Tiernan claimed that he had killed the acid-crazed Immel because Immel was planning to set up his own, personal harem among the female devotees in contravention of the rules laid down by Prabhupada. Tiernan was convicted of murder and committed to a mental institution.

Bhagwan Shree Rajneesh

The most notorious of the new-style Indian *swamis* was Bhagwan Shree Rajneesh. Born Rajneesh Chandra Mohan, to a wealthy, middle-class family, he was brought up by his grandparents, who spoiled him.

Rajneesh became an honours student at the University of Jabalpur, going on to become a professor of philosophy. In 1966 he quit, claiming that he had attained enlightenment without the help of either a *guru* or any form of rigorous religious discipline. He invented 'dynamic meditation', which involves catharsis – usually in the form of expressions of anger or sexual intercourse. This was just one of the many forms of meditation that he devised during his lifetime.

In 1969 he moved the centre of his operations to Bombay, where he was besieged by young Western drop-outs searching for enlightenment. He took them on as his pupils, and in exchange for everything that they owned he gave them lectures and rose-coloured robes. They were encouraged to chant mantras, kick, bite, scream and punch each other in order to release their pent-up emotions, to romp naked and to have as much sex as they could handle. Rajneesh took the title *Bhagwan* – which means 'Master of the Vagina' – and maintained his own state of enlightenment with a string of young female initiates, some of whose seduction was little short of rape, as the *guru* took it upon himself to teach them the spiritual benefits of sexual submission.

The nude romps on the beach that were carried out under the auspices of the Bhagwan attracted the hostility of the locals of Bombay and the cult consequently moved to Poona. In order to support the *ashram* (the religious community), the Bhagwan's followers took to smuggling drugs. The proceeds were then funnelled back into the Bhagwan's coffers. When a BBC documentary exposed this practice, the Indian authorities began an investigation of the cult's activities. The Bhagwan accordingly moved his operations to Antelope, a small town in Wasco County, Oregon, in the USA, in order to escape the consequences of the charges of fraud and tax evasion that had been brought against him. There he bought a desert property called Big Muddy Ranch for $6 million and renamed it Rajneeshpuram.

While his followers toiled at the ranch, enduring a state of squalor, the Bhagwan lived in opulence: he had a fleet of 90 Rolls-Royces, 4 aircraft, a private arsenal and an endless supply of submissive young women. The regime grew stricter for his followers and they were marshalled by the cult's police force. All expressions of individuality were stamped out and the outside world, including members' friends and families, was derided as being worthless and meaningless.

Cult members infiltrated Antelope's local council and thus effectively took over the town. Buildings were erected on the ranch without planning permission and when state officials protested their offices were firebombed. The ensuing federal investigation discovered laboratories containing chemical and biological agents on the ranch. Then several of the Bhagwan's senior lieutenants – including his secretary, Ma Anand Sheela – turned against him and the Bhagwan fled. He headed for Bermuda, but when his private jet set down at Charlotte-Douglas International Airport in Carolina to refuel he was arrested and taken to jail in chains. Convicted on fraud charges for making false visa applications, he was fined $400,000 and deported. However, India refused him residence. He then headed to Nepal, before hopping around the globe for two years until the Indian government finally let him settle in Poona in 1987.

There followed a time of confusion. The Bhagwan insisted that he was not a teacher, although his teachings already ran to 500 volumes. Then he rejected the title Bhagwan; some of his followers thought that Bhagwan meant 'God', he said. He was not God; he did not even believe in God: like Buddha and Lao-Tzu, he was an atheist. From now on he was to be known as Gautam the Buddha, he proclaimed. Two days later, however, he announced that he was not Gautam the Buddha after all, but Maitreya the Buddha (Maitreya means 'friend'). Two days after that, he declared that he was to be known as Shree Rajneesh Zorba the Buddha. 'Zorba the Buddha simply means the synthesis between materialism and spiritualism – that is my contribution', he explained.

He managed to remain Zorba the Buddha for a week before he announced 'Shree Rajneesh is enough to indicate me'. One month later he became Osho Rajneesh; Osho means the 'whole man'. Seven months after that he dropped Rajneesh – his given name – and became simply Osho. A few months afterwards, in 1989, he died, possibly of poisoning, but more probably of AIDS, which had struck down a number of his senior aides.

At the height of his popularity the Bhagwan had run 600 meditation centres around the world; only 20 were left when he died. The cult, which now operates under the name Osho, was taken over by the Canadian real-estate magnate Michael William O'Bryne, who is known to the devout as Swami Prem Jayesh. His slimmed-down operation still nets some $45 million a year by 'de-stressing' business executives. Two followers who were not de-stressed, however, were the British women Sally-Anne Croft, or Ma Prem Savita, an accountant from Devon, and Susan Hagan, or Ma Anand Su, a Hertfordshire aromatherapist. In 1995 they were extradited from England to Oregon, where they were tried for conspiring to murder a lawyer who had been investigating the activities at the cult's ranch in Antelope. They were convicted and sentenced to five years' imprisonment.

Followers still promote the Bhagwan's Mystic Rose Meditation, which the he claimed was the 'greatest breakthrough in meditation in 2,500 years', and of all the meditations that he had invented, he said that it was 'perhaps the most essential and fundamental one'. The director of the Mystic Rose Meditation programme has claimed that 'If everyone on the planet did Osho's Mystic Rose, all wars would cease immediately'.

21 ❖ The People's Temple

When it comes to mass murder, it is hard to beat the record of cult leader Jim Jones, the founder of the People's Temple, who was responsible for the deaths of over 900 of his followers. A precocious cultist, he began his career in religion at the age of 12, delivering hellfire-and-damnation speeches at mock funerals for dead cats. But some saw a more sinister side to his interest in felines: 'Some of the neighbours would have cats missing and we always thought he was using them for sacrifices', a childhood acquaintance recalled. There may have been something to this because Jones' mother believed in spells, omens, black magic and the transmigration of souls.

Jones was brought up in the small town of Lynn, in Indiana, which depended for its livelihood on one thriving local industry – coffin-making. Jones' father had been gassed in France during World War I. Back in Lynn, he became the local barfly. He was a dyed-in-the-wool, redneck racist and a lifelong member of the Ku Klux Klan. Jones' mother shocked small-town Indiana by smoking in the street. She subscribed to the *National Geographic* and made up bedtime stories for her son which featured imaginary journeys up the Amazon and her life with the head-hunters there. She believed that dreams were visions of the future and predicted that her son would one day be the champion of the poor and the weak. He was destined to be a man who left his mark on the world, she said.

While his contemporaries left school in order to make their way in the white-dominated worlds of banking, business, farming or teaching, Jones worked in a hospital in Indianapolis, where his colleagues were mainly poor and black. There he met and married a student nurse who was five years his senior. Jones wanted to become a doctor, so he enrolled at the University of Indiana, in Bloomington. He dropped out after a year, however, being now intent on becoming a preacher. He began his religious career as a door-to-door recruiter for a Methodist mission before becoming an unordained supply preacher. But his ministry was not a success: the largely white congregation at his first church did not like the black people that Jones was bringing in. Neither did they like his hell-and-damnation sermons, and they certainly did not like being told by Jones that he had met God one day on the train to Philadelphia. He was thrown

Jim Jones founder of the People's Temple cult

out and the church was closed down, as if it had been desecrated.

At the age of 22, unfinanced and unordained, Jones founded the Community National Church in a rundown area of Indianapolis. It was operated very much on a shoestring and Jones supported it by importing and selling monkeys at $29 a piece.

Jones was not the prototypical American tele-evangelist preaching God, the flag and the American way – quite the opposite. In 1953 he joined the Communist Party. In that year, too, he conceived of the idea of 'revolutionary death' when the spies Julius and Ethel Rosenberg were executed. Their deaths, he concluded, shattered the illusion that the USA was the 'last best hope of mankind'. Jones described himself privately as a 'socialist', although his political philosophy seems to have owed more to Robin Hood than to Karl Marx. The poorer and weaker his followers the more the attention that he lavished on them. One early member of the church recalled 'He had a lot of them, the kind of people most folks don't want to have anything to do with. Fat, ugly old ladies who didn't have nobody in the world. He'd pass around hugs and kisses like he really loved them, and you could see on their faces what he meant to them.'

His success at building a truly multi-racial congregation – one of the first in the USA – attracted unwelcome attention. Segregationists called him a 'nigger-lover' and threw dead cats into his church; his windows were smashed and explosives were detonated in his garden. But the more opposition that he faced the harder he tried. He even adopted eight Korean and black children. His unwavering stand against racism led, in 1961, to his appointment to the newly created City Human Rights Commission, which reported directly to the mayor.

By 1957 Jones and his wife, Marceline, had amassed $50,000 and they established the first People's Temple in a lavishly converted synagogue on North Delaware Street, Indianapolis. At around that time Jones made several pilgrimages to the Peace Mission of Father Divine, the most successful ministry to the urban poor in the country. He learnt at the master's feet. The keys to 'Father Divine's' success were his absolute insistence on his own divinity and his extravagant demonstrations of the power of faith. Jones quickly learned his lessons and began putting on his own displays of healing. In carefully contrived, theatrical settings, he got believers to spew up chicken's livers, claiming that they were cancers. He raised up perfectly fit young people, who had been made up to look like wheelchair-bound geriatrics, and astounded his congregation with his mind-reading powers. These were also trickery: he had a photographic memory and kept detailed files on all his followers. Jones also noted that Father Divine, although he was black and had an almost exclusively black following, surrounded himself with an inner circle of attractive, middle-class, white women. Father Divine furthermore compensated himself for his long hours of selfless devotion to his flock with Cadillacs and a 40-room mansion.

Jones followed a different path, however. He took his young family off for two years of missionary work in the *favelas* of Belo Horizonte, in Brazil. There he met hardened Marxists for the first time and consequently added a fresh dollop of communist dogma to his gospel of social change through Christian love. On his way back to the USA, Jones stopped off in British Guiana, which was soon to become the independent country of Guyana.

Back in the USA, society was changing. Jones' battle to unite black and white people was no longer being fought single-handedly. Martin Luther King, Jr, for example, was now expounding his vision of a future USA in which race would no longer be an issue. But what made a more powerful impact on Jones were the words of Malcolm X, who asked 'What has Christianity done for black people – except oppress them?'

The Vietnam War, civil-rights marches in the south and race riots throughout all of the major cities of the USA convinced Jones that he must take his followers to a 'promised land'. He decided that Redwood Valley, near Ukiah, in California, was the ideal place and accordingly relocated the People's Temple there, bussing his followers across the country to their new home. Some stayed behind in Indiana, but those who followed Jones sold all of their property and gave it to the church. From then on they were totally dependent on the People's Temple. The People's Temple spread from Redwood Valley to San Francisco and Los Angeles, where Jones opened food kitchens and day-care centres. Soon he was wielding considerable political power.

Indeed, Jones could deliver the vote of the several thousand black members of his People's Temple. Virtually every liberal office-holder in the state – from lieutenant governor down to district attorney – was offered the chance to address his congregation. They quickly became beholden to Jones and in gratitude for his support San Francisco's mayor, George Moscone, appointed Jones chairman of the city's housing authority. Even national politicians cultivated him: during the 1976 presidential campaign Jones was invited to dine with Rosalynn Carter, the wife of presidential hopeful Jimmy Carter. For his part, Jones used his influence to secure the preferential treatment of his congregation at welfare agencies, housing authorities and even in court.

In the affluent Redwood Valley Jones attracted an educated, white, middle-class congregation, members of which he installed as an upper echelon of his church to organise the People's Temple's activities. One of these was an ambitious young lawyer named Tim Stoen. Like the rest of his generation, Stoen had become politically disillusioned following the assassination of John F Kennedy and the Vietnam War and was looking for a revolutionary way ahead. Jones promised just that: his multi-racial congregation and freewheeling Christian/Marxist philosophy seemed to represent a democratic future. Jones' growing political influence secured Stoen the plum job of assistant district attorney in San Francisco, but his price was access to the body of Stoen's attractive young wife, Grace. In 1972 Grace gave birth to a son, John-John. The birth certificate named the father as being Tim Stoen, but in a later affidavit Stoen stated that he had requested Jones to sire a child by his wife 'in the steadfast hope that the said child will become the devoted follower of Jesus Christ and be instrumental in bringing God's kingdom here on Earth, as has been his wonderful natural father'. Jones, Stoen said, was the 'most compassionate, honest and courageous human being on Earth'. The affidavit was witnessed by Marceline, Jones' wife; Grace Stoen's opinion was not recorded.

Jones began treating his congregation as a harem, and his young women followers seemed to consider it a privilege to satisfy his sexual cravings. Jones' secretary kept a separate appointments' book for these pastoral liaisons, and Jones boasted of his sexual prowess, claiming that he possessed almost superhuman sexual endurance, technique and potency.

At one time he even asked for psychiatric advice on how to bring his libido under control. Jones used sex not just for pleasure, but for gaining power. By seducing members of his congregation he loosened the bond between them and their regular sexual partners and thereby bound all the parties concerned closer to the People's Temple. Jones banned all sexual contact with outsiders, while sexual relations between members of his congregation required the People's Temple's specific approval in advance; it was seldom forthcoming. One woman had an abortion rather than bear Jones' child, but at least three of Jones' congregation carried his children to term.

Jones did not only sleep with the women: male members of his congregation were also encouraged to have sex with him. This, Jones explained, was a 'revolutionary act'. But he entered into the spirit of things with a little too much zest. In 1973 he was detained for making flagrant homosexual overtures to an undercover policeman in the toilet of a cinema during a matinée screening of *Jesus Christ Superstar*. Jones claimed that his arrest was part of a police vendetta against him and the People's Temple. If it was, it failed: Jones wielded enough influence not only to get the charges dropped, but also to have the record of his arrest sealed by a Los Angeles judge.

Sex was a frequent topic of discussion for the People's Temple's all-important Planning Commission, the inner circle of around 100 members largely consisting of the better-educated, middle-class whites. Meetings would drag on into the early hours, with Jones railing against bourgeois sexual attitudes. He would force members to confess their sexual fears and fantasies publicly. Sometimes Jones would sentence those who were less than forthcoming to long periods of celibacy. They should follow his example, Jones said: he took no sensual pleasure in sex; for him it was a tool of revolution. During one meeting Jones forced one white man to perform cunnilingus on a black woman in order to prove that he harboured no racial prejudice. Sexual candour and urination in public, Jones maintained, were symbolic representations of the People's Temple's openness (Jones, it appeared to some, took an unhealthy pleasure in exposing himself).

While things were becoming more 'open' inside the community, Jones began to take an increasingly paranoid view of the outside world. He believed that his phone was being tapped by the FBI and that he was being followed by government agents. People who had left the People's Temple were watched by the cult's members to make sure that they were not talking to the FBI or to hostile journalists. Their private lives – and sometimes even their rubbish – were combed for material with which to blackmail them and thus ensure their silence. The Mertle family was a typical victim of this practice.

In 1968 Elmer and Deanna Mertle were invited to visit the People's Temple in Redwood Valley. They found there a feeling of friendship and sense of community that they had not experienced before. Both of them came from fatherless homes and saw a potential father figure in the shape of Jones, was already styling himself 'Dad'. Deanna had been brought up as a Seventh-day Adventist and Jones challenged many of her fundamental beliefs. Christianity was a 'slave religion', she was told; the Bible was full of illogical contradictions, Jones pointed out, so she read it again and found that this was so. Elmer was more attracted by Jones' politics. And he liked the way in which, after their first visit to the People's Temple, everyone greeted them by name. The Mertles and their children were fussed over like they already belonged to the cult.

One night Deanna had a dream in which she and Elmer were threatened by a terrible monster, but Jones saved them. Soon afterwards they sold their home and gave their money to the People's Temple. They then moved into a farmhouse that Jones had rented for them nearby. By 1975 the Mertles had become members of the Planning Commission, but were becoming increasingly disturbed by Jones' bizarre behaviour. And when their 16-year-old daughter was spanked for a minor infraction they decided to leave the cult.

This was not as easy as they thought, however. Two of their children lived in the homes of other cult members and felt more loyalty to Jones than to their parents. The Mertles' home, and everything in it, belonged to the People's Temple. It was also their only source of income; they had been completely supported by the People's Temple for five years during, which they had had almost no contact with the outside world. But they were also lucky: Elmer's mother was rich. They contacted her and she gave them a profitable rest home that she owned in Berkeley, as well as the money with which to buy a house.

When Deanna called one of Jones' aides to tell him that they were leaving the cult all hell broke loose. A delegation of members visited them and tried to persuade them to change their minds. They were accused of stealing incriminating documents from the church and their home was searched. Jones threatened to accuse Elmer of being a child-molester, to which the Mertles responded by saying that they would take their lurid tales of the meetings of the Planning Commission to the press. The Mertles finally escaped and changed their names. They deposited documents that were damaging to the People's Temple, as well as sworn affidavits charging Jones with all manner of indecent behaviour, in a safe-deposit box.

After the Mertles had left the People's Temple, Jones denounced them as traitors who had abandoned the task of building a better world in favour of enjoying worldly pleasures. They had sold out their brothers and sisters, Jones told his followers, 'for a pocketful of credit cards and a fancy car'.

In the same year as the Mertles left the cult Jones was named 'Humanitarian of the Year' by the *Los Angeles Herald-Examiner*, while the Foundation for Religion in America selected Jones as one of its '100 Outstanding Clergymen in America'. Jones was then invited to speak at an anti-suicide rally in San Francisco on Memorial Day in 1977. The purpose of the rally was to put pressure on the city fathers to build a barrier along the Golden Gate Bridge – a favourite jumping-off point for the depressed and disturbed. Although Jones' speech began as a sternly moral statement of his disapproval of suicide, halfway through he suddenly changed tack: his initial condemnation of suicide became a blanket endorsement for it.

Jones had first mentioned the idea of 'revolutionary suicide' to Grace Stoen in 1973. At that time he planned that his followers should die, but said that he would remain alive in order to explain to others why they had done it. In 1976 he began to put his plan to practice: on New Year's Day he coerced his followers into drinking what he told them was poison. He railed against the 'traitors' who had left the People's Temple and told the members of his congregation that if they loved him they could only prove it by drinking the poison. Some became hysterical, but following the mock shooting of a member who had tried to run away Jones' followers meekly did what they were told. Forty-five minutes later he told them that the 'poison' was innocuous and they thanked him for testing them. This was the first of a series of suicide rehearsals that Jones called 'white nights'. Each time the members of the congregation were told that they were swallowing poison – and they could never be sure that they were not. But they gradually got used to the prospect of laying down their lives for 'Dad' – who was by now claiming to be God, or at the very least from another planet, like Superman. At around the same time Jones relinquished all of his belief in Christianity, even hurling his Bible to the ground during a sermon in order to reinforce a point.

Then things started going wrong for the People's Temple. *New West* magazine published an article attacking Jones. Once free, the Mertles had dedicated themselves to fighting the People's Temple and had told the *New West* reporter about the sexual and physical abuse that they had witnessed. The magazine had furthermore unearthed evidence of extortion, embezzlement and blackmail on the part of the cult. (Jones had begun diverting the People's Temple's money into off-shore investments). The article also outlined Grace Stoen's relationship with Jones.

Grace had by now run away from the People's Temple and now began suing for the custody of her son, John-John. Jones was determined that she should not have him, however: John-John was one of the new breed of followers born into the People's Temple which Jones said would inherit the Earth. Tim Stoen was still Jones' legal adviser and told him that there was no point in fighting Grace by means of the courts. They were bound to return John-John to his natural mother, especially when Grace and the Mertles were called to the witness box and started to outline Jones' bizarre sexual practices. There was only one way in which Jones could hold on to John-John, said Stoen: by taking him abroad. The process of fighting for custody of the boy in a foreign court could be strung out for years, perhaps forever, and Jones knew exactly where to go.

Seven years after his first, fleeting visit to Guyana in 1963, Jones had formulated plans to build a Utopia there. The Guyanese government was immediately receptive to his idea: because Guyana was an underdeveloped country it welcomed any scheme that would bring in foreign capital – especially from a source as politically sympathetic as Jones'. Jones' proposal for clearing the jungle and then turning over the virgin land to agriculture also coincided with the Guyanese government's development aims. It therefore leased him land along the Venezuelan border in an area that had long been disputed. Establishing a large colony of Americans there, it believed, would prevent the Venezuelan Army from annexing the region and would help to establish the claim that the land belonged to Guyana. Guyana was also perfect from Jones' perspective. Although the majority of the people in the country were ethnically east Indian, since its independence from Britain in 1966 Guyana had had a socialist government that was run by the descendants of African slaves.

In 1974 Jones paid $1 million for 27,000 acres of jungle in Guyana. By 1976 Jonestown was still an experimental agricultural outpost, but in 1977, when Jones came under pressure in the USA, large amounts of building material were shipped up the river to nearby Port Kaituma. Some 380 cult members then applied successfully for visas and headed for Guyana; John-John was among them. In the following year another 700 set off for Jonestown. The entry fee to Jones' Utopia was everything that his followers owned or earned. Many chose to pay it, but others had no choice. An unknown number of children – perhaps as many as 150 – had been handed over to the People's Temple, along with their welfare cheques, by probation officers and welfare agencies in Ukiah and San Francisco.

Briefly free from Jones' tyrannical discipline, the cult members went wild on the trip to Jonestown. They got drunk in the grog shops of Georgetown and the party continued on board the boat travelling up the river. One teenage girl, full of rum, had a brief fling with one of the Guyanese boatmen; when he heard about it Jones furious.

Once inside the compound, a regime of iron discipline was reimposed upon the cult members. Casual sexual encounters were banned and the Relationships Committee imposed a three-month waiting period on any couple which applied to have a serious relationship. Such prohibitions did not apply to Jones himself, of course, who moved into a hut with two of his mistresses while his wife lived nearby. One young girl who refused his advances was forcibly drugged and taken from Jonestown's hospital to Jones' hut each night. And when one member, Debbie Blakely, left the cult, Jones openly confessed that it was his fault. She had wanted bourgeois sex – for pleasure! For him, sex was a political act, so he had nobly refused her and that was why she had left.

Those who found favour with Jones were given special privileges. The Jonestown doctor, for example, who supported Jones' claim that non-revolutionary sex caused cancer, was indulged with a succession of teenage girls. Those who opposed Jones fared less well: beatings were commonplace for minor offences or merely because Jones thought that the offender's 'head was between their legs' – that is, they were thinking about sex rather than socialist work. He was especially hard on any male who was interested in a girl whom he himself fancied. Adults were caned or forced to fight each other until 'right prevailed', or were simply beaten into bloody submission. Children were particularly harshly treated, even for minor breaches of discipline. They were taken before a microphone at 2am and beaten with a board – for as many as 75 strokes – while their cries echoed via the PA system throughout the compound. Others were lowered down a well and were pulled into the water by a waiting assistant.

Meanwhile, Jones was becoming increasingly paranoid. He claimed to have killed a burglar whom he had caught breaking into his hut and to have served up the man's flesh in a stew to his followers. While cult members toiled in the fields from sun-up to sundown, Jones stayed in his hut, taking drugs and monitoring the news from San Francisco and the People's Temple's outpost in Georgetown. He controlled his followers' radio-listening and doctored the news from the outside world. He claimed that Jonestown was about to be attacked by a force of mercenaries that had been trained by the CIA and which was being mustered in a staging area across the Brazilian border. Armed guards were posted around the compound, ostensibly to protect the compound from attack, but they were actually there to stop disaffected cult members from escaping.

The members who had left the People's Temple in the USA could not be controlled, however. They told the press bizarre tales of the goings-on in Guyana. The bisexual Jones sexually abused his flock, they claimed; he forced his followers to undertake gruelling manual labour in appalling physical conditions; they were disciplined by means of humiliating rituals and were not allowed to leave. A support group, the Committee of Concerned Relatives, was formed. One of these relatives, Sam Houston, a journalist with the Associated Press, accused the cult of murdering his son. The boy had left the People's Temple following a blazing row with Jones. The next day he had died in a grisly railway accident near the waterfront in San Francisco. One of Houston's drinking buddies was Congressman Leo Ryan. Several of the People's Temple's members came from Ryan's congressional district in southern San Francisco. Houston persuaded Ryan to investigate the cult to find out what was really going on in the People's Temple's South American settlement.

On 24 October 1978 Ryan received authorisation from the US House of Representatives' Foreign Affairs Committee to go to Guyana. With legal action pending which threatened to cut off cult's funds, Jones had no choice but to let Congressman Ryan visit Jonestown. But he nevertheless tried to lay down conditions: he would not allow Ryan into Jonestown if he brought any 'traitors' or members of the press with him. The feisty congressman would have none of this and travelled to Guyana with four members of the Committee of Concerned Relatives, as well as reporters and photographers from the San Francisco daily papers and the *Washington Post* and an NBC film crew. Ryan informed Jones that if he was not allowed into Jonestown film footage of him being turned away would be broadcast by NBC from coast to coast in the USA. A full-scale Congressional investigation would be sure to follow.

On the afternoon of 17 November Ryan's party flew to the airstrip at Port Kaituma, a few miles from Jonestown. The group was collected by one of Jones' adopted sons, Johnny. Congressman Ryan, the relatives and the party of journalists entered Jonestown just before sunset on a Jonestown dump truck. Their reception was surprisingly friendly: although Jones retired scowling to his hut, the cult members had been instructed to smile. Dinner was served at 8pm and afterwards the Jonestown band began to play. Congressman Ryan then made a speech which exhibited pure political genius: he told the cult members how much he had enjoyed the band and said that Jonestown looked like a pretty nice place in which to live. 'From what I have seen,' Ryan said, 'there are a lot of people who believe this is the best thing that ever happened to them.' There was only one thing wrong with Jonestown as far as he was concerned, he continued: it wasn't in his Congressional district, so its inhabitants could not vote for him.

The cult members, who, despite their smiles and Sunday-best clothes, were deeply resentful of this perceived instance of outside interference, broke into spontaneous applause. The tension was dispelled and the band struck up again. The young people took to the dance floor while the older ones joined in the clapping. Everyone seemed happy. But as the dance floor emptied later that night a young black woman named Monica Bagby passed a note to NBC journalist Don Harris. It asked him to arrange for her and her friend, Vern Gosney, to leave Jonestown with Congressman Ryan the next day.

On the following morning things began to fall apart for Jones. At daybreak nine sect members seized their chance to escape and set off through the jungle towards the village of Matthew's Ridge, some 20 miles (32km) away. Avoiding taking the official tour of Jonestown, some journalists furthermore started poking around on their own and almost provoked a riot. For his part, Harris began interviewing Jones on camera. Jones talked openly about his mistresses and denied press reports that there was a ban on sexual intercourse among his followers: it was 'bullshit', he said. 'Thirty babies have been born since the summer of 1977.'

But this was not the smooth, polyester-suited Jones who had once charmed politicians in California. He was now fat, pale and sweaty. After only a few minutes of the reporter's persistent questioning Jones began to crack. 'The only thing I regret is that somebody hasn't shot me', he ranted. 'We're only a small community, we're no threat to anyone, but they won't rest until they destroy us. I wish they would just shoot me and get it over with. But I guess the media smear is what they use now – in the long run it is as good as assassination.'

Other reporters began pressing Jones about John-John, whom Jones still refused to return to his mother. (By this time Tim Stoen had also defected from the People's Temple and had been reconciled with his wife. Together they were trying to get John-John back, but as Stoen had so accurately predicted the case was being stalled in the Guyanese courts.) The journalists asked why the Jonestown security guards carried weapons, and why threats were made to those who wanted to leave. 'It's all lies', responded Jones wearily. But then he was immediately caught out in a lie himself: one of his henchmen brought news that Edith Parks, the grandmother of a family that had been planning to escape for some time, had asked Congressman Ryan to take them out of Jonestown. Jones went to see them. 'I am betrayed', he wailed. 'It never stops.' Seizing their opportunity, another 20 people asked Ryan to take them with him. By this time Jones was hysterical. 'I've given my life for my people', he cried.

His aides calmed him down and persuaded Jones to let the 'traitors' go. It was such a small number of defectors – 30 compared with the 1,000 who were staying – that it was not important, they said. Even so, the atmosphere in Jonestown began to turn ugly. As the defectors left, Don Sly, a burly young man in his late 20s, pulled a knife from his pocket and grabbed Congressman Ryan. Two of Jones' aides pulled Sly off, cutting his arm in the process; the blood spurted over Ryan.

At the last moment another cult member, Larry Layton, announced that he was 'pissed off with Jonestown' and joined the departing party. The other defectors were terrified because Layton was known as 'Robot', the strictest of all Jones' security guards. Layton was searched before he boarded the plane at Port Kaituma, but he somehow managed to smuggle a gun on board. Before the plane could take off the Jonestown tractor appeared and blocked the runway; in its trailer were 20 armed men. Inside the plane Layton started shooting, hitting Bagby in the chest. The men from the trailer also opened fire and three of the defectors were hit. On the runway, the congressman and three of the NBC crew, including Harris, were caught in a hail of bullets. After they had fallen to the ground the Jonestown gunmen made sure that they were dead by delivering a shot to the head. Three other journalists were wounded. Then the tract and trailer pulled away.

Meanwhile, back at Jonestown, Jones called his followers together. He sat on a crude, wooden throne, surrounded by nearly 1,000 cult members. He had bad news for them, he announced: they were all about to die. He explained that one of their number, Layton, had shot the pilot of Ryan's plane in the head and that the plane had consequently crashed in the jungle. (That had been the original plan; the 20 men in the trailer had been sent in case anything went wrong.) Jones said that the CIA would force the left-wing government in Georgetown to send the soldiers of the Guyanese Defence Force to attack the People's Temple. These soldiers were their black, socialist brothers, so they could not fight back. The only answer to the conundrum was a solution that they had long been prepared for – they would kill themselves. One of the cult members then asked whether it was not too late to escape to the Soviet Union. The Soviets would not take them now, Jones replied, although he had already dispatched two of his aides to the Soviet Embassy in Georgetown with a suitcase containing $500,000 in cash.

Jonestown's medical staff then prepared two 50-gallon (190l) drums of the soft drink Kool-Aid laced with Valium and cyanide. His followers were well prepared. for what would happen and Jones assured them that they would 'meet again in another place'. The cult members queued up for the deadly cocktail in an orderly fashion. Mothers gave the cyanide-laced drink to their children; it was squirted into infants' mouths by means of a syringe. Jones' own children were also happy to take the poison. Indeed, the congregation had long been told that swallowing poison would lead to a painless death. But when the children went into convulsions panic broke out. Jones managed to calm the congregation, however: 'They are not crying out of pain', he said. 'It's just a little bitter-tasting.' So the adults calmly drank their poison from paper cups. They then went out into the fields, lay down and died. It was the turn of the armed guards next; they, too, took their poison without resistance. When they were all dead Jones seized a pistol and blew out his brains. Annie Moore, one of Jonestown's nurses, shot herself in the head with the same gun moments later.

Jones had left a ghoulish suicide note in the form of a tape recording of that final cult meeting. It did little to help to explain to a shocked world how the charismatic leader had driven over 900 people to kill themselves. On the tape Jones can be heard reassuring his followers: 'I don't care how many screams you hear . . . how many anguished cries; death is a million times preferable . . . Take the potion like they used to take it in ancient Greece. It is a revolutionary act.' The children, in particular, were anxious. 'Can some people assure these children of the relaxation of stepping over into the next plane?' Jones was heard saying. But despite the fact that he was about to commit mass murder, Jones was full of self-pity. 'The world is not ready for me', he lamented on the tape. 'The best testimony we can make is to leave this goddamn world.'

When the Guyanese Defence Force arrived in Jonestown it estimated that there were only about 600 dead; it was hard to tell, as bodies were piled on top of bodies. And, like most ordinary Guyanese, they had not really been interested in these new settlers and had left them to their own devices. There had been two Guyanese soldiers at Port Kaituma when the shooting started who had done nothing to defend Congressman Ryan and his party. They later said that if two lots of crazy Americans wanted to shoot each other what business was it of theirs? Days after the murders a US Army mortuary team arrived in Jonestown. It was only then that the death toll was finally fixed at 914. Among the dead was Grace Stoen's son, John-John.

The mortuary team, along with the Guyanese coroner, Dr Leslie Mootoo, examined the bodies for blisters on the upper arms. They were looking for evidence that the cyanide had been forcibly administered to unwilling victims. But, with the exception of a few feeble older people, there were no signs of any telltale blisters. Although the crowd of Jones' followers had been ringed by armed guards, there did not seem to have been the need to coerce the cult members into killing themselves. In fact, the victims seemed not just willing, but eager to drink the poison. According to one witness, the first victim, Ruletta Paul, walked up to the dais with her child and took the cyanide without even being asked to. 'She just poured it down the baby's throat. And then she took the rest herself', said one witness. 'It didn't take them right away. She had time to walk outside . . . then the next women, Michelle Wilson, she came up with her baby and did the same thing.'

And when Jones had radioed to the People's Temple's office in Georgetown that liaised with the Guyanese government and had instructed his followers there to commit suicide, too, the public-relations officer had taken her three small children into the bathroom, had killed them and had then slit her own wrists. The other members failed to follow suit, however.

Although one could argue that the suicides were voluntary, Jones had spent years cowing his followers into total submission. Not only would they do whatever he said, they would also anticipate whatever he wanted and then do it before he even asked them to. Had he lived, it would therefore have been hard for Jones to have denied responsibility for the deaths of those who had gulped the cyanide down – and had given it to their children – at his behest.

But not everyone perished: the day after the massacre Guyanese soldiers entering Jonestown found two survivors. Grover Davis was hard of hearing and had missed the summons to the pavilion. When he finally went to investigate the commotion he saw the first children suffering their death throes and hid in a dry well. The next day he climbed out and went back to his hut to sleep. He woke when the soldiers arrived and was nearly shot because they thought that he was a corpse coming back to life again. The other survivor, Hyacinth Thrush, had slept throughout the whole tragedy. She was frail and bedridden. When her breakfast was not delivered the next morning she hobbled outside to find out what was happening. By the time that she reached the door the terrible smell explained everything. Later she said that she was sorry to have missed the opportunity to die with her brothers and sisters.

Others had escaped. One of them was Odell Rhodes, who had been a heroin addict when he first encountered the People's Temple. It had turned his life around by weaning him off drugs and putting him in charge of the children. He became a teacher and, for the first time in his life, had some social status. He had been happy to go to Guyana. When Jones had said that the CIA was going to attack them he did not mind the prospect of fighting and dying for the People's Temple – he was a Vietnam veteran. But he had become fed up with the nightly meetings; after a long day in the fields he could not stand the hysteria, the sermonising, the sexual humiliation and the 'white nights'. So he had volunteered to work in the nursing cottage, which had allowed him to skip the meetings. Not having been as indoctrinated as the others he had not been prepared to take the poison on Jones' say so. At the final meeting Rhodes had found himself at the front, unable to move without drawing attention to himself. He had been shocked at how readily the others took the poison. When the children had started dying he had volunteered to go to the hospital to get a stethoscope. He had then slipped away, into the jungle. When he reached Port Kaituma he found it difficult to convince the police that everyone at Jonestown was dead. But eventually the police put him on the phone to Georgetown, where a sceptical police inspector said that he would be down the next morning with the army.

Another escapee was Stanley Clayton. He had been working in the kitchen on that evening when he had been told to forget about dinner; there had been 'white nights' before, but no one had ever said 'forget dinner'. When he had reached the pavilion he had seen the children dying. But he had not been prepared to take his own life just because a few people had left the People's Temple; he would rather have risked getting a bullet in his back. He had pretended that he was looking for someone, had slipped past the backs of the guards and had made off into the jungle. He had found a house nearby and had told the occupants what had happened. They did not believe him, but when he told them that they would be able to help themselves to the tools and supplies in Jonestown they had decided to check out what he was saying. They had come back with their arms full of stolen goods and a glazed look of horror in their eyes. When Clayton finally made it into town he was arrested. News of the massacre had spread and it was rumoured that one of Jones' last acts was to send out assassination squads; it was thought that Clayton belonged to one of them. He eventually managed to convince them otherwise.

Others survived because they were absent from Jonestown at the time. One of them was Jones' 19-year-old son, Stephan. He could not forgive his father for what had happened. 'I can almost say I hate the man. He has destroyed everything I have to live for', he said.

There was a final, terrible irony in Jones' death. Despite the fact that his father had been a member of the Ku Klux Klan, Jones had spent his whole life fighting against racial prejudice. He had established his ministry in the ghettos and had preached to a largely black congregation. Until the time of People's Temple it had been rare to see black and white people worshipping together in the USA. He took black junkies off the street, helped black, unmarried mothers, educated black children, helped to house black people and provided day-care centres and food kitchens for black, inner-city residents. He and his wife had even adopted black children. He saw himself as a great revolutionary leader in the mould of Martin Luther King, Jr, and Malcolm X. In order to identify more closely with his black congregation he claimed to have Cherokee Native American blood, which had given him his swarthy complexion. Death had played a little trick on him: the cyanide that his followers had taken had turned the skin of even the white cult members black, while Jones, who had shot himself, had been drained of blood and had turned a deathly white colour.

Even with Jones dead his former followers were not safe. After the Jonestown massacre the Mertles and their teenage daughter were found murdered. No one was arrested and the police had no suspects and no active leads. Although the police said that they had no reason to believe that the Mertles' murders had anything to do with the People's Temple, other defectors did. Many lived for years in fear of the People's Temple's assassination squads.

Only one person went to trial for complicity in the Jonestown massacre: the 35-year-old former Quaker Larry Layton. Extradited to the United States, he was charged with injuring the US diplomat Richard Dwyer and with conspiring to kill Congressman Ryan. But the jury in San Francisco could not reach a verdict.

22 ❖ Wacko at Waco

Victor Houteff was a Bulgarian immigrant to the USA. He was also a Seventh-day Adventist preacher until 1930, when he was defrocked for not adhering to the strict line that had been laid down by the church. So he started his own cult – the Davidians.

Houteff believed that there was a hidden meaning contained in the Bible that could be unlocked by breaking a series of scriptural codes. Once he had done this, perhaps unsurprisingly, he discovered that the apocalypse was at hand and that he, Victor Houteff, had been chosen personally by God to lead a band of the elect who would rule the Earth, along with Jesus Christ, in the thousand years that followed.

Earning his living as a part-time washing-machine salesman in California, Houteff began to gather a band of followers around him. He bought 200 acres of low-cost farmland in Texas, near a small town called Waco, where he established a Bible school that taught his own, eccentric interpretation of the scriptures. Houteff's great task, he believed, was to cleanse the world of wickedness prior to God's coming. His 40 devoted followers were not in the slightest bit fazed, however, when their leader died before this had been accomplished.

Another self-styled prophet, Ben Roden, then took over the cult. He wisely avoided making the same mistake of other apocalyptic cult leaders and did not set a date for the Second Coming, which so often leads to disappointment. Instead he enforced compulsory daily worship and began publishing religious pamphlets; one claimed that the pope had masterminded the Watergate Affair. When Roden died, in 1978, his wife, Lois, took over while their son, George, waited patiently in the wings for his mother to die. He was extremely fat and the Davidians therefore wittily dubbed the heir apparent the 'prince of whales'.

Three years later, the 23-year-old Vernon Howell joined the cult. Howell was the illegitimate son of a Dallas schoolgirl; his mother, Bonnie, had been just 14 when she gave birth to him. Even so, she was allowed to keep the child. He was a slow learner and dropped out of school in the ninth grade. He also failed to develop physically, despite his efforts as a body-builder, and was furthermore an excruciatingly bad heavy-metal guitarist by all accounts. The only thing that he was good at was memorising the Bible: he knew the whole of the New Testament by heart by the time that he was 13. He joined the Seventh-day Adventists, but was later expelled for ranting and raving during services. Then, following a series of menial jobs, fate led him to Waco.

By the time that he arrived on the Davidians' doorstep Howell was already an accomplished conman. His comprehensive knowledge of the Bible now stood him in good stead, as did his understanding of human nature. He told Lois Roden that he wanted to join the Davidians as part of a spiritual quest. Then he threw himself on her mercy: he was in the grip of a terrible vice, he confessed – excessive masturbation. She approved his application.

The conservative cult members were somewhat wary of Howell at first, regarding him as a hippie and a wastrel. But he soon won them round with his quick smile and willingness to lend a hand. He worked hard at fixing the Davidians' ramshackle ranch buildings, repairing the cult members' cars and running errands. And they could not have failed to have been impressed by his knowledge of the scriptures and by his religious zeal.

After two years Howell was ready to make his bid for power. Lois Roden was 70 years old and her grip on the cult was slipping. The 25-year-old Howell approached her and told her that he had had a vision in which God had told him that they must conceive a child together; their son would be the last prophet. Even though her age precluded any possibility of conception, Lois was flattered by Howell's vision and set about trying to fulfil the prophecy: they became lovers. When news of the relationship spread among the Davidians there was disquiet. 'Our Mother,' quipped one cultist, 'who art in heaven . . .'

Howell used his enhanced status to instigate a religious revival. He was a natural showman and his hellfire-and-damnation sermons put new life into the cult. He also told cult members what they wanted to hear – that the apocalypse was at hand and that they must cleave to the new prophet. Lois Roden had now been marginalised and Howell dumped her and took a 14-year-old bride who bore him two children. He also had sex with other girls in the cult, some as young as ten. The reason for his actions was simple, he told his flock: he was the ultimate sex machine.

All this was too much for Lois Roden, and she died at the age of 71. Her son, George, stepped into her shoes and rounded on Howell, accusing him of being a worshipper of Satan. His passion for heavy metal was proof of this, George said, and he expelled Howell and his offspring from the cult 'unto the tenth generation'. To everyone's surprise, Howell accepted this judgement and left. But he took with him 25 cult members, including most of the young ones. Because they had split from the Davidians they called themselves the Branch Davidians.

A period spent in the wilderness is *de rigueur* for a *bona fide* prophet. Howell and his followers accordingly wandered around the Midwest in a couple of beaten-up trucks, supporting themselves with social-security cheques and odd jobs. In fact, they did rather well and soon had enough money to send Howell to Israel, where his status as a prophet was apparently confirmed. He came back saying that he was indeed God's chosen leader who would fight the world's last great battle again Satan. His next trip was to Australia, where he recruited more followers. Back in the USA, he gathered around him a core of mediocre rock musicians. Taking his inspiration from Houteff, Howell realised that there were hidden messages from God encoded in rock songs, especially the blues classic 'The House of the Rising Sun'.

Howell had built up a following of over 60 before he moved back to

Texas. His inner circle consisted of body-builders who called themselves the 'mighty men'. It was they who seized control of the Davidian ranch at Waco. In a last-ditch attempt to retain his authority, George Roden issued what can only be regarded as a Satanic challenge. On Hallowe'en 1987 he had the dead body of an 85-year-old Davidian disinterred; Howell could only call himself a prophet, Roden said, if he could raise the corpse from the dead. But Roden was no match for Howell, who simply accused Roden of being Satan himself. After all, he had dug up a corpse; what further proof was needed? So, claiming that they were doing God's will, Howell and his mighty men simply took over. There was a brief altercation, during which Roden was shot; it was only a flesh wound, but it was enough for Roden, who fled. (Although Howell and his men were later legally charged with the shooting they were acquitted.) They then fortified the compound at the Waco ranch to prevent Roden from staging a counter-coup. Howell's Branch Davidians now numbered well over 100.

Howell changed his first name (Vernon) to David – after King David – and took the surname Koresh, the Hebrew name of the Babylonian king, Cyrus, who had allowed the Jews to return to Palestine after their exile. The ranch at Waco was renamed Ranch Apocalypse; according to Koresh, it would be the battlefield on which Armageddon would begin. Satan, Koresh told his followers, would attack them there, probably under the guise of the US Army.

Koresh's rule became absolute. The sense of paranoia at Waco was increased by his nightly harangues about what a hostile place the outside world was, as well as a diet of war videos. Discipline was rigidly enforced: everything, even the children's games, was regulated and any hint of dissent was snuffed out. The Branch Davidians were the army of God and now lived under martial law.

Everything in the commune belonged to him, Koresh maintained, including his followers' underwear: if he came into their quarters and demanded their possessions in the name of God they were to strip naked. Naturally, all of the women also belonged to Koresh because the prophet had to multiply. His numerous wives – who were picked from among the wives and daughters of his followers – wore the Star of David. Many of the girls whom he took as lovers were underage. The other men in the compound were denied sex altogether. They were housed in separate dormitories, and in order to ease their sexual frustration they were encouraged to drink heavily. The men somehow managed to rationalise their situation: sexual intercourse was aggressive and incursive, they said; it was an assault on the physical integrity of women and they expressed their gratitude to Koresh for taking that burden upon himself. But then they also believed Koresh when he said that God was going to come down to Waco in a spaceship and take them up to heaven in it.

While the bulk of his followers were kept corralled in Ranch Apocalypse steeling themselves for the battle ahead, Koresh and his mighty men were having a good time in the local bars and restaurants. Meanwhile, they were amassing a huge arsenal of weapons at the ranch Apocalypse, managing to stockpile over 11 tonnes (11,176kg) of small arms, grenades and tactical weapons, such as anti-tank guns.

The US authorities were not unaware of what was going on at Waco, largely due to the courage of one man: Mark Breault. Breault was one of Koresh's original mighty men and was no longer happy about the way in which things were going. His wife had already quit the sect and had returned to her native Australia. Now he himself was beginning to feel uneasy about the situation: Koresh had just taken up with a 13-year-old girl who was lording it about the place. This was too much for Breault, who managed to slip out and phone his wife. She promised to send him the air fare to Australia. All that remained was for Breault to go to Los Angeles, where he could board a plane for Melbourne. Claiming that the mixing desk in the commune's recording studio needed replacing, he therefore said that he would have to drive to Los Angeles to buy a new one. Koresh, however, replied that he would come along, too, and brought his 13-year-old lover and a Kalashnikov assault rifle with him. The Branch Davidians had a house in California, where the three of them stayed. The existing inhabitants had somehow got wind of Breault's plans and told Koresh, who ordered Breault to fly back to Waco, where he would be punished. Instead, however, Breault seized his chance and flew to Australia.

Breault had kept a detailed diary of his time at Waco. In Australia, he and a group of other defectors got together and warned the US authorities that Waco was potentially another Jonestown. Australian TV picked up on the story and devoted an edition of a current-affairs programme to the goings-on at Ranch Apocalypse. But it still took the US authorities two years to do anything about Koresh and his apocalyptic army.

The US Bureau of Alcohol, Tobacco and Firearms – the ATF – eventually responded to the reports of the huge amount of arms that the Branch Davidians had accrued. They tried to infiltrate the group, but any ATF agent stood out like a sore thumb. Indeed, the ATF's activity only served to increase the Branch Davidians' paranoia. Now they were ready to die – and kill – for Christ.

On 28 February 1993 members of the ATF covertly moved in on Ranch

Apocalypse, concealed in cattle trailers. Certain of success, the bureau's press office had already optimistically prepared a press release trumpeting the successful capture of Koresh. When the AFT arrived at Ranch Apocalypse the place was eerily quiet: it was a Sunday, and the Branch Davidians were at prayer. Seeing no guns at the windows, the ATF officers were given the go-ahead, streamed out of the cattle trucks and they tried to scale the walls of the main building using ladders. Then they suddenly came under a hail of gunfire from all around the compound; some ATF agents fell. They had clearly been expected.

In fact, nearly everyone in the county knew that a raid was imminent: you cannot assemble hundreds of law-enforcement officers in a sparsely populated area of Texas without anyone noticing. The ATF had furthermore hired a van to supply coffee and doughnuts to its men. Even the local TV station had been given advance warning, and its film crew was spotted setting up its camera before the raid.

The first battle lasted for nearly an hour. The ATF was hopelessly outgunned. Four ATF men were killed and twenty-four were wounded. The Davidians lost six; one wounded cult member was shot by his colleagues 'to put him out of his misery'. Koresh called the police headquarters to complain that the ATF had killed some of his children; then he launched into a sermon. Later he called his mother, telling her that he had been shot and would see her really soon, 'in the skies'.

The ATF's advance publicity had backfired on it and it was seen on network TV to have bungled the operation. The FBI was now put in charge instead. it knew that the Branch Davidians had stockpiled food which would keep them going for a year, as well as enough firepower with which to defend themselves indefinitely. Worse still, they were led by a madman. So the FBI called in its hostage-negotiators. This conciliatory approach at first seemed successful, and after a week two older women and twenty-one children were allowed to leave the compound. But the authorities knew that there were still probably a hundred people left inside, of which at least seventeen were children.

The real problem was that the FBI hostage-negotiators had been trained to deal with Muslim fanatics, criminal gangs and politically motivated terrorists. They did not understand the jargon of the apocalyptic Christians. When Koresh talked of the seven seals of the Book of Revelations the FBI thought that was a militant environmentalist who was concerned about the clubbing of baby seals. Breault tried to put them straight: in Koresh's theology, the fifth seal was mass suicide, he told the bureau. But the FBI's psychological-profilers did not consider this a possibility. Koresh, they concluded, was a physical coward, and they furthermore did not believe that he inspired the same kind of fanatical devotion as Jim Jones.

As the siege dragged on, psychological tactics were employed. Spotlights were played on the ranch's windows to try to disrupt the cult members' sleep. Loudspeakers blasted the compound with the chanting of Tibetan monks, the screams of dying rabbits and loud rock music. The Branch Davidians simply countered these assaults by blacking out the windows of the ranch and deadening the sound by piling bales of hay against the walls. Weeks of these FBI tactics brought no results and a more gung-ho faction within the FBI therefore began to find favour. To complicate the picture, there was now a new US attorney general, Janet Reno, who was concerned about the welfare of the children in the ranch. She knew that they had been sexually abused and was worried about the insanitary conditions that they were now having to endure. She told President Bill Clinton that she intended to authorise the FBI to use tear gas with which to flush out the Branch Davidians.

At 4am on 19 April 1993, after fifty-one days of the siege, two tanks fitted with battering rams rumbled into position. As they moved forward, the FBI called the compound and told the Branch Davidians that this was not an armed assault: holes were going to be knocked into the outer walls and tear gas would be injected into the compound, but if they came out with their hands held up they would not be harmed. Instead of complying, the Branch Davidians put on their gas masks and prayed. Loudspeakers repeated the FBI's message, but the advance of the tanks was met with gunfire. The tanks nevertheless reached the compound unscathed, knocked holes into the walls and began pumping in the tear gas. After half an hour Koresh refused to negotiate any more, so extra tear gas was used. Three hours later the process was repeated. But Koresh still did not want to make peace and was briefly glimpsed inside the ranch while adjusting his followers' gas masks.

The FBI had high-tech listening devices that picked up some of what was going on inside Ranch Apocalypse. At around midday the eavesdroppers heard instructions being given to start fires. Wisps of smoke were seen before the wind suddenly whipped across the prairie, turning the ranch into a conflagration. A few cult members managed to run clear of the burning watchtower as it collapsed. Then the ammunition dump detonated in a series of huge explosions. The FBI eavesdroppers next heard one member inside ask 'What is the plan?' Koresh replied, with sardonic humour, 'Well, you always wanted to be a charcoal briquette.'

Eight members of the cult managed to escape the flames, some with their clothes ablaze; they were arrested. Over 100 people perished, not all of them voluntarily: 25 of the charred bodies that were dug out of the ashes of Ranch Apocalypse belonged to children, of whom 12 were Koresh's. A two-year-old boy had been stabbed to death and a woman had been shot in the back. Another 17 members had died of gunshot wounds; 5 of them were children. Koresh had shot himself through the forehead.

One survivor, Kathryn Schroeder, turned state's evidence and testified that the Branch Davidians had planned to kill anyone who tried to storm the compound. Murder and conspiracy charges were laid against 11 surviving members of the cult. However, the jury found that the ATF had bungled the raid so comprehensively that it was largely responsible for the deaths of its own agents. Five Branch Davidians were found guilty of involuntary manslaughter; two more were convicted of firearms offences and four walked free.

The faith of the Branch Davidians did not die in the all-consuming flames of Ranch Apocalypse, however. One member, who was absent from the ranch when the siege began, regarded Koresh's departure from the Earth as a sign from God and eagerly awaited Koresh's resurrection. Another, who lost a son, two daughters and four grandchildren in the conflagration, continued to believe in Koresh's prophecies of the Second Coming. Perhaps even more frighteningly, there are many who think that the deaths of Koresh and his followers were avenged by the Oklahoma bombing of 1995, which took place on the second anniversary of the ending of the siege.

23 ❖ The Solar Temple

Unlike the People's Temple and the Branch Davidians, the Solar Temple was not an off-shoot of a more conventional, Christian sect: its apocalyptic vision instead claimed that its roots lay in the Knights Templar. Some 50 of its members lost their lives in a mass suicide in October 1994.

The cult's founder, Luc Jouret, was born in the Belgian Congo in 1947. Following a period spent in the Belgian Army he studied medicine at Brussels University. He had intended to specialise in obstetrics, but during his course he became interested in New Age ideas, especially homeopathy. His interest gradually began to spread to mysticism and the occult. During the 1970s he joined the Renewed Order of the Templars, a neo-Nazi organisation led by the former Gestapo officer Julien Origas. When Origas died, in the mid-1980s, the Renewed Order fell apart as a result of a squabble over its finances and Jouret left to form the International Chivalric Order of the Solar Tradition in Switzerland, which peddled a mixture of environmentalism, homeopathy and mysticism. This group was soon amalgamated with a cult called the Foundation Golden Way, which was led by Joseph DiMambro, who believed in a New Age approach to high finance. Together Jouret and DiMambro formed the Solar Temple, a cult that seemed to have the answer for everything during the 1980s.

Jouret was the cult's high priest. He preached that the apocalypse was at hand and that it would come in the form of an ecological disaster. This being the era of the yuppie, cult-membership fees were high, and followers were served chilled champagne at cult meetings. The Solar Temple was not interested in recruiting the drop-outs and hippies that were lured into other cults: they wanted to attract people with money. Jouret recruited new members through his up-market homeopathic clinic in Geneva. He also toured the world lecturing on environmental politics, which gave him access to prominent people who would swallow anything as long as it was wrapped up in the politically correct, 'green' packaging.

The Solar Temple did not approve of the type of heavy-handed discipline that other sects employed: its members were far too sophisticated for that. But Jouret had also mugged up on all the latest management techniques. He freelanced as a corporate motivator and perfected his elegant techniques of control and coercion.

In 1986 Jouret and DiMambro branched out and formed a Canadian wing of the Solar Temple. They bought an old monastery north of Montreal and established an organic farm there. Meanwhile, Jouret continued his corporate career, giving lectures and seminars on man-management, motivation and self-realisation to large Canadian corporations. These activities gave him the chance to recruit corporate high-fliers. He picked up other followers by travelling around small towns speaking on homeopathy and wholefoods. He furthermore sold inspirational tapes through New Age shops. Using such methods Jouret managed such people such as Robert Ostiguy, the mayor of the town of Richelieu, Quebec, and Robert Falardeau, an official in the finance ministry of Quebec, into the Solar Temple.

Membership of the Solar Temple cost $50 a week. That sum allowed a cult member to attend lectures and seminars. For $150 a week they received 'Club Arcadia' membership, which entitled – or rather obliged – members to work on the organic farm, recruit new members and participate in the Solar Temple's religious rites. And $200 bought membership of the inner 'Golden Circle'. Members were then allowed to take part in the

Luc Jouret, founder of the Solar Temple cult

Solar Temple's secret, occult rituals. Naturally, they were also expected to donate all of their savings and property to the Solar Temple; enlightenment did not come cheap.

While members of the Solar Temple toiled in the fields producing organic vegetables, Jouret and DiMambro maintained a playboy lifestyle, skiing and travelling the world. Jouret slowly tightened his grip on the group, assuming the right to approve marriages and arbitrarily to dissolve existing unions. And he maintained discipline by claiming that only 100 cult members – the elect – would survive the apocalypse. It was Jouret, of course, who would decide who those 100 would be.

One of the cult's most prestigious converts was Princess Grace of Monaco, the former film star Grace Kelly. According to an article that appeared in Britain's *Sunday Times* newspaper after her death in 1982, her initiation into the cult had involved nude massage and ritual sex.

Details of the cult's activities began to come to the notice of the outside world when a member left it in disgust and went to the papers, claiming that they had handed over $500,000 to the sect. Then, in 1993, Jouret was fined $750 for weapons offences. By that time there was growing disquiet within the Canadian branch of the Solar Temple. During the 1980s DiMambro had invested much of the cult's funds in property, but now the real-estate market was in decline. The yuppie dream was over and so, it seemed, was this New Age religion: soon Jouret began to talk of mass suicide.

In the hope of generating a spiritual revival, Jouret visited sympathetic groups in Australia with a view to holding religious rites at Ayers Rock. However, the Aborigines who controlled the rock and the surrounding Uluru National Park refused him permission to do so. There were also rumours of Jouret's links with right-wing terrorist groups and stories that the Solar Temple was stockpiling weapons. Then it suddenly all came to an end.

On the night of 5 October 1994 a farmhouse in the agricultural village of Cheiry, in Switzerland, caught fire. A neighbour raced to the scene and broke into the burning house to find its owner, the retired businessman Albert Giacobino, dead in a bedroom. He had been shot. When the fire-fighters had quenched the flames they searched the farm and discovered that the spacious barn had been converted into a temple of sorts. A pentagram had been drawn on the floor. Over a triangular pulpit was a picture of Christ holding a chalice, but the face in the painting was that of Jouret. Around the base of the pulpit, spread out in a sunburst shape, were 23 dead bodies – 10 men, 12 women and DiMambro's 12-year-old daughter. The men were wearing robes of white, black and red; the women wore white and gold. The cult members seemed to have been well prepared for their send-off from Earth, for empty champagne bottles were strewn around them. Around half of the bodies had plastic bags tied over their faces; some also had their hands tied together; others had been shot up to eight times. Although three rifles were found in the barn the cult members had been despatched with a pistol – a .22. Over 50 shell casings were found on the floor.

Four hours later, three chalets in Granges-sur-Salvan, 50 miles (80km) away from Cheiry, caught fire. Inside, were found 25 bodies, 5 of them belonging to children. The bodies had been badly burned, but plastic residue indicated that they had died with bags over their heads. None had been shot, although some had been badly beaten. The remnants of drugs and syringes indicated that they had been heavily sedated before they were killed. The .22 handgun that had been used in the barn-temple at Cheiry was also found in the ashes.

Later that day, in Canada, an explosion occurred in a house in Quebec that was owned by the Solar Temple. In a bedroom the fire-fighters found the bodies of a man and a woman; around their necks were medallions depicting a double-headed eagle. They were members of the Solar Temple. In the basement the bodies of Antonio Dutoit, DiMambro's Swiss chauffeur, and his British wife, Nicki, were discovered. They had been dead for some time before the fire had started. Wedged behind the immersion heater was their three-month-old son, Christopher. The child had had a plastic bag tied over his head and a stake had been driven through his heart.

Investigators soon identified the cause of the fire: a crude timer had been set to ignite cans of petrol. Former cult members claimed that DiMambro had been annoyed when the Dutoits had had a baby without the Solar Temple's permission. The child, DiMambro said, was the Anti-Christ, and cult members had therefore been ordered to kill it in a blood-curdling ritual a few days earlier. Jouret and DiMambro were seen leaving the house early on the day before the fire. They seem to have taken the 10am flight to Geneva and then to have gone about finishing off the rest of the cult in Switzerland.

At first it was thought that Jouret and DiMambro had been involved in a financial swindle and that they had escaped to live a life of luxury on the proceeds. Rumours circulated that they had more than the equivalent of £90 million salted away in a Swiss bank. However, dental records subsequently revealed that Jouret and DiMambro were among the victims of the fire at the chalets in Granges-sur-Salvan. They had been telling their followers for some time that the cataclysm was imminent, and two days before the murders DiMambro had taken out 12 members of the cult out to an expensive restaurant for a last supper. Apparently, they believed that they would be reborn on a distant planet called Sirius if they underwent a fiery death on Earth.

In December 1995 16 more members of the Solar Temple were found dead near Grenoble, in France. And on 23 March 1997 the charred bodies of three women and two men were discovered in a house that was owned by a member of the Solar Temple in Saint Casimir, Quebec. They had burned themselves alive.

24 ❖ Heaven's Gate

Marshall H Applewhite, the founder of Heaven's Gate, called his sect the 'cult of cults'. In order to prove it, Applewhite and 38 of his followers – who described themselves as angels – committed suicide in March 1997. They were convinced that their bodies were mere containers and that

Marshall H Applewhite, founder of the Heaven's Gate cult who along with his 38 followers comitted suicide in March in 1997

by destroying them their souls would be released and beamed up to an alien spacecraft that was passing near the Earth's atmosphere in the wake of the comet Hale-Bopp, which was visible from the planet at that time.

Applewhite, as it turned out, was a repressed homosexual. The son of a Presbyterian minister, he had once been a professor of music and had had a wife and son. But during the early 1970s he had checked himself into a psychiatric hospital in Houston, Texas, and had asked to be 'cured' of his homosexual condition. In 1975 he met a psychiatric nurse named Bonnie Lu Nettles. Together they set up a cult called Human Individual Metamorphosis (HIM) in California.

Applewhite and Nettles were known as Bo and Peep, or 'the two', by members of HIM. They claimed to have been sent to Earth by a spaceship in order to teach humans how to attain an elevated level of existence beyond Earth. Followers had to give up their names and property and become celibate. However, HIM fell apart after its prophecies failed.

For a while, Applewhite and Nettles supported themselves by stealing cars and credit-card fraud. They moved back to Texas, where Applewhite took out a full-page advertisement that invited people to join his UFO-related cult. It used the names Total Overcomers Anonymous and Higher Source. Those who responded were sent a video showing Applewhite and two zonked-out followers, who appeared to hang on every word that issued from the *guru*'s lips.

UFO Magazine published a feature on the cult. In it, Applewhite referred to himself as 'Do' and to Nettles as 'Te'. It is thought that these names were taken from the notes that were played in the film *Close Encounters of the Third Kind*. However, there may have been another influence. Whatever he called himself – Do, Father John Doe or even King Do – Applewhite had a special affection for *The Sound of Music*. In that film 'Te', like the poison that the suicide cult later took, was a 'drink with jam and bread, which takes you back to Do'. Other cult members were called Re, So and Fah.

Yet Applewhite was serious and he and some of his senior lieutenants had themselves castrated. Living in Arizona, the cult outlined its beliefs in a screenplay called *Beyond Human: Return of the Next Level*. The US TV network NBC expressed interest in it.

The cult moved into a $1.3-million mansion in San Diego County, which had once been the home of Douglas Fairbanks, Jr. Set in three acres on a hilltop, the lavish retreat was leased to the cult by its owner, Sam Koutchesfahani, a convicted fraudster who had run a scam bribing colleges to enrol students from the Middle East who had already entered the USA illegally. When the cult members moved in they had no contact with their millionaire neighbours. They slept on bunk beds. They were not allowed to drink or smoke and they severed all contact with their families. In order to earn money, they turned to the Internet and designed websites. The mansion was packed with computers and the cult's own website advertised their wares. 'Higher Source is very much "in tune" with the current pulse and future direction of technology', it boasted. What's more, its leaders had worked closely together for over twenty years. During those years each of us has developed a high degree of skill and know-how through personal discipline and concerted effort. We try to stay positive in every circumstance and put the good of a project above any personal concerns or artistic egos. This crew-minded effort, combined with ingenuity and creativity, have helped us provide advanced solutions.

One of the cult's clients was the San Diego Polo Club, which asked Higher Source to do some more work for it early in 1997. It then received got an e-mail saying that Higher Source could not undertake any projects after Easter because of a 'religious festival'.

Cult members wore badges proclaiming that they were 'Heaven's Gate Away Team'. They were an 'away team' in the *Star Trek* sense – a group of crew members that had been beamed down to the surface of a planet in order to visit alien life forms. Members thought of themselves rather like caterpillars: their bodies were 'vehicles', or 'containers', that they could leave behind on Earth. The comet Hale-Bopp was the 'sign we've been waiting for'. Following unseen behind the comet, they believed, would be the 'spacecraft to take us home'.

The cult's departure from the planet was announced on the Internet: 'RED ALERT – Hale-Bopp brings closure to Heaven's Gate', its home page said. By way of an explanation, Applewhite added 'I am in the same position in today's society as was the One that was in Jesus then . . . If you want to go to Heaven, I can take you through that gate – it requires everything of you'. The approach of Hale Bopp meant that 'Our twenty-two years of classroom here on planet Earth is finally coming to conclusion – "graduation" from the Human Evolutionary Level. We are happily prepared to leave "this world" and go with [the spaceship's] crew.' The website also contained a warning: 'Planet about to be recycled – Your only chance to survive – Leave with us'.

The cult prepared for its imminent departure by sending videos to former cult members explaining what they were going to do. 'By the time you get this we'll be gone – several dozen of us', said a note accompanying the video. 'We came from the level above human in distant space and we have now exited the bodies that we were wearing for our earthly task, to return to the world from whence we came – task completed.' 'We couldn't be happier about what we're about to do', said one cult member on the video. 'Maybe they're crazy, for all I know', said a woman cultist. 'But I don't have any choice but to go for it, because I've been on this planet for 31 years and there's nothing here for me.' Another female follower, who apparently believed – groundlessly, as it turned out – that Applewhite had terminal cancer, said 'Once he is gone . . . there is nothing left here on the face of the Earth for me . . . no reason to stay a moment longer'.

All 39 of the suicide victims appeared on the tape. Everyone of them had their hair cut short, leading the police to believe that they were all young men. In fact, their ages ranged from 26 to 72, and 21 of them were women.

In a second tape Applewhite presented a long and rambling manifesto of their beliefs. 'We came for the express purpose to offer a doorway to the Kingdom of Heaven at the end of this civilisation, the end of the millennium', he said. 'Your only chance to evacuate is to leave with us. I guess we take the prize of being the cult of cults.'

The videos having been dispatched, the 39 members of the cult went out for a final meal in a local restaurant. They then divided themselves into three groups and committed suicide in shifts over the next three days. Applewhite had helpfully written out suicide instructions for each member:

'Take pudding or apple sauce and mix it with the medicine' – phenobarbitone – 'drink it down with a vodka mixture and relax'. His instructions were plainly ineffective: most of the cult members died of suffocation, and the last two suffocated themselves by putting plastic bags over their heads.

One of the Heaven's Gate farewell videos had been sent to a Beverley Hills businessman, who employed a former member of the cult. The two of them drove to the San Diego estate, where they found 39 bodies lying on their backs 'as if asleep'. They had their hands by their sides and their lifeless eyes were staring at the ceiling through a 3-foot- (90-cm-) square of purple silk, which had been folded into a triangle pointing downwards. They wore identical black trousers and trainers. Their bags were packed and they carried identification details in their shirt pockets.

The businessman called the police. The first two deputies to arrive were rushed to hospital and a Hazard Materials team was sent into the mansion to test for poisonous gases. The noxious fumes were eventually discovered to have come from the victims' bodies, which were removed using a refrigerated lorry and a fork-lift truck.

With their 'containers' having been disposed of by the San Diego Mortuary Department, the cult members' spirits presumably reached the spaceship which took them home. Applewhite – 'Do' – had left a chilling message for the world on the Internet, which was still there in 1999. It read

Do's Intro: Purpose – Belief

What our Purpose is – the Simple "Bottom Line"

Two thousand years ago, a crew of members of the Kingdom of Heaven who are responsible for nurturing "gardens," determined that a percentage of the human "plants" of the present civilization of this Garden (Earth) had developed enough that some of those bodies might be ready to be used as "containers" for soul deposits. Upon instruction, a member of the Kingdom of Heaven then left behind His body in that Next Level (similar to putting it in a closet, like a suit of clothes that doesn't need to be worn for a while), came to Earth, and moved into (or incarnated into), an adult human body (or "vehicle") that had been "prepped" for this particular task. The body that was chosen was called Jesus. The member of the Kingdom of Heaven who was instructed to incarnate into that body did so at His "Father's" (or Older Member's) instruction. He "moved into" (or took over) that body when it was 29 or 30 years old, at the time referred to as its baptism by John the Baptist (the incarnating event was depicted as ". . . the Holy Spirit descended upon Him in bodily form like a dove" – Luke 3:22). [That body (named Jesus) was tagged in its formative period to be the receptacle of a Next Level Representative, and even just that "tagging" gave that "vehicle" some unique awareness of its coming purpose.]

The sole task that was given to this member from the Kingdom of Heaven was to offer the way leading to membership into the Kingdom of Heaven to those who recognized Him for who He was and chose to follow Him. "The Kingdom of Heaven is at hand" meant – "since I am here, and I am from that Kingdom, if you leave everything of this world and follow me, I can take you into my Father's Kingdom." Only those individuals who had received a "deposit" containing a soul's beginning had the capacity to believe or recognize the Kingdom of Heaven's Representative. They could get to His Father only through total reliance upon Him. He later sent His students out with the "Good news of the Kingdom of Heaven is at hand," and His followers could then help gather the "flock" so that the "Shepherd" might teach others what was required of them to enter His Father's House – His Father's Kingdom – the Kingdom of Heaven – in the literal and physical Heavens – certainly not among humans on Earth. Leaving behind this world included: family, sensuality, selfish desires, your human mind, and even your human body if it be required of you – all mammalian ways, thinking, and behavior. Since He had been through this metamorphic transition Himself from human to Level Above Human – under the guidance of His Father – He was qualified to take others through that same discipline and transition. Remember, the One who incarnated in Jesus was sent for one purpose only, to say, "If you want to go to Heaven, I can take you through that gate – it requires everything of you."

Our mission is exactly the same. I am in the same position to today's society as was the One that was in Jesus then. My being here now is actually a continuation of that last task as was promised, to those who were students 2000 years ago. They are here again, continuing in their own overcoming, while offering the same transition to others. Our only purpose is to offer the discipline and "grafting" required of this transition into membership in My Father's House. My Father, my Older Member, came with me this time for the first half of this task to assist in the task because of its present difficulty.

Looking to us, and desiring to be a part of my Father's Kingdom, can offer to those with deposits that chance to connect with the Level Above Human, and begin that transition. Your separation from the world and reliance upon the Kingdom of Heaven through its Representatives can open to you the opportunity to become a new creature, one of the Next Evolutionary Level, rightfully belonging to the Kingdom of Heaven.

Why it is Difficult to Believe or Accept Us

We don't know if you believe in the real existence of negative or "lower" forces. If you do, then you may be able to understand or relate to some of what we are about to say. It seems that how your "programing" permits you to see or identify those forces, determines the limit of your acceptance or understanding. Many believe that there are "evil" acts or even "evil" individuals, but would draw the line before they would believe in evil spirits, evil discarnates, negative influences, malevolent space aliens, "Luciferians," or Satan and his fallen angels.

The generally accepted "norms" of today's societies – world over – are designed, established, and maintained by the individuals who were at one time "students" of the Kingdom of Heaven – "angels" in the making – who "flunked out" of the classroom. Legends and scriptures refer to them as fallen angels. The current civilization's records use the name Satan or Lucifer to describe a single fallen angel and also to "nickname" any "evil presence." If you have experienced some of what our "classroom" requires of us, you would know that these "presences" are real and that the Kingdom of God even permits them to "attack" us in order for us to learn their tricks and how to stay above them or conquer them. The space aliens, or Luciferians, use the discarnate spirits (the minds that are disembodied at the death of a body) as their primary servants – against potential members of the Kingdom of God. These "influences," or discarnates, are constantly "programing" every human "plant" (vehicle or body), to accept a set of beliefs and norms for behavior during a lifetime. From our point of view, this "programing" finds that body, and the vast majority of all human bodies, barely usable by students of the Kingdom of Heaven.

As the above example can serve to testify, the "lower forces" would – through their "norm" concept – what is "socially acceptable," what is politically correct – have you not believe in spirits, spirit possession, negative space aliens, Satan, etc. They would have you believe that to even dabble in these ideas is of the "occult," satanic, or at the least, giving credence to "fringe" topics. That's where they would also categorize any mental search of Eastern religions, astrology, metaphysics, paranormal, UFOs, etc., etc. In other words, they (these space aliens) don't want themselves "found out," so they condemn any exploration. They want you to be a perfect servant to society (THEIR society – of THEIR world) – to the "acceptable establishment," to humanity, and to false religious concepts. Part of that "stay blinded" formula goes like this: "Above all, be married, a good parent, a reasonable church goer, buy a house, pay your mortgage, pay your insurance, have a good line of credit, be socially committed, and graciously accept death with the hope that "through His shed blood," or some other equally worthless religious precept, you will go to Heaven after your death."

Many segments of society, especially segments of the religious, think that they are not "of the world," but rather that their "conversion" experience finds them "outside of worldliness." The next statement that we will make will be the "Big Tester," the one that the "lower forces" would use to clearly have you discredit or disregard us. That statement is: Unless you are currently an active student or are attempting to become a student of the present Representative from the Kingdom of Heaven – you ARE STILL "of the world," having done no significant separation from worldliness, and you are still serving the opposition to the Kingdom of Heaven. This statement sounds – to humans who have been so carefully programed by the "lower forces" – arrogant, pompous, or egotistical at the least – as if by taking this stand we had something to gain – as if we were seeking recognition as "Deity" or as self-appointed prophets.

That Luciferian programing has truly been effective, for we don't even want to voice to you the statement in question. However, believe it or not, it is only for your sake – the sake of prospective recipients of the Kingdom of Heaven – that we must "tell the truth," openly identify to you as Representatives of the Kingdom of Heaven, well aware of the "fallout" of that position.

The hard facts or bold statements in a nutshell, that are so difficult to accept or "digest" – come down to: If you want to or ever expect to go to Heaven – here is your window. That window opportunity requires: 1) an incarnate (as human) Representative of the Kingdom of Heaven; 2) that all who hope to enter Heaven become active students of that Representative while the Representative is present; 3) those who endure the "transition classroom" until it ends (adequately bonding or "grafting" to that Representative) will go with that Representative – literally LEAVE the human kingdom and Earth as He is about to do. Staying behind, for any significant period, could jeopardize that "graft." That window to Heaven will not open again until another civilization is planted and has reached sufficient maturity (according to the judgement of the Next Level).

We can't blame you for "buying into" the "Luciferian" program. What else has been available during those periods when no Representative was present? Almost nothing – save some warnings in the Scriptures, i.e., Luke 20:34–36, Luke 21:23, Mark 12:25, and Mark 13:17–19. Check these out.

Another fact is that what someone is into during the time a Representative is not present really doesn't matter that much, except that they are found unprepared when One comes – the only time when the Kingdom of Heaven can be offered to you.

The dilemma is we are here and most humans are thoroughly "hooked" to humanity. However, the same "grace" that was available at the end of the Representative's mission 2000 years ago is available now with our presence. If you quickly choose to take these steps toward separating from the world, and look to us for help, you will see our Father's Kingdom.

It is clear to all of us, that to the Anti-Christ – those propagators of sustained faithfulness to mammalian humanism – we are, and will be seen as, their Anti-Christ. This is certainly to be expected, and it will not delay our return to our Father's Kingdom. It might even accelerate that return.

We will, between now and our departure, do everything we can for those who want to go with us. But we cannot allow them to interfere with or delay our return to Him.

The Present Representative

Do

If you are convinced by that, and feel the urge to shed your 'container', remember that Heaven's Gate is closed. Hale-Bopp is on its way to the furthest corner of the solar system and won't be coming back near Earth until 6210 – and you are going to be dead by then anyway.